JEWS, SPORTS, AND THE RITES
OF CITIZENSHIP

EDITED BY JACK KUGELMASS

Jews, Sports, and the Rites of Citizenship

UNIVERSITY OF ILLINOIS PRESS

URBANA AND CHICAGO

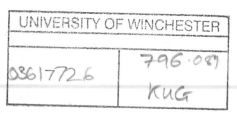
Publication of this volume was supported in part by the
Lucius N. Littauer Foundation and the William and Ina
Levine Family Foundation.

© 2007 by the Board of Trustees
of the University of Illinois
Manufactured in the United States of America
I 2 3 4 5 C P 5 4 3 2 I

∞ This book is printed on acid-free paper.

Library of Congress Cataloging-in-Publication Data
Jews, sports, and the rites of citizenship / edited by
Jack Kugelmass.
p.   cm.
Includes bibliographical references and index.
ISBN-13: 978-0-252-03082-6 (cloth : alk. paper)
ISBN-10: 0-252-03082-6 (cloth : alk. paper)
ISBN-13: 978-0-252-07324-3 (pbk. : alk. paper)
ISBN-10: 0-252-07324-X (pbk. : alk. paper)
I. Jews—Sports—History. 2. Jewish athletes—History.
I. Kugelmass, Jack.
GV709.6.J48   2007
796.089'924—dc22   2006000322

Contents

Preface

Ever since I became director of Jewish studies at Arizona State University, it was my intention to sponsor events that enabled people working in diverse fields to think about seemingly familiar material in new ways. The jewel in the crown of these endeavors was an annual spring conference on modern Jewish history and culture drawing on scholars from universities throughout North America, Europe, and Israel and leading to a published volume. Our first conference, "Key Texts in American Jewish Culture," stimulated eighteen scholars to do close readings of Jewish-authored texts and their reception in order to unpack their significance for the social, economic, and political history of American Jewry. Shortly after the conference, two of my colleagues, Charles Dellheim and Gordon Weiner, had lunch at Phoenix's Biltmore Hotel (a fabulous deco-era resort designed by Frank Lloyd Wright) with Ezra Mendelsohn, one of the participants. All three are sports aficionados—Ezra is a great fan of basketball—and the chatter eventually drifted to the question of Jews in sports. When the conversation was relayed to me, I thought the topic might work well as a conference. The response to the call for papers proved me right.

It was never my intention to organize the conference and certainly not to edit this volume. Given the initial enthusiasm, I assumed others would pick up the ball, so to speak. But when concept moved to actualization, some combination of unforeseen circumstances, either research leaves or lack of interest on the part of available manpower, placed this project in my lap. Given my interests—or, better put, lack of interest in sports—it seemed somewhat inappropriate, to say the least. Fortuitous circumstances proved much to my benefit because after working on this project, I have become, if not quite a sports fan, then at least intrigued by sports as a fertile subject of study with particular significance for the field of Jewish studies.

There is of course considerable discrepancy between the conference presentations and this volume. Various essays could not be included because of space and the limited number of themes that could be effectively explored here. Wherever possible, I have included observations by these participants in my introductory essay.

Acknowledgments

I would like to thank William Levine for the gift that enabled this conference to take place. Benefactors like him have helped project the Jewish studies program at Arizona State University into the national spotlight. I'd also like to thank Naomi Goodell, with whom I worked in the ASU development office; my colleagues, Professor Allison Coudert, Provost Milton Glick, and Professor Gordon Weiner, for receiving the participants; and Aaron Baker and Ruthy Stiftel for assistance during the conference. I'd like to thank my assistants, Dawn Beeson, Sandy Quinn, and Kristen Ungrodt, for keeping track of the comings and goings of participants and ultimately of the submissions and revisions of the papers.

I am particularly grateful to my mother, Fanny Kugelmass, who helped see this conference through at a very difficult time. She was a lover of books, so I dedicate this volume to her memory and to the memory of my father, David Kugelmass, who loved sports and communicated even to me the passion that all Montrealers share for Les Habitants. *Zikhronam l'vrakha.* And, of course, to Eliahu and Tamar.

PART I

Entering the Arena

JACK KUGELMASS

1   Why Sports?

Athletic Jews

Why a book on Jews and sports? Wouldn't common sense speak for an inverse relationship between the two, for the *unathletic Jew as normative*?[1] John Hoberman, both a sport historian and a critic of organized sports, is rather blunt about the negative ramifications of sports culture for American Jews, arguing that it contradicts some very basic Jewish values.[2] Biblical literature hardly celebrates the man of brawn. Jewish lineage is traced through Jacob, not Esau. Nor did physicality for its own sake strike much resonance with the Jews of late antiquity, a time when they were just as likely to be warriors, tillers of the soil, and laborers as any other people. We know from Josephus that the ruler of first-century Judea who veered far from Judaic belief and practice in committing himself to Hellenistic pursuits of leisure was reviled by his subjects. Herod's support of the Olympic games may seem to us as noteworthy, perhaps even admirable, but this and related enthusiasms hardly made him a paragon of virtue in the eyes of his Jewish contemporaries, many of whom took this as evidence that the man was not a Jew at all.[3]

Although there are ample social and historical reasons to support Jewish cultural abhorrence of certain games, the overall Jewish relationship to physicality is complex. Charges that Jews abhorred all physicality were particularly evident during the past century when sports and nationalism became closely linked. Given the political culture of the period, with mass movements bent on creating a new man[4] and the virulent anti-Semitism that the most successful of these movements espoused, from the 1920s until the 1940s, Jews touted achievements in sports as an apologetics against accusations of racial degeneracy. Nor was the need to defend Jews confined to Europe. Joel Gereboff's conference presentation argued that American Jewish popular writings from the 1930s onward cite the plethora of Jewish participants in sports throughout history. In doing so, they assert the fit between Jews as citizens and America as a nation. Times have changed. The more recent books are concerned about assimilation and, consequently, attempt to combat it by instilling a sense of group pride through the achievements of Jewish athletes.

Andrew Handler begins his short monograph on Jews in Hungarian sports by noting disfavorably one popular text on Jewish history and its dismissal of Jewish achievement in the field of athletics: "I would dearly love to see the facial expression of any of the Jewish Olympic, world, European, or national champions upon reading these words."[5] Considerable research supports Handler's thesis; as a group, Jews have been prominent in boxing, basketball, and fencing and individual Jews have won recognition in various other endeavors. But even before the professionalization of sports, it's simply incorrect to assume—whatever the inherent cultural bias that traditional Judaism brings to physical culture—that the unvirile male of the *yeshive bokher* is characteristic of all or even the majority of Jews, and certainly not so outside the confines of the Pale.

How could it be otherwise given the broad, diverse, and enduring social and economic history of Jewry? In various places and at various times there were Jewish soldiers, farmers, coachmen, porters, and strongmen. There was always, therefore, a muscular segment of the Jewish population, and it was a segment that could be called upon for communal self-defense.[6] At the same time, sport itself did figure in Jewish daily life, in part as a consequence of contact with, and observation of, the non-Jewish majority. In parts of Medieval Europe, for example, some rabbis were inclined to giving dispensations for ball games and other athletic activity on Saturday afternoons and they did so as well for activities connected to wedding festivities. In thirteenth-century France, groom and guests competed in riding and in a kind of tournament.[7] According to Yehiam Soreq, "numerous rabbis from Spain, France, Italy, etc. were well aware of the importance of physical culture to body health. And thus did not resent, and sometimes even encouraged, in certain cases, physical activities."[8] Maimonides considered physical exertion "a means towards a wholesome and worthwhile life" and "a wholesome and 'complete' body is the wish of God."[9]

Just as rabbinic sources indicate a complex and sometimes positive relationship between sports, physicality, and Jews, historians also note a complex and evolving relationship between sports and non-Jews. The data is particularly rich in regard to the processes of professionalization and the popularization of various types of games across Europe. According to Eric Hobsbawm, in Britain and the continent, the adoption of soccer as a mass spectator sport occurred toward the latter part of the nineteenth century and, along with it, the replacement of middle-class players with working-class professionals. Bicycling also emerged in this period as a mass spectator sport promoted by the commercial interests of manufacturers.[10] The factors that produced a frenzy for sports in the United States during this same period are somewhat different and have been cogently summarized in an essay by Stephen Riess. In the latter part of the nineteenth century, the United States was undergoing very substantial economic and political transformations. These included the rise of big business and the expansion of the federal government with the concomitant diminishment of individuality, the bureaucratization of the workplace, and the new demand for managerial workers and sales staff. This new middle class was less autonomous than an earlier era's and the transformation created one level of identity crisis. A second was the emergence of a post–Civil War generation living with the memory of the struggle that just ended and keenly aware that their own courage would not be forged in anything nearly so dramatic. A third crisis was the increasing feminization of American culture with Protestant preachers advocating values such as meekness and humility. As Riess argues, a fear existed among members of the old elite that the Anglo-Saxon male was "becoming frightened, had become effete, was losing his sexual identity and was becoming impotent."[11] The antidote for middle-class men was vigorous physical activity and one of the preeminent advocates of the "strenuous life" to hone one's masculinity was Theodore Roosevelt, who during the 1890s articulated his view in periodicals such as *North American Review* and *Harper's Weekly*. What is particularly important for our subject is that the cult of masculinity and the attendant role of sports was the zeitgeist of America at the time of mass migration of East European Jews to the United States, and it must have had a significant impact both upon the civilizing process by which ill-mannered foreigners were transformed into citizens (and subject to the same disciplinary processes that were transforming Americans in various other cultural domains into commodities)[12] as well as on the hybrid culture Jews would fashion for themselves in the New World. Fast-forward two generations and we arrive at the sports-addicted Potemkin family of *Goodbye Columbus*.

In disputing the disconnection between Jews and sports, one runs the risk of emulating compilations of Jewish sporting achievements—some rather dubious, as Mordecai Richler maintains in an acerbic review of one such volume, including sometimes the ethnic provenance of their achievers.[13] My intention is not to do that but rather to force us to think of sports and athletics as a unique window onto Jews and their modernization, relations with their coterritorial populations, and expressions of group pride. The intention of this volume is to consider the Jewish link to sports through the twin lenses of social history and cultural anthropology rather than the usual ones of sports history and hagiography. Moreover, because the conference upon which this book is based joined historians with anthropologists and because the essays roam from Europe to the Middle East and finally to North America, the window it opens on Jews and sports is much wider both intellectually and geographically than any of the existing collections on this subject.[14]

Borrowing some of the concerns of the anthropology of sports as framed by Noel Dyck, one could summarize the academic interest in Jewish athletics in broader questions about the observation, establishment, maintenance, transgression, dismantling, and redefining of boundaries between Jews and the coterritorial populations among whom they reside—hence the focus here on citizenship.[15] These same processes are observable in many other aspects of cultural production and performance—certainly in the performing arts and literature (an argument I made in *Key Texts in American Jewish Culture*), but nowhere are they so concretized via the body as in sport, at the same time nowhere are they so spectacularized either through mass spectatorship in stadia or through print and electronic media. Spectacle undoubtedly lies beneath the significance of sports in collective memory as Harvey Goldberg suggests in his essay. Add to this the element of the heroic—made manifest typically via the rhetoric of record breaking or sheer endurance and of beating the odds—and we can readily comprehend the importance of sports for any minority, colonial, or postcolonial people for whom power and agency have special connotation given the prevailing social or political order. So why not for Jews whose poetics of gender would make them seem the very antithesis of heroic?[16]

Identity

Given the plethora of major-league teams and national and international competitions, and the hoopla that surrounds them, it's not surprising that sports in the modern world is a significant contributor to local identity.

Mega sports events in particular help "people to reanimate their sense of the world as involving spatial distances and differences," providing a counterbalance to the "destructurations of lived space in late modernity." Mega events make local places meaningful within a global context, transforming mundane entities into international host cities.[17] But even more localized events contribute to filling the world with sites of significance. As has been argued for European soccer, both the field and the teams that play on it join sentiment and place, thereby spectacularizing urban social relations;[18] hence the public investment in wooing major-league teams, in building new and grander stadia, and the tendency for politicians to use sports metaphors in asserting their agenda.[19] By the same token, team ownership allows enterprising individuals, some Jews included, not only to invest, but also in a very visible way to establish themselves as pillars of local communities (and, of course, to be players at the national level) and, in so doing, to fulfill one's civic duties.[20] It's interesting to note that substantial Jewish support sometimes leaves certain clubs with a reputation of being Jewish and, according to Franklin Foer, some of the greatest prewar European soccer clubs were considered that way. The Dutch soccer team Ajax attracted a number of Jewish supporters who had survived the war and prospered in business. The team also had Jewish players, much-admired Jewish physiotherapist Salo Muller, and philo-Semitic star player Johann Cruyf. As Simon Kuper writes:

> The non-Jewish players of the great Ajax (and there were a few) inhabited a Jewish environment that was almost unique in the post-war Netherlands: the chairman, the sugar-daddies, the masseur, a couple of teammates, journalists, Arie Haan's agent, the player's favourite baker—why, you'd almost think there were a lot of Jews in Holland.
> Salo Muller says the changing-room "was a wonderful environment for an Amsterdam Jew." Jews and gentiles alike would tell Jewish jokes and use Amsterdam-Jewish expressions. When the other players teased Salo Muller, the big goalkeeper Heinz Stuy would shout, "Don't let those *goyim* get to you!," and the masseur would correct his pronunciation of "*goyim*."[21]

Despite its tie to commercial entertainment and despite globalization (think of how many sports teams change their host cities, how unlikely it is to have athletes play for their hometown team, or how many athletes now play for teams outside their countries of origin),[22] sport is intricately linked to popular culture and offers a good example of the continued transmogrification of mass culture into something local, oppositional, and subversive of official culture. Since the outcome of any athletic contest is rarely predetermined but is contingent on various factors including individual excellence, teamwork, and often enough luck, the possibility of victory against a more powerful opponent offers players and spectators a dramatization of the struggle and possible perseverance of the weak against the mighty. Edward Shapiro in his essay cites the former coach of the CCNY basketball team who argued that "the small and undernourished boys" of his squads were "so many Davids doing battle with the Goliaths of collegiate sports." Little wonder that so many in New York and elsewhere identified with that team.

Transmogrification into the popular occurs partly through sport's ability to absorb and carry the culture of resistance, but also through the transmission of lore and legend of heroism and villainy. The latter is particularly evident in professional wrestling because of its highly articulated theatrics, but it is present in all sports because of the explicit code of sportsmanlike behavior and the endless ways in which it is, or is believed to be, violated. Moreover, in various settings, including international competition, the impartiality of referees and judges is not always a given—at least not from the perspective of the losing side.[23] André Levy's chapter discusses the need for Arab referees in Jewish sports competitions in Casablanca precisely because as outsiders, they are presumed to be impartial. Even so, disputed calls provoke the charge that a referee has been bought by one side or another. In America during the first half of the twentieth century, a sport such as boxing was particularly known for the tendency to "fix" or "throw" a game. One of the more compelling American sports films is the 1947 *Body and Soul* starring John Garfield, which is loosely based on the story of Barney Ross, a Jewish boxer hounded by his promoter to do precisely that. The film ends on a very upbeat note—the hero walks away from the ring, his reputation intact. Less upbeat was the conclusion to the 1951 CCNY basketball point-fix scam, which scandalized college sports and led to the prosecution and imprisonment of those involved. One noteworthy aspect of the scandal, as Edward Shapiro suggests, was the lack of anti-Semitic reverberation, in part because so many non-Jews were involved in it as well. Although clearly the same could be said for sports gambling in general, the Jewishness of a gambler as prominent and successful as Arnold Rothstein did not go unnoticed. As Michael Alexander notes, Rothstein and his cronies—ministering to the middle-class and nouveau riche rather than high-end casino types—earned the epithet "the Delicatessen Decades" for this period of Jewish dominance of the industry. Perhaps no one was more put off by Rothstein's crassness than August Belmont II, the creator of Belmont Park racetrack and the son of August Belmont I, born August Schonburg in the Rhineland, who began his career as a small-time Jewish merchant. Belmont was particularly offended by Rothstein's behavior because he had "built the exquisite racetrack," according to Alexander, "to honor the refurbished memory of his father."[24] One can only wonder whether these two men, clearly each other's nemeses, did not in a sense act as mirrors, each reflecting to the other both dream and nightmare fantasies about the self. Moreover, if sport serves the purpose of civilizing the Jews, of transforming the Jewish body into that of an ideal sportsman, would it not "at some point betray the Jew . . . and reveal its inherent weakness?"[25] Could building an exquisite racetrack really refurbish the memory of a more humble Jewish background? Clearly, for Belmont, more was at stake in such refurbishing than class origins, and the very disreputability of gambling brought that to the fore.

Citizenship

Writing in 1964 in *Sports Illustrated*, Robert Kennedy argued, "Part of a nation's prestige in the cold war is won in the Olympic games." The attorney general saw athletic contests as an increasingly important factor in international relations given the then nuclear stalemate. Lamenting the fact that "in this quadrennial conflict the U.S. has skidded steadily for 16 years," he went on to outline a national initiative to reverse the trend.[26] Kennedy was harping on a theme already articulated by his brother just before he assumed the presidency in 1960. Also writing in the same magazine, the president-elect made clear the association between national salubrity and physical fitness. Moreover, Kennedy connected national defense to an initiative on sports participation. Arguing that throughout U.S. history, the struggles against aggressors "have been won on the playgrounds and corner lots and fields of America," Americans' "increasing lack of physical fitness . . . is a menace to our security."[27] God knows what he would say today!

Estimates indicate that at least one out of every three human beings tuned in to the 1976 Olympics[28] and an even higher proportion—3.5 billion people—tuned in to the Barcelona games of 1992.[29] Sport in the modern era, particularly as national and international spectacles, is a referendum on the nation, and political leaders are particularly explicit about the stakes involved in such competition. That concern is in the minds as well of the players themselves. "Until I scored that [final] goal," reflected a key player in the Canadian national hockey team that beat the Russians in 1972, "I didn't know the difference between democracy and communism."[30] It is also in the minds of organizations bent on addressing international audiences—sometimes boycotts or protests for one cause or another, most occurring in response to the Olympic Games.[31] Other times, global attention tempts spectacular assaults on the games or individual teams; the fate of the Israeli wrestling team at the Munich Olympics is a case in point. Highly cognizant of the appeal of soccer's World Cup, Osama bin Laden apparently planned an attack on British and American players at the 1998 games in France.[32]

Ethnic visibility within the referendum speaks a great deal to whether the nation is to be imagined as inclusive or exclusive. Recent studies make much of the body in representing political formulations and their attempts at utopian social transformation. George Mosse's work on fascism pioneered the study of masculinity and national regeneration, and he applied these considerations much more widely late in his career, including Zionist poetics of physicality.[33] Other scholars note the significance of the Viennese physician Max Nordau's call for a muscular Judaism at the Second Zionist Congress and its impact on modern Jewry. And yet, how masculine (in the colloquial sense) are these muscular Jews? Stephen Whitfield's essay offers a sobering perspective on the rediscovery of Jewish athleticism, citing Irving Howe to argue that a distinguishing feature of American Jews and certainly of those a generation or two ago who constitute the subject of *World of Our Fathers* is a "suspicion of the physical, fear of hurt, anxiety over the sheer 'pointlessness' of play."[34]

A good deal of evidence supports that view, including comments made by exemplary Jewish athletes. According to the manager of Vienna's HaKoah soccer team, which toured the United States in 1926 (some 46,000 people came to see them play in New York's Polo Grounds),[35] the players disliked the game "but played to demonstrate to the world that Jews possessed physical as well as spiritual power and that they would not take a back seat in the sport world."[36] Or consider the case of the reportage on one of the most outstanding of modern athletes, Sandy Koufax. Some reports suggest a certain ambivalence on his part toward the career in which he excelled. He summed this up pithily after winning the final game of the 1965 World Series: "I'm just glad it's over and I don't have to do this again for four whole months."[37] Moreover, what kind of an athlete sets out to become an architect (he would ask his professor at Columbia for permission to be absent when a World Series victory party conflicted with class schedule; Koufax had not yet become a household name, so his professor assumed he was a fanatic sports fan)[38] and is described in a *Time* profile as a fan of classical music[39] or in a *Saturday Evening Post* profile as a "brown-eyed and darkly handsome bachelor" who "reads Thomas Wolfe, George Santyana, Aldous Huxley and other writers of substance"?[40] Koufax's modesty is strikingly apparent in his self-deprecating comments on his reputed talents—athletic, cerebral, and amorous—in a profile he did with Milton Gross for *Look*.[41] This is a type—whether constructed by the press or truly the character of the man—that hardly breaks the mold of Jewish masculinity. If anything, it anticipates the sensitive male that emerged in the late 1960s—a masculinity in which Jews feature prominently either as actors in films and/or as subjects.[42] But here we're dealing with a double oxymoron: the Jewish athlete, the athlete intellectual.

Of course, from the other side one might ask how Jewish are these muscular Jews? Jeffrey Gurock's essay documents the struggle to integrate sports into the curriculum of Orthodox Judaism's premiere academic institution—Yeshiva University. The effort was part of outreach and a partial accommodation to the tastes and preoccupations of American Jewry. But that accommodation was generally greeted with a degree of ambivalence if not outright contempt by some within the university. More traditionalist students and faculty were leery of the athletic students. Typically drawn from outside the Orthodox day school, they were unable to hold their own in Talmud or Hebrew-language classes and, therefore, required a special program in general Jewish studies. Despite this accommodation to athletics, clearly the bulk of the university's students retained traditional Orthodox Judaism's disdain for physicality.

Circumscribing the Nation

Koufax's resolve not to play on Yom Kippur like Hank Greenberg, the Detroit Tigers home-run hitter a generation before him, underlines the larger public drama enacted through sports: Explicit is a certain poetics of gender because male and female athletes are almost always relegated to separate and rarely equal competitions.[43] And quite typically it is in the international male athletic competitions that one comes to see over time "an overlap of practical and symbolic constructions of national characteristics, national values, and national pride and sorrow."[44] Therefore, the nation is defined through the embodiment of ideal specimens of male and (more problematically and less forcefully) female bodies[45] whose beauty, prowess, and dexterity are highly eroticized[46] and subject to public adulation or derision (especially through scandals and unsportsmanlike behavior or simply on account of poor performances); then there is the epic dimensions of sports contests, offering ordinary mortals the opportunity to witness the heroic, to "see history in the making," thereby transforming simple turf into mythic landscapes. Such epic contests are not exclusive to international competition, but are also evident in the

performance of the national pastime.[47] Indeed, there are those who argue
that playing fields are already inscribed as mythic. Asked why he decided
to write a novel about baseball, Philip Roth replied, "Because whaling has
already been used";[48] finally, there is the question of whose bodies figure
within that physical representation of the nation. Through the spectacle
of sport, the nation is an immanent biological entity. Sometimes seen as
exclusive, the nation's strength derives from "pureness"—an idea that
negatively affected the careers and opportunities of minority athletes in
this country until it was publicly exposed and discredited. Other times,
the nation is seen as inclusive and greater than the sum of its parts. The
latter, at least for Jews, is famously reflected in the *Detroit Free Press*'s
front-page encomium during the 1934 pennant race when on Rosh Hasha-
nah Hank Greenberg scored two home runs: "And so to you, Mr. Greenberg, the Tigers fans say, *'Leshono tovo tikosayvu!'*"[49] Or some thirty
years later, a bumper sticker that reads, "You don't have to be Jewish to
love Sandy."[50] The very same surge of inclusiveness occurs when Jews
themselves are the majority. Take, for example, the case of Sakhnin, a
soccer club (with Arab, Jewish, and some foreign players) representing an
Arab town in the Galilee, whose victory over HaPoel Haifa earned the
team the State Cup, which qualified the squad to represent Israel in a
major European tournament. Calls of congratulation came in both from
Ariel Sharon and Yasir Arafat while coverage of the game in the Israeli
press temporarily displaced much more depressing news about the ongoing military conflict in Gaza. As the *New York Times* reported, "For one
night, said Aryeh Maliniak, a sports columnist, the Arab minority felt
'they were equal members of society,' while Jewish Israelis 'felt free to
express appreciation of the Arab team without dragging the question of
"who's right?" into the issue.'"[51]

Who watches sports? And how much does sport literacy define membership in various collectivities—from cohort to class and nation? In this
respect, sports speaks directly to the question of citizenship: How nations
select and deselect their ideal physical representatives. But it also speaks
to how individuals and collectivities within states use sports literacy
and fandom as a self-administered test of citizenship. In a wonderful
and much cited essay, Philip Roth discusses his youthful enthusiasm for
baseball, a sport he describes as "a kind of secular church that reached
into every class and region of the nation and bound millions upon millions of us together in common concerns, loyalties, rituals, enthusiasms,
and antagonisms." The loyalty baseball elicits is less time-bound and
ephemeral than that incited by state authority. Unlike the patriotism
nourished by war "that fixes a bayonet to a Bible," baseball puts one "in

touch with a more humane and tender brand of patriotism, lyrical rather than martial or righteous in spirit, and without the reek of saintly zeal."[52] Anyone who has accompanied a child to a weekend softball game can vouch for the veracity of that statement.

However benign the patriotism of baseball, viewed from the standpoint of the power bloc, fandom may be seen not as a self-administered referendum, but as a test of loyalty. As Pierre Bourdieu argues, the popularization of sport, increasingly organized through aid from public authorities, was an extremely economical means of controlling adolescents and very useful in "the mobilization and symbolic conquest of the masses."[53] Indeed, turn-of-the-century American public and private agencies saw in sports the possibility of instilling ideas of teamwork and cooperation in immigrants that would serve them well in the industrial workplace while learning, as one play activist put it, "a higher standard of civic duty."[54] German Jews, well established in the country by the 1880s and concerned about remaking East European immigrants into proper Americans, saw in sport the same possibility. They also saw it as a means of fending off accusations that these newer immigrants were "unassimilable because they belonged to a weak and alien race whose people historically rejected physical pursuit in favor of religious and intellectual study."[55] In many cases, similar attention was placed on boys as well as girls, as Linda Borish argued in her conference presentation, but often, too, substantial differences existed regarding the types of activities toward which each sex would be channeled. Describing this division in New York City's playgrounds during the early part of the twentieth century, Cary Goodman writes, "Activity and competition were the bywords of the space allocated for boys. Conversely, the watchwords for the girls' space were relaxation and cooperation."[56] Elsewhere, in Germany for example, many Jewish women turned to sports in the early part of the twentieth century to keep up with fashion and trim down their bodies. The results, according to one Jewish magazine, were "catastrophic" for women's sports.[57]

Any American Jewish historian will be familiar with the graphic *Forverts* piece dating to the early part of the twentieth century that explains the game of baseball to the Yiddish-speaking public.[58] And fans of *Sesame Street* and *Chicago Hope* probably know the CD *Mameloshn*, in which Mandy Patinkin sings a Yiddish rendition of "Take Me Out to the Ball Game." Both items speak directly to the avid fandom among members of a population we're not accustomed to thinking of as sports people. In some respects, they were not. Or, at least, their fandom was something new, distinguishing one generation from its antecedents and giving it a sense of membership in a world outside the confines of the Jewish street.

In regard to aspiring Jewish athletes, not all immigrant parents were delighted with their sons' achievements. As Irving Howe relates in *World of Our Fathers*, one Jewish hoopster recalls the striking lack of interest: "All they understood were books, books, books, knowledge, knowledge, knowledge."[59] Others were deeply concerned about what their children were turning into, "whether we were Jews or a new kind of shagitz."[60]

If Howe is correct about the negative attitudes toward play of these first-generation Americans, then from the standpoint of commercial interests, fans had to be created and, where they already existed, fostered and their numbers increased. The prospect of enlarging the numbers of Jewish spectators motivated some promoters to include Jews (like any other ethnic player in areas with significant concentrations of a particular population) in their teams' rosters. The clubs' managers weren't always concerned about their ability to play because a mediocre athlete could simply be relegated to the bench.[61] In the case of the New York Giants of the 1920s, the baseball team's manager John McGraw really wanted his Jewish player Andy Cohen to succeed. After one particularly bad day for Cohen, McGraw headed to the racetrack where he bet on a horse ridden by a Jew. When the horse did not win, McGraw exclaimed, "They can't ride either."[62]

Some observers felt that this exploitation of Cohen's ethnicity may have been good for business, but was not very helpful to the player. "Every time Andy comes to bat," wrote one commentator, "he feels he must make a hit, not only for John McGraw, his teammates and the City of New York, but for the Jewish race as well, which is a large order."[63]

However, fans responded well to ethnic players. A 1928 story in *Baseball Magazine* describes Andy Cohen's fans as dressed in long coats, hats, sideburns, and beards and saying "Oy, oy, Endy." And one folk bard composed the following accolade, which ends in a tribute to "Casey at the Bat":[64]

> Then from the stands and bleachers the fans in triumph roared.
> And Andy raced to second and the other runner scored.
> Soon they took him home in triumph amidst the blare of auto
>   honks.
> There may be no joy in Mudville, but there's plenty in the
>   Bronx.[65]

Cultural Production

The ditty about Cohen underlines the close connection between sports and other popular entertainments, most notably vaudeville, both of which were born in their professional form shortly after the Civil War.[66] Of course, both were popular among immigrants and constituted a means to socialize them to the rules and nuances of the New Country and its complex multiethnic urban culture. Vaudeville's stock in trade was the lampooning of immigrants' learning the intricacies of the New Country, sports included. The skits allowed those already at home in America to relive, minus the trauma, the bewildering experience of encountering the new. One of the greatest of the Yiddish vaudevillians was the monologist Michel Rosenberg whose beloved character Getsl attends a baseball game quite by chance. After learning about a new cantor performing somewhere in the Bronx, Getsl hops onto an uptown train and follows the crowds exiting at "Yankl Stadium." Seated in the bleachers, Getsl observes the following:

> From one hole emerges some kind of a man with a blue suit and a strange yarmulke. This is certainly the choir leader. Following him comes a colleague with woolen socks, long underwear and a sweater and on the sweater is written "Yankl." That's my cantor? They begin praying. Suddenly I feel such a slap on my back that my right lung feels like it's going to collapse. "Hello, buddy!" I take a look it's the same guy with ____. He gives me such a greeting with "Ata boy!" that I almost pass out. I say, "What is it here?" He says, "Buddy, it's going to be some game!" I say, "Who is the man with the long suit and the yarmulke?" He says, "That is the oompire." I say, "And the one with the freezing hand who wears a glove?" He says, "That is the peetcher." And immediately emerges someone with a mattress on his belly and something on his face that looks like a strainer for noodles. He says, "This is the catcher." I say, "What does he catch other than a cold if the pitcher spits in the glove and throws the ball and there's tossing from pitcher to catcher and catcher to pitcher. Neither one wants the ball and they stand there![67]

Skits such as this point to the fact that Jewish involvement with sports may be far more evident off than on the field. America's most popular sport song, "Take Me Out to the Ball Game," was written by a Milwaukee Jew, Albert Von Tilzer, who apparently had never seen a major-league game.[68] At least three major American novels about baseball were written by Jews—Bernard Malamud's *The Natural*, Mark Harris's *Bang the Drum Slowly*, and Philip Roth's *The Great American Novel*. Certainly an area that needs to be explored is the Jewish link to the professionalization of sports in the United States. Ever-increasing spectatorship via the mass media—from newspaper to television (by 1908, even the New York Yiddish press carried boxing results)[69]—not only has enabled athletes to use their skills to advance economically but has given rise to a professional class of aficionados: the writers and newscasters who mediate sports for the interested public. Jewish sportswriters and newscasters have played a prominent role in North America—so much so that no history of modern sports could be written without paying some attention to them.[70] How much some Jewish commentators allow themselves to speak with a minor—that is, Jewish—voice is always conjecture, but a case can be made for it in the close relationship between a once-despised boxer, Muhammad Ali, and "an acerbic Jewish social critic," Howard Cosell. Indeed, as Hoberman argues, "It did not take a semiotician to detect the estrangement of this Jewish non-athlete from his well-muscled colleagues in the broadcasting booth."[71] And perhaps Cosell did precisely what Whitfield suggests in his essay Jewish writers typically do: Identifying physical weakness as a distinctively Jewish trait, they exalt toughness or athleticism by turning to non-Jewish street toughs as the subject of their creative output.

Cultures in Conflict

Long before the twentieth century, European thinkers considered the value of sports on national salubrity. Conservatives in particular conceived of athleticism as an antidote to modernity's nervousness. Extremists saw in the body something collective or public while Nazism called for the political education of the body.[72] As John Hoberman argues, sport, in totalitarian regimes, had to conform to ideological norms and because for Nazism sheer aggressiveness was a norm, "boxing was Hitler's idea of a politically wholesome sport—an antidote to 'peaceable aesthetics and bodily degenerates.'" By contrast, international sport "was a 'pacifist-international' plot concocted by Jews to soften up the German male and substitute sport for war on behalf of global reconciliation."[73]

Sometimes sports are seen as salubrious or insalubrious based on their particular national associations. English colonists in Ireland, for example, were forbidden to play certain Irish sports lest they develop the degenerative habits of the people whose land they occupied. Some five hundred years later, Irish games were reinvented in order to bolster that nation and fend off the degenerative habits of the English.[74]

When groups do disengage from larger national collectivities and express aspirations for political and/or cultural autonomy,[75] the symbolic weight of individual sports may come under special scrutiny. Just as exhibiting excellence in some sports is considered by elites as a sign of pedigree and, therefore, a possible route to social acceptance for select individuals from minority groups, others within the group may consider participation in those very sports an indicator of domination. German

Jewish turners, according to Joshua Shanes, replicated non-Jewish athletic forms, but in Galicia, the same societies considered those activities foreign, and they viewed fencing in particular as a symbol of assimilation. At the same time, the Galician turners' competitive matches with non-Jewish teams were important for asserting Jewish national pride. Jewish clubs typically attributed losses in such competitions to the fact that that their squad was still in its infancy (an excuse used for quite some time). Indeed, one report on the continued losses argued that the mere appearance on the field of a Jewish sports club forced non-Jews to treat Jewish sportsmen with respect.

Nations engage and disengage in sports as part of a complex maneuver in the politics of identity, often appropriating foreign sports and transforming them into national pastimes. Japanese and Latin American baseball are cases in point, as is the striking attachment to cricket among various countries in the former British Empire. In the latter case, many former colonials have managed to transform the sport into something scarcely recognizable to British fans of the game.[76] For ethnic and other social groups within larger states as well, engaging or not engaging in particular sports is intricately connected to the politics of identity. Early twentieth-century European socialists articulated a poetics of sports very much in opposition to the elitism, competitiveness, and blatant militarism of bourgeois athletics.[77] Jack Jacobs's essay shows that various stripes within the Jewish Left of interwar Poland emphasized different kinds of physical contests based on values such as mass participation versus individual "masters" or "sport acrobats." Soccer and boxing were both eschewed by the Jewish Labor Bund's sport club Morgnshtern. The group eventually relented, possibly, as Jacobs argues, in response to the desires of some of the movement's rank and file. By contrast, Anat Helman's analysis of Mandate-era Tel Aviv indicates no distinction in sports played by left-wing and bourgeois clubs HaPoel and Maccabi. Interestingly, to this day, some Israeli fans pick their allegiances according to political affiliation.

Often enough, the fierce rivalry between groups, the very physicality of athletic competitions, and the tensions they provoke—which either dissipate at the game's conclusion or are exacerbated by mistrust of the sportsmanlike behavior of rival players and referees—foments a violence just beneath the surface, especially where volatility exists in other aspects of the social arena. Violent flare-ups among sport audiences, argues Norbert Elias, "may be seen in a wider context as a symptom of some defect in society at large rather than simply in that particular section which enjoys committing acts of violence."[78] The defect, of course, is social inequality. That defect exists not only within nations but between them as well. Warring states rarely put forth teams sufficiently disengaged from one another emotionally so that the reality of the outside world is temporarily suspended as it must be for a game to be a game. Witness, for example, the bloody water polo match between Hungary and the Soviet Union at the 1956 Olympics.[79] In less volatile situations, where the rules of the game, so to speak, prevail and social cleavages are less a matter of struggle than acquiescence, athletic contests between rival groups may serve to give expression to hostility in a controlled manner, adding to the excitement of the encounter. For that reason, teams drawn from the same social group may not produce much by the way of conflict, leading to a rather dull contest, while other groups openly opposed to one another in other domains of social life may provide the fuel through which the sporting encounter ignites into a serious breakdown of social order.[80] As Janet Lever puts it, "Where societies have numerous or intense internal cleavages, the conflict dramatized is so real that the spectacle is enhanced, but only up to the point where hostilities are so intense that playing together becomes impossible."[81]

A case in point is André Levy's study of soccer matches between Casablanca's Arabs and Jews. The material illustrates the delicate etiquette of engaging in competitive matches between a dominant and a numerically reduced subordinate group. And particularly so during the eruption of international crises in which both parties have very different stakes. Sometimes a game is not just a game and the subordinate group understands quite well the risk it faces if it performs well on the field—even without explicit threats.

Not all social cleavage is conflict ridden and certainly not when various groups accept the existing social order. In Harvey Goldberg's analysis of nineteenth- and early twentieth-century Jewish athletic displays in Tripoli, volatility is not present and Jewish muscularity rather than challenging social hierarchy dovetails with it. Sometimes, as Goldberg argues, sports and Jewish prowess signify not the possibility of social achievement but "are anchored in the unchallenged assumption of the fixity of the place of the Jews."

More typically, at least in the modern world, sports are used by groups as a means of individual mobility and collective integration. As Tamir Sorek shows in his essay, Arab soccer teams in Israel are careful to include at least one Jewish player, use Hebrew as their public language, and consider the sport an opportunity for integration. Sorek's findings show that soccer fandom affects the political orientation of some of its participants, but no evidence exists to show comparable ecumenical spillover among Jewish-Israeli soccer fans. Sometimes, and clearly in less schismatic societies than Israel, minority athletic achievements attain the national spotlight, are celebrated by all social segments, and act as a kind of utopian reframing the nation as far more inclusive than the realities of the political economy would otherwise suggest. (One of the peculiar features of spectacle, as John MacAloon notes, is that it both converts reality into appearances and "simultaneously rescues 'reality' from mere 'appearance' and represents it in evocative form as the subject for new thought and action.")[82] Some argue that this is very much the case in the United States where sports and entertainment create an illusion of black acceptance and social achievement much less true in other social domains. The same holds true, albeit in a much more naïve and probably cynical vein, for how Avery Brundage as president of the U.S. Olympic Committee treated the issue of Jewish representation in the 1936 Berlin Olympics. Falsely convinced that Jews could qualify for the German team, Brundage was perfectly content (and familiar) with a system of "separate but equal" and could dismiss the significance of German exclusionary policies outside of the Olympics with his observation that, "In my club in Chicago, Jews are not permitted either."[83] But, from the standpoint of minority players and fans, because of its indirectness, its ability to challenge without threatening, this reframing the nation via minority inclusion in national teams is a vehicle for asserting their rights as citizens (just as for the events' organizers, intentional inclusion of diversity constitutes the rites of citizenship). One can only wonder what she meant by it when the half-Jew Helene Mayer, invited to join the German team at the 1936 Berlin Olympics, raised her arm in a Nazi salute after winning the silver medal in fencing.[84] Was this a disassociation from her Jewish half, a symptom of her political naïveté,[85] or a plea for acceptance despite her "racial" status (she herself did not identify as a Jew) and for a more inclusive new Germany? We will never know for certain. But it underlines the fact, as Steven Riess and George Eisen reminded us in their presentation at the conference, that "Jews were excluded from the German gymnastic movement, barred from country clubs, discriminated in ski-resorts and hotels, and, finally, murdered in Auschwitz—in spite of winning Olympic medals for their countries—all through the twentieth century." So however important the relationship between achievement on the field and acceptance in other social domains, sport cannot be isolated from the larger social, political, and cultural matrix affecting Jewish citizenship.

Cultural Capital

A sport may be meaningful to certain groups despite or because of the fact that the game itself is either ignored or even disparaged by the dominant culture. Soccer among Latinos in the United States, boxing among the lower classes, and cockfighting among Puerto Ricans in New York are some examples. Nor is the subaltern status of a group always a factor in taking to an unpopular sport. Soccer in the United States, for example, thrives among suburban kids because it is not associated with many of the things that characterize modern American sports—violence, money, domination by men, and African Americans.[86] Of course, moving up the social ladder, the dominating classes have used sports to define their own culture and inculcate that to their children—typically at elite schools— and thereby secure and reinforce the exclusiveness of their position. In doing so, they glorify sport as a training ground for character and put forward, as Pierre Bourdieu argues, "other criteria of 'achievement.'" Bourdieu goes on to argue that the dominant class relates to the dominated fraction such as intellectuals and artists in terms of male/female, virile/effeminate oppositions. Hence the "implications of the exaltation of sport and especially of 'manly' sports like rugby."[87] Hence, also, the unheroic feminized Jew.

Class bisects ethnicity and the nation in the type of pursuit or non-pursuit of athletic activity. Pierre Bourdieu notes that activity in sports declines with age as one moves down the social ladder while spectatorship in the most popular sporting events declines as one moves up the social ladder.[88] Of course, a meta-spectatorship associated with movement up the social ladder is team ownership. Stables have a special place in the culture of old money, hence their appeal to the newly monied. Hence, too, the audacity of Arnold Rothstein, who appropriately (given the English translation of his surname) dubbed his Belmont stable Red Stone. Or, as John Hoberman notes in his essay, the recent obituaries of Anglo-Jewish businessmen, which included material on their passion for horse racing. Citing one account of a Jewish financier who attended the racetrack and examined his company's finances while seated underneath images of his racehorses: "A tableau from *The Economist* that offers . . . a striking, and no doubt unintentional contrast between healthy animal vitality and bloodless Jewish finance" and "a fair warning that the Jewish relationship to the horse remains, as we say, 'problematic.'"

Clearly, team ownership by wealthy Jews reveals less about the unique inclinations of Jewish entrepreneurs and their unfettered ability to purvey the new than the very opposite: the search for social distinction that makes certain Jews faithful imitators of their non-Jewish economic peers. Indeed, there may be some peculiar aspects to such pursuits as well. A number of years ago, I joined a prominent New York Jewish veterinarian on a three-day yacht trip. His running joke was the comments of non-Jewish friends about what a Jew is doing owning a yacht (a gag put to good use in Jackie Mason's *The World According to Me*). On our return trip, we docked at a local country club with a substantial Jewish membership. Although many of those present dressed in the regalia of upper-class yachtsmen—plaid cotton pants and blue, green, or red blazers—the club's distinction is that it has the highest percentage of non–boat ownership of any yacht club in the country. So much for Jews as sportsmen.

Who one plays with and who refuses to play tells us much about a group's acceptance. Much has already been written about the exclusion of Jews from German fencing clubs earlier in the twentieth century. It is still rather striking to note that a 1962 survey shows that out of 803 country clubs in the United States, more than half barred Jews completely and more than one in ten had quotas.[89] Today, such figures ring as rather odd. Less odd are the reasons for the formation of exclusively Jewish clubs. Although they were frequently founded because Jews were excluded from elite non-Jewish clubs, they also served to promote Jewish endogamy by bringing eligible Jewish men and women together.[90] Not only did some of these clubs bar non-Jews as members, they sometimes excluded categories of Jews. In Atlanta, for example, the Capital City Club barred German Jews, who then founded the Standard Club in 1905, which in turn barred Russian Jews from membership.[91]

At the same time, at the uppermost end of the social spectrum where Jewish presence would have been highly contested, there was a degree of Jewish hyperemulation of their financial peers' recreational pursuits. Indeed, the most exclusive American Jewish country clubs established earlier in the twentieth century not only distinguished the Jewish elite from less established coreligionists, but also served to notify non-Jews that the wealthy German Jews who built these clubs "were no different from their gentile counterparts . . . thus doing away with any logical reason for their exclusion."[92]

Exclusionary policies vis-à-vis Jews, women, and minorities show how caste has long played a role in the world of athletics, sometimes relegating individuals to certain kinds of activities as a redeployment of other social divides. Witness, for example, the undue emphasis given to athletics as *the* paragon of black genius.[93] Note how useful Bourdieu's notion of achievement is in understanding former exclusionary policies in elite American academic institutions in regard to Jewish participation in certain sports. One case that made the national press followed the Yale basketball team's disastrous 1922 season. An inquiry set up by the university noted the absence of any Jewish players on the team. Given the prominence of Jews in basketball at that time, the absence was noteworthy and, once corrected by a new coach, the squad went on to win the title.[94] The reason for Jewish exclusion in the first place probably stems from the negative attitudes toward Jews in elite schools during the same period. Interestingly, a survey of Harvard students favored restrictions on Jewish enrollment on account of "their poor hygiene, competitiveness, and 'disdain for athletics.'"[95]

Environment versus Predisposition

Theories abound as to why Jews excelled in basketball during the first half of the twentieth century. The quintessential urban game, it required limited space and could be played indoors or out. Baseball, by contrast required open playing fields. The problem with this ecological theory is that there are many other sports that could be played within the confines of the city, and the absence of suitable space and certain facilities may hamper but not necessarily completely curtail the pursuit of excellence. Indeed, some 80 percent of the first professional baseball players came from urban areas despite the fact that only 25 percent of Americans lived in cities at that time.[96] Stereotypes aside, the fact is that not all New York Jews lived in densely populated tenement districts, nor did all of America's Jews live in urban areas as dense as the Lower East Side. Sandy Koufax hailed from Brooklyn. The borough's parks and playgrounds may have been a better incubator for baseball than lower Manhattan's crowded streets, although in Bensonhurst, too, basketball was the preferred sport for athletic Jews. And it was the one in which the young Koufax first excelled.[97] Although environment plays a role (the South is not known for its hockey players), it is mediated by other factors. Among them are the meaning of specific sports for national, regional, or ethnic cultures; the economic possibilities versus the importance of amateurism of sports for various groups according to the strategies individuals within them pursue or eschew for social mobility; and the constraints imposed by various social agencies and variously accepted by members of a group who if they see themselves as upwardly mobile might therefore be inclined to abide by them. Certainly, in this case one would have to consider the role of the settlement houses and institutions both public and communal in channeling immigrant children off the streets and into supervised play—on courts and in swimming pools.

Achievement of American Jews in basketball led to some interesting speculation about the suitability of specific athletic activity to particular ethnic groups. One sports aficionado of the 1930s attributed the affinity of Jews for shooting hoops to the sport's "premium on an alert, scheming mind . . . flashy trickiness, artful dodging and general smart aleckness," qualities that appealed to "the Hebrew with his oriental background."[98] Baseball, by contrast, is a gentleman's game and how would immigrants of an East European Jewish provenance and their children be able to master the nature of the game? Jews were conditioned through centuries of petty commerce, so the mid-1930s argument went, to be sharp of wit and quick with the hand. The Jew was suited for an individualist sport like boxing, but not a team sport like baseball.[99] Others saw the Jewish physique as unsuitable to some sports—the reputed tendency toward flatfootedness early in their careers would impede the Jew's ability to run the bases swiftly, according to one observer who also noted the same physical defect among Italians. In the case of Jews, the cause, at least as reported to him from a Jewish player, was that "his people got that way centuries ago because they had had to trudge through the desert on their flight from Egypt."[100] On a more positive note, intelligence is often attributed to the Jewish athlete and his or her effectiveness. That same cunning was used deftly by Jewish hoopsters while their reputed unique sense of balance and speed made them formidable challengers on the court. One Jewish sports commentator attributed Jewish excellence in basketball specifically to the Jewish mind, arguing in a CCNY editorial that no other sport necessitated "the characteristics inherent in the Jew . . . mental agility, perception . . . imagination and subtlety."[101]

Even if the Jewish mind is not the source of Jewish excellence in select sports, cultural values (or social values imbued with cultural ones) may in fact channel athletes away from some avenues and into others. George Eisen considers the abhorrence of blood sport one reason for Jewish prominence in European fencing, especially in Hungary where they dominated the field. "What suits Jewish middle- and upper-middle-class sensibilities is that the participants retain the ability to control violence."[102] The *Forverts's* *bintl brif* respondent promoted baseball among Jewish youth precisely because it was physical, but not "the really wild . . . aristocratic game in the colleges" football.[103]

Clearly, class plays as much of a role in regard to culturally prescribed or proscribed sports as does inherent cultural sensibility. And where and among whom Jews lived and how they positioned themselves and their aspirations within the social hierarchy would have considerable effect on Jewish physicality. Early twentieth-century immigrant areas were often tough neighborhoods and turf rivalry among ethnic groups made physical strength a desirable attribute. At the very least, it provided a community-serving role for Jewish toughs[104] and sometimes for Jewish teams and fans when threatened by anti-Semitic hooligans. Franklin Foer devoted a whole chapter in his book on soccer and globalization to Jews and sports, paying particular attention to the early twentieth-century Viennese soccer club HaKoah. The club ran wrestling and boxing clubs as well, some of whose members were drawn upon to provide the team with security—a service they eventually provided for community institutions.[105] But even where ethnic rivalry was less of a factor, Jews shared some of the tastes and leisure pursuits of other members of their socioeconomic class as Todd Endelman indicates in his account of Jews and prizefighting in late eighteenth- and early nineteenth-century London.[106]

For many, the physical prowess of the exceptional Jew was a point of pride, offering a sense that "we could do that too." The half-Jewish boxer Max Baer made much of his Jewishness by wearing a star of David on his trunks when he fought Hitler's favorite boxer Max Schmelling. Philip Roth, convinced that the memory of pogroms had fostered among Jewish families of his youth "the idea that our worth as human beings, even perhaps our distinction as a people, was embodied in the *incapacity* to penetrate the sort of bloodletting visited upon our ancestors."[107] But he recalls a fascination with boxing as an adolescent and hearing about the prowess of famous Jewish boxers from his father and friends. Then he notes the following:

> And yet Jewish boxers and boxing aficionados remained, like boxing itself, "sport" in the bizarre sense, a strange deviation from the norm and interesting largely for that reason: in the world whose values first formed me, unrestrained physical aggression was considered contemptible everywhere else. I could no more smash a nose with a fist than fire a pistol into someone's heart. And what imposed this restraint, if not on Slapsie Maxie Rosenblum, then on me, was my being Jewish. In my scheme of things, Slapsie Maxie was a more miraculous Jewish phenomenon by far than Dr. Albert Einstein.[108]

Roth isn't the only observer to compare Einstein unfavorably to Jewish pugilists. Commenting on the spectacular success of Benny Leonard, one Jewish pundit declared Leonard greater than the Jewish mathematician "for he was not only known by millions but understood by them as well."[109]

Roth's comments point to one of the characteristics of sport as play: In reversing some aspect of everyday reality, it confirms the very reality it overturns.[110] For a group such as American Jews simultaneously undergoing Americanization and embourgeoisement, Jews in the ring must have provided substantial relief from the inner pressures to conform—and how much more so during the period of rising anti-Semitism. At the same time, there was clearly something liberating in this mastery of a physicality that ought to be the very antithesis of Jewish masculinity, suggesting an ability of Jews (as in European fencing) to hijack the ultimate symbols of a dominating culture, and, in so doing, reassuring themselves collectively of their physical potential whether or not members of the group chose to actualize it.

So, I answer the question, why sports? with the following observation: Why not? It's a rich enough subject, particularly so when viewed through the lens of citizenship. Indeed, this volume is as much about Jews and sports as it is about Jews and modernity and their place within the public sphere. Given the increasing significance of sports in the modern world—and there is much evidence of a search for self-determination among many people through sports communities[111]—I cannot think of a better window, and one less adequately considered, onto the modern Jewish experience. And for those who scoff at the significance of topics such as this for Jewish studies, I'll close with Saul Lieberman's aphorism about the work of Gershom Scholem: "Nonsense is nonsense, but the study of nonsense is science."

Notes

1. John Hoberman, "Why Jews Play Sports," *Moment* (April 1991): 34–39, 42.

2. Hoberman, "Why Jews Play Sports," 42.

3. Manfred Laemmer, "King Herod's Endowment to the Olympic Games," in *Proceedings of the Pre-Olympic Seminar on the History of Physical Education and Sport in Asia* (Netanyah: Wingate Institute, 1972), 31–50.

4. Manfred Laemmer, "Physical Education and Sports in the Jewish History and Culture," in *Proceedings from an International Seminar on Physical Education and Sport in the Jewish History and Culture* (Netanyah: Wingate Institute, 1973), 63.

5. Andrew Handler, *From the Ghetto to the Games: Jewish Athletes in Hungary* (Boulder, Col.: East European Monographs, 1985), v.

6. Ben Khayim, "The Porters of Warsaw," in *From a Ruined Garden: The Memorial Books of Polish Jewry*, ed. Jack Kugelmass and Jonathan Boyarin (Bloomington: Indiana University Press, 1998), 84.

7. Yehiam Soreq, "Rabbinic Aspects of Physical Culture and Sport among Medieval and Renaissance Jewry," in *Proceedings from an International Seminar* (Netanyah: Wingate Institute, 1981), 39–45.

8. Yehiam Soreq, "Rabbinic Aspects of Physical Culture and Sport among Medieval and Renaissance Jewry, 44.

9. Uriel Simri cited in Danny Rosenberg, "Maimonides on Physical Exercise," in *Proceedings, 5th Canadian Symposium on the History of Sport and Physical Education* (Toronto: University of Toronto, 1982), 267–74.

10. Eric Hobsbawm, "Mass-Producing Traditions: Europe, 1870–1914," in *The Invention of Tradition*, ed. Eric Hobsbawm and Terrence Ranger (Cambridge: Cambridge University Press, 1983), 288–90.

11. Steven A. Riess, "Sport and the Redefinition of Middle-Class Masculinity in Victorian America," in *The New American Sport History: Recent Approaches and Perspectives*, ed. S. W. Pope (Urbana: University of Illinois Press, 1997), 185.

12. John Kasson, *Rudeness and Civility: Manners in Nineteenth-Century Urban America.* (New York: Hill and Wang, 1990), 256.

13. See Mordecai Richler's very funny review of Bernard Postal, Jesse Silver, and Roy Silver's *Encyclopedia of Jews in Sports* (New York: Bloch, 1955) in Mordecai Richler, *Hunting Tigers Under Glass: Essays and Reports* (London: Weidenfeld and Nicolson, 1968), 54–57.

14. Three important ones to note were published in *Sport History*, which has a strong historical and international perspective to the essays; two separate collections appeared in *American Jewish History* and these obviously with a strictly American focus.

15. Noel Dyck, "Games, Bodies, Celebrations and Boundaries: Anthropological Perspectives on Sport," in *Games, Sports and Cultures*, ed. Noel Dyck (New York: Berg, 2000), 31.

16. Daniel Boyarin, *Unheroic Conduct: The Rise of Heterosexuality and the Invention of the Jewish Man* (Berkeley: University of California Press, 1997).

17. Maurice Roche, *Mega-Events and Modernity: Olympics and Expos in the Growth of Global Culture* (London: Routledge, 2000), 224.

18. Richard Giulianotti and Gary Armstrong, "Introduction: Reclaiming the Game—An Introduction to the Anthropology of Football," in *Entering the Field: New Perspectives on World Football*, ed. Richard Giulianotti and Gary Armstrong (New York: Berg, 1997), 6.

19. David Kertzer, *Ritual, Politics, and Power* (New Haven, Conn.: Yale University Press, 1988), 74. See also Dale A. Herbeck, "'Three Strikes and You're Out': The Role of Sports Metaphors in Political Discourse," in *The Cooperstown Symposium on Baseball and American Culture*, ed. Peter Rutkoff (Jefferson, NC: McFarland, 1999), 133–46.

20. Peter C. Neuman, *Bronfman Dynasty: The Rothchilds of the New World* (Toronto: McClelland and Stewart, 1978), 265–68.

21. Simon Kuper, *Ajax, the Dutch, the War: Football in Europe During the Second World War* (London: Orion, 2003), 187.

22. For globalization and Latin American baseball, see Alan Klein, *Sugarball: The American Game, The Dominican Dream* (New Haven: Yale University Press, 1991). For a quirky discussion of soccer and globalization with an interesting chapter on Jews and soccer, see Franklin Foer, *How Soccer Explains the World: An Unlikely Theory of Globalization* (New York: HarperCollins, 2004), esp. 65–88.

23. See, for example, Janet Lever, *Soccer Madness* (Chicago: University of Chicago Press, 1983), 124–30.

24. Michael Alexander, *Jazz Age Jews* (Princeton: Princeton University Press, 2001), 37.

25. Sander Gilman, *Fat Boys* (Lincoln: University of Nebraska Press, 2004), 210.

26. Robert F. Kennedy, "A Bold Proposal for American Sport," *Sports Illustrated,* July 1964, 13.

27. John F. Kennedy, "The Soft American," *Sports Illustrated,* December 1960, 16.

28. John J. MacAloon, "Olympic Games and the Theory of Spectacle in Modern Societies," in *Rite, Drama, Festival, Spectacle: Rehearsal Toward a Theory of Cultural Performance,* ed. John MacAloon (Philadelphia: Ishi, 1984), 241.

29. These figures are very hard to corroborate and more detailed analysis proves them an exaggeration. Nevertheless, they do point to the remarkable size of the Olympic audience and to the role of global television in expanding that audience. For an analysis of the figures, see Miquel de Moragas Spa, Nancy K. Rivenburgh, and James F. Larson, *Television in the Olympics* (London: John Libbey, 1995), 213.

30. Toby Miller, Geoffrey Lawrence, Jim McKay, and David Rowe, *Globalization and Sport: Playing the World* (London: Sage Publications, 2001), 55.

31. For a description of the counter-Olympics in 1936, see Edward Shapiro, "The World Labor Athletic Carnival of 1936: An American Anti-Nazi Protest," *American Jewish History* 74, no. 3 (March 1985): 255–73.

32. Simon Kuper, "The World's Game Is Not Just a Game," *New York Times Magazine,* May 26, 2002, 39.

33. George Mosse, *The Image of Man: The Creation of Modern Masculinity* (New York: Oxford University Press, 1996), esp. 151–53.

34. Irving Howe, with Kenneth Libo, *World of Our Fathers* (New York: Harcourt Brace Jovanovich, 1976), 182.

35. Foer, *How Soccer Explains the World,* 74.

36. Gerald R. Gems, "Sport and the Forging of a Jewish-American Culture: The Chicago Hebrew Institute," *American Jewish History* 83, no. 1 (1995): 25.

37. Richler, *Hunting Tigers Under Glass,* 61.

38. Milton Gross, ed., "I'm Only Human," *Look,* December 31, 1963, 55.

39. "The Kid from Brooklyn," *Time,* September 14, 1959, 56.

40. Melvin Durslag, "Sandy Koufax: The Strikeout King," *Saturday Evening Post,* July14–21, 1962, 69.

41. Gross, "I'm Only Human," 51–56.

42. Esther Romeyn and Jack Kugelmass, *Let There Be Laughter: Jewish Humor in America* (Chicago: Spertus Press, 1997), 66–72.

43. For feminist critiques of the coverage of women in *Sports Illustrated,* see Gina Daddario, *Women's Sport and Spectacle: Gendered Television Coverage and the Olympic Games* (Westport, Conn.: Praeger, 1998), 17–18.

44. Eduardo P. Archetti, "Masculinity and Football: The Formation of National Identity in Argentina," in *Game Without Frontiers: Football, Identity and Modernity,* ed. Richard Giulianotti and John Williams (Vermont: Ashgate, 1994), 236.

45. It was not until the 1920s that women entered the Olympics in a significant way. Earlier, cultural assumptions considered the ideal female body—of the middle and upper classes—as too delicate to attain the physical prowess and agil-

ity necessary to compete. The emergence of female athletes did not eliminate such assumptions, and consequently the muscular female body was linked with lesbianism; as S. K. Cahn notes, "'female athleticism' became culturally coded as 'contrary to heterosexual appeal, which appeared to rest on women's difference from and deference to men.'" Such ideas clearly link sports and masculinity while significant events such as paired figure skating spectacularize "normative heterosexuality, 'pairing' a masculine male with a feminine female in routinized rituals of romance." Cited in Kay Schaffer and Sidonie Smith, "Introduction," in *The Olympics at the Millennium*, ed. Kay Schaffer and Sidonie Smith (New Brunswick, N.J.: Rutgers University Press, 2000), 11.

46. Arguing against critics of sports who see in such exhibitions the disciplining of the body to the spectators' gazes, Guttmann believes the evidence is overwhelming "that men's and women's sports experiences can be and often have been suffused with a sense of erotic pleasure." Allen Guttmann, *The Erotic in Sports* (New York: Columbia University Press, 1996), 172.

47. G. Ralph Strohl III, "The 1913 World Series and the Epic Imagination," in Rutkoff, *Cooperstown Symposium on Baseball and American Culture*, 41–55.

48. Cited in Mark Harris, "Horatio at the Bat, or Why Such a Lengthy Embryonic Period for the Serious Baseball Novel," *Aethlon: The Journal of Sport Literature* 2 (Spring 1988): 1–11.

49. Jane Leavy, *Sandy Koufax: A Lefty's Legacy* (New York: Harper Collins, 2002), 174.

50. Leavy, *Sandy Koufax*, 172.

51. Alan Cowell, "Israeli Arabs Exulting in a Rare Triumph," *New York Times*, May 20, 2004, A8.

52. Philip Roth, *Reading Myself and Others* (New York: Penguin, 1985), 181.

53. Pierre Bourdieu, "How Can One Be a Sports Fan?" in *The Cultural Studies Reader*, ed. Simon During (New York: Routledge, 1993), 348.

54. Peter Levine, *Ellis Island to Ebbets Field: Sport and the American Jewish Experience* (New York: Oxford University Press, 1992), 15.

55. Levine, *Ellis Island to Ebbets Field*, 15.

56. Cary Goodman, *Choosing Sides: Playground and Street Life on the Lower East Side* (New York: Schocken Books, 1979), 111.

57. Gertrude Pfister and Toni Niewerth, "Jewish Women in Gymnastics and Sport in Germany 1898–1938," *Journal of Sport History* 26, no. 2 (Summer 1999): 293.

58. "*Der iker fun di beysbol 'geym,' erklert far di nit-keyn sportslayt*," *Forverts*, August 27, 1909.

59. Harry Litwack cited in Peter Levine, "Basketball and the Jewish-American Community 1920s-1930s," in *Major Problems in American Sport History: Documents and Essays*, ed. Steven Riess (Boston: Houghton Mifflin, 1997), 306.

60. Milton Klonsky cited in Levine, "Basketball and the Jewish-American Community," in Riess, *Major Problems*, 306.

61. In his essay on Lester Harrison, the Jewish owner of the Rochester Royals basketball team from 1945–57, Donald Fisher relates an episode in which Harrison hired a player named Levane, assuming that the man was a Jew. When he found out otherwise, Harrison told him, "Get me a Jewish player. I don't care if he can play or not. Just make sure he's a Jew." Players who sat on the bench but were hired for audience appeal were called "sticks." Donald M. Fisher, "Lester Harri-

son and the Rochester Royals, 1945–1957: A Jewish Entrepreneur in the NBA," in *Sports and the American Jew*, ed. Steven A. Riess (Syracuse, N.Y.: Syracuse University Press, 1998), 228.

62. Tilden G. Edelstein, "Cohen at the Bat," *Commentary* 76, no. 5 (November 1983): 55.

63. Paul Gallico quoted in Levine, *Ellis Island to Ebbets Field*, 114.

64. "Casey at the Bat, A Ballad of the Republic," a poem by "Phin" (Ernest L. Thayer), *Daily Examiner of San Francisco*, June 3, 1888, 4.

65. Edelstein, "Cohen at the Bat," 54.

66. Richard Pioreck, "Baseball and Vaudeville and the Development of Popular Culture in the United States, 1880–1930," in Rutkoff, *Cooperstown Symposium on Baseball and American Culture*, 83.

67. Michel Rosenberg, "Getsl at the Ball Game." *Getzel bay a beyzbol geym* (New York: Banner Records, 193[?]).

68. Stephen Provizer cited in Riess, *Sports and the American Jew*, 56. Interestingly, the same story is told about another reputed creator of this song, Jack Norworth. Pioreck, "Baseball and Vaudeville," 93.

69. Goodman, *Choosing Sides*, 89.

70. Riess, *Sports and the American Jew*, 56.

71. Hoberman, "Why Jews Play Sports," 39.

72. John M. Hoberman, *Sport and Political Ideology* (Austin: University of Texas Press, 1984), 163.

73. Hoberman, *Sport and Political Ideology*, 166.

74. Mike Cronin, *Sport and Nationalism in Ireland: Gaelic Games, Soccer and Irish Identity Since 1884* (Dublin: Four Courts Press, 1999), 70.

75. Dag Tuastad, "The Political Role of Football for Palestinians in Jordan," in Giulianotti and Armstrong, *Entering the Field*, 105–21.

76. Arjun Appadurai, "Playing with Modernity: The Decolonization of Indian Cricket," in *Consuming Modernity: Public Culture in a South Asian World*, ed. Carol A. Breckenridge (Minneapolis: University of Minnesota Press, 1995), 42.

77. Roni Gechtman, "Socialist Mass Politics through Sport: The Bund's Morgnshtern in Poland, 1926–1939," *Journal of Sport History* 26, no. 3 (Summer 1999): 326–52.

78. Norbert Elias, "Introduction," in *Quest for Excitement: Sport and Leisure in the Civilizing Process*, ed. Norbert Elias and Eric Dunning (London: Basil Blackwell, 1986), 54.

79. Schaffer and Smith, "Introduction," in *Olympics at the Millennium*, 6.

80. Erving Goffman, *Encounters: Two Studies in the Sociology of Interaction* (New York: MacMillan, 1986), 71–72.

81. Janet Lever, *Soccer Madness*, 148.

82. MacAloon, "Olympic Games and the Theory of Spectacle in Modern Societies," in MacAloon, *Rite, Drama, Festival, Spectacle*, 275.

83. Arnd Kruger, "'Once the Olympics Are Through, We'll Beat Up the Jew': German Jewish Sport 1898–1938 and the Anti-Semitic Discourse," *Journal of Sport History* 26, no. 2 (Summer 1999): 358.

84. Allen Guttmann, "The 'Nazi Olympics' and the American Boycott Controversy," in *Sport and International Politics*, ed. Pierre Arnaud and James Riordan (New York: E and FN Spon, 1998), 46.

85. Pfister and Niewerth, "Jewish Women in Gymnastics and Sport," 317.

86. Kuper, "The World's Game Is Not Just a Game," 39.

87. Bourdieu, "How Can One Be a Sports Fan?" 344.

88. Pierre Bourdieu, "Sport and Social Class," *Social Science Information* 17, no. 6 (1978): 828.

89. George Eisen, "Jewish History and the Ideology of Modern Sport: Approaches and Interpretations," *Journal of Sport History* 25, no. 3 (Fall 1998): 500.

90. Anthony Hughes, "Sport in the Australian Jewish Community," *Journal of Sport History* 26, no. 2 (Summer 1999): 381.

91. James M. Mayo, *The American Country Club: Its Origins and Development* (New Brunswick, N.J.: Rutgers University Press, 1998), 30.

92. Peter Levine, "The American Hebrew Looks at 'Our Crowd': The Jewish Country Club in the 1920s," *American Jewish History* 83, no. 1 (1995): 35.

93. John Hoberman, *Darwin's Athletes: How Sports Has Damaged Black America and Preserved the Myth of Race* (Boston: Houghton Mifflin, 1997), xxv.

94. Dan A. Oren, *Joining the Club: A History of Jews and Yale* (New Haven, Conn.: Yale University Press, 1985), 85–86.

95. Eisen, "Jewish History and the Ideology of Modern Sport," 514.

96. Steven Riess, "Professional Sports as an Avenue of Social Mobility in America: Some Myths and Realities," in *Essays on Sport History and Sport Mythology,* ed. Allen Guttmann, Richard D. Mandell, Steven A. Riess, Stephen Hardy, and Donald G. Kyle (College Station: University of Texas at Arlington Press, 1990), 103.

97. Leavy, *Sandy Koufax,* 37.

98. Paul Gallico cited in Levine, "Basketball and the Jewish-American Community," in Riess, *Major Problems,* 299.

99. Edward G. White, *Creating the National Pastime* (Princeton: Princeton University Press, 1996), 258.

100. Edelstein, "Cohen at the Bat," 55.

101. Stanley Frank cited in Levine, "Basketball and the Jewish-American Community," in Riess, *Major Problems,* 299.

102. Eisen, "Jewish History and the Ideology of Modern Sport," 495.

103. Irving Howe and Kenneth Libo, *How We Lived: A Documentary History of Immigrant Jews in America* (New York: R. Marek, 1979), 52.

104. Gems, "Sport and the Forging of a Jewish-American Culture," 23.

105. Foer, *How Soccer Explains the World,* 72–73.

106. Todd M. Endelman, *The Jews of Georgian England 1714–1830: Tradition and Change in a Liberal Society* (Philadelphia: Jewish Publication Society, 1979), 219–26.

107. Philip Roth, *The Facts: A Novelist's Autobiography* (New York: Farrar, Straus & Giroux, 1988), 28.

108. Roth, *The Facts,* 28.

109. Gems, "Sport and the Forging of a Jewish-American Culture," 23.

110. For a summary of the arguments on play and counterculture, see Brian Sutton Smith, "The Idealization of Play: The Relationship between Play and Sport," in *Sport and Social Theory,* ed. C. Roger Rees and Andrew W. Miracle (Champaign, Ill.: Human Kinetics, 1986), 85–106.

111. Giulianotti and Armstrong, "Introduction: Reclaiming the Game—An Introduction to the Anthropology of Football," in Giulianotti and Armstrong, *Entering the Field,* 12.

JOHN HOBERMAN

2 "How Fiercely That Gentile Rides!": Jews, Horses, and Equestrian Style

Not many modern readers are likely to be familiar with the idea that a Jew cannot properly ride a horse. When it became known, for example, during the New York mayoral campaign of 2001, that candidate Michael Bloomberg's children were equestrians, the salient point was not whether they could ride with the requisite skill, but rather that this hobby placed their only vaguely Jewish father, as the *Forward* phrased it, "at the assimilated end of the spectrum." The latent cultural problem, at least for those Jews who were old enough to remember it, concerned not the Jews' ability to ride, but the propriety of their riding at all. As the *Forward* headline put it: "Bloomberg's Test: Will New York Vote for a Jew Who 'Rides Horses'?"[1] In fact, New York did, although this result certainly had little to do with the future mayor's willingness to pay for his children's riding lessons. What is of interest here is that the forgotten role of equestrian ambition in promoting the assimilation of American Jewry had reappeared long after its relevance to American social life had disappeared. Defying the odds against the survival of racial folklore that has outlived its time, the idea that there is a problematic relationship between Jews and horses had demonstrated its ability to survive in public life into the twenty-first century.

The purpose of this essay is to show how ideas about Jews and horses can contribute to our understanding of the Jewish experience over the past two centuries. More specifically, we will see how ideas about the Jew's estrangement from equestrian experience can help us understand the

Jewish male predicament that developed in Europe during the nineteenth century.[2] For it was during this time that Jews moved out of their European ghettos and began to mix, and compete, with the gentile majority in a broad range of public and professional venues. This gradual process of social assimilation was accompanied by many conflicts, both overt and subtle, between Jewish norms and those of the societies Jews were now entering as professional men, along with their claims to civic and social status and the masculine dignity such roles implied. In a social world in which foxhunting on horseback or military service in the cavalry served as evidence of manhood and social respectability, equestrian skills played an important role as evidence of masculine virtue and the requisite affiliations with people of distinction.

But if equestrian skill and experience could do much to make a man, then a lack of rapport with horses could do as much to disqualify him from authentic manhood and social respectability. One perspective simply disassociated Jews and horses as a fact of nature. "Arabs," the great nineteenth-century explorer Richard Burton remarked, "are just Jews on horseback."[3] More frequently, however, the anti-Semitic observer makes it clear that the aesthetic effect presented by the combination of Jew and horse is distasteful, and that a dignified norm has somehow been violated. Numerous recorded opinions testify to the unpleasant effects of the Jews' equestrian deficit.[4] As that sickly adulator of physical vitality, Friedrich Nietzsche, once put it: "The way a Jew mounts a horse is worth thinking about."[5] At a time when the body language of the Jew was being read as evidence of racial difference and pathology, the Jew's alleged inability to establish rapport with a horse stood out as a kind of anthropological defect that confirmed his alien and deficient essence. A similar exploitation of the grotesque disparity between the caricatured Jew and noble horse appears in a Frenchman's retrospective account of the triumphal German march through a humiliated Paris in 1871 following the Franco-Prussian War: "Behind the Centaurs, covered with armour and gleaming metal, there advanced like pairs of tongs astride their horses, a strange group of persons dressed in long, padded brown great-coats. They had drawn faces and golden spectacles, long hair, dirty auburn beards twirled into cork-screws, wide-brimmed hats. These were the Jewish bankers . . . following the German army like vultures." The obscene incongruity that results from putting these unmartial shylocks on horseback is, of course, an anti-Semitic provocation on the part of the author, one René Lagrange, who published this reminiscence in *Figaro* in 1883.[6] In this scene, the aesthetic offense against the partnership of man and horse accentuates the racial contrast between the Germanic conquerors, whom the admiring Frenchman calls "aristocratic warriors," and the distasteful Jews, who are cast as physically awkward parasites who feed on Frenchman and German alike. Putting them on horses was calculated to give the observer's indignation a sharper edge.

The exclusion of Jews from the world of equestrian experience is also an exclusion from the realm of nature itself. The fact that many Eastern European Jews lived in rural communities and engaged in rural occupations such as farming and woodcutting was not incorporated into the predominant Jewish stereotype. Centuries of confinement in the urban ghettos of Europe persuaded the Western imagination that Jews had always been exiled from the countryside and its fertile soil, from the rhythm of the seasons, the rituals of planting and harvesting, the bonds with animals who lived and died by the farmer's hand. This inexhaustible universe of life in all of its forms became a prodigious source of ideas about the ways in which Jewish mind and bodies were different from other men. "Always the newcomers, Jews didn't love humus, or the soil, or the exaltation of forests. They understandably mistrusted a pastoral lyricism and nationalist impulse invoked to shut them out."[7] As this passage suggests, Jews could embrace as well as resent the exile from the natural world that Christian Europe had imposed on them. We might call this withdrawal from nature one Jewish response to exclusion, whose tiny echoes would eventually include early twenty-first-century gossip about Michael Bloomberg's children and their horses. In the meantime, Jews might simply resign themselves to their unnatural condition and leave the outdoor life to the *goyim* who were better adapted to its ordeals. This retreat from nature was described by Walter Lippmann in 1922 with a dry detachment that conveyed a certain scorn for communing with nature at all: "It happens that the Jews, for good or evil, have no court or country-house tradition of high living, and little of the physical grace that just barely makes that mode of life tolerable."[8] This country-house tradition included, of course, that ritual bonding with the animal kingdom known as foxhunting, and we will see how Anglo Jewry dealt with this English ritual in its own way.

But the idea of a Jewish estrangement from nature could also be presented as a matter of Jewish principle. "Might it be that Judaism and nature are at odds?" Steven S. Schwarzschild asked in 1984, and his answer was an unhesitating yes. "The main line of philosophy (in the exilic age) has paradigmatically defined Jewishness as alienation from and confrontation with nature. . . . We can, therefore, quite peremptorily dismiss the notion that nature is sacred." Here the Jewish retreat from nature has acquired the status of a wisdom that further accentuates Jewish cultural difference. Although well aware that "a back-to-nature thrust inheres in the Zionist enterprise," this Jewish ecologist and vegetarian insists on the priority of morality over aesthetics. From this perspective, it is a Jewish obligation to resist the pantheism that confers sacred status on the natural world.[9] In a similar vein, Judaism refuses to grant divinity to animals while preserving their status as feeling creatures deserving of respect. The mystique of the symbiosis between horse and rider is, for this reason, incompatible with the Jewish sensibility of the transatlantic Diaspora. Even the "back-to-nature" movement cultivated by the early Zionists was tempered by the idea that, for the Jews, nature was an urgent form of therapy rather than an opportunity for exuberant or reverent emotion.[10] Jewish reluctance to be absorbed into the experience of nature is also expressed in the shtetl saying that "even when he turns farmer, a Jew is not a peasant."[11]

The commandment to practice abstinence from the beauties and profundities of the natural order has never prevailed among modern Jews. The Romantic heritage, National Geographic, and the lure of assimilation throughout the Diaspora have made sure of that. What do persist, however, are cultural memories of the conflict between the seductive appeals of nature and the internalized restraints, born of principle or culturally acquired inhibition, that have made Jews self-conscious about surrendering to the charms of the natural creation. Jewish unfamiliarity with or disorientation within the natural world thus became a part of a racial folklore that has been absorbed both by the Jews it purports to describe and by non-Jews who take an interest, for whatever reason, in what it means to be Jewish. By the second half of the twentieth century, Jewish novelists had acquired sufficient perspective on the sources of such unease to understand the comic or pathetic scenarios such Jewish discomfort with nature offered to the literary imagination.

The novels of Aharon Appelfeld, who was born in Bukowina and later emigrated to Israel, are filled with strange or uncomfortable encounters between his Central European Jewish characters and the natural world around them. In The Slave (1962), Isaac Bashevis Singer's Jewish protagonist Jakob is enslaved into a natural paradise to which he adapts even as it is darkened by the perversities of the peasant savages—the true nature dwellers—among whom he lives. "He had been here so long now and had become so acquainted with the plants that he could detect the odor of each flower and each variety of grass."[12] Only abduction into this landscape had revealed this sensual knowledge to the Jewish city dweller, who now is awed by the grandeur of the mountain landscape and the flora and fauna it sustains. The anxiety-ridden protagonist of Bruce Jay

Friedman's novel *Stern* (1962), a black comedy of Jewish adaptation to suburban life, is haunted by his inability to keep plants alive. "Stern was sickened by the diseased shrubs; it was not so much their appearance that troubled him but the feeling that he had betrayed a sacred trust," a failure witnessed by gentile neighbors who, he assumes, live in effortless harmony with the natural creation.[13] Bernard Malamud's novel *A New Life* (1961) follows a shy New Yorker to a rural college town located in the forests of Oregon. In this wilderness setting, Malamud explores not a Jewish disability vis-à-vis nature, but rather a Jewish yearning for nature that stops short of ecstatic pantheism because it is tempered by an older Jewish unease about nature's hard laws and dangerous creatures.[14] Twentieth-century Jewish experience will not, in the last analysis, abolish this tension. Although fictional Jews who leave Europe for the New World do acquire a new freedom to appreciate the wonders of nature, they cannot entirely escape their own apprehensions about nature's violence and the shame implied in a surrender to the pagan ecstasies of nature worship.

More than any other natural domain, it was the animal realm that provided many opportunities for speculating about the strangeness of the Jews and their special powers or weaknesses. Given the uncanny or fiendish roles that Jews had played in the European imagination over many centuries, it is not surprising that German folklore encouraged the belief that Jews could understand the language of the animals, or that Richard Wagner described Jews as "calculating beasts of prey."[15] Contrary to the anti-Semitic Wagner, Jews often adopted the animal metaphor to identify themselves—not as predators, but as prey in a hostile world. This dramatic convention, which exposes the Jew to the cruel impulses of the hunter, appears repeatedly in *Ivanhoe* (1819). "Think not so vilely of us, Jews though we be," says Isaac of York; "the hunted fox, the tortured wild-cat loves its young—the despised and persecuted race of Abraham love their children!" In a similar vein, the violent knight Front-de-Boeuf advances slowly "towards the Jew, upon whom he kept his eye fixed, as if he wished to paralyse him with his glance, as some animals are said to fascinate their prey." These scenes of terror point to Scott's interest in the psychology of the Jew's fear, hence his analysis of Isaac's state of mind as the latter hopes to be "delivered as a prey from the fowler."[16]

The sadistic amusement the hunter-prey scenario makes possible reappears in many venues in which Jews are hunted by their enemies, including the work of an obscure English anti-Semite who titles his insulting tract *The Jew at Bay* (1933). Jewish writers have also employed this drama of the hunter and the hunted from their own perspectives. In

"Crusade," a short story by Israeli writer Amos Oz, the narrator attributes to medieval Jews the same ambiance of paralysis and animal-like fear that inspired such keen interest in Sir Walter Scott: "Outwardly they were calm, but a closer inspection would have betrayed a nervous muscular spasm in their faces, like the ripples on the skin of a deer standing in feigned repose, poised for flight."[17] Heinrich Heine's feelings of empathy for hunted animals belonged to a traditional Jewish sensibility that felt horror at every manifestation of the predatory impulse: "The taste for hunting is in the blood. . . . My ancestors, however, belonged not to the hunters but rather to the hunted, and my blood would revolt if I were to shoot at the descendants of their former colleagues [Kollegen]." Shmuel Almog points out that Heine's "solidarity with the victim" and his "disgust for aristocratic pleasure" are two aspects of his Jewish sensibility.[18] For Jews, the obscenity of hunting lay in "the desire to hunt for its own sake," a desire that revealed a shameful capacity to take "a noble pleasure in hunting."[19] Indeed, Jews associated nobility itself with predatory instincts and behaviors, while the nobility often adopted for their heraldic signs "birds of prey or the rampant postures of aggressive animals."[20] Here, too, animal symbolism dramatized profound differences between a Jewish ethos of mercy and the harder sentiments of the wider European world in which Jews attempted to find their place.

Purging oneself of the predatory instinct was an obligation that extended beyond the hunting of animals to include the hunting of human beings in war. The same Jewish abhorrence at taking pleasure in killing is evident, for example, in the memoir of a German field rabbi who served during the Great War. The Jewish soldier, he says, must overcome more powerful inhibitions than his gentile counterpart before he can kill, and he "never fires just for sake of firing," or simply because it gives him pleasure to do so.[21] The inflicting of pain and suffering must always serve an urgent need and must never serve to gratify the instincts or the senses. Jews frequently attributed a taste for sadistic pleasure to the aristocracy that was not above unleashing dogs against Jews, a form of terror that left a lasting mark on Jewish memories of Europe.[22]

This sensibility has proliferated in Jewish life over the past couple of centuries. A German-Jewish text on "The Suffering of Animals" (1928) reports that the sadistic treatment of animals is not addressed in Jewish religious literature because such acts have been regarded as too unimaginable for Jews to require proscription.[23] One of the recent manifestations of this Jewish doctrine is the influential animal rights philosophy of Peter Singer, whose commitment to the moral dignity of animals was stimulated by his asthmatic father's sympathy for the gasping victims of recreational fishermen he and his son would encounter during their river walks in England.[24] More than a century earlier, an extreme Anglo-Jewish distress at the spectacle of animal suffering had prompted Lewis Gompertz to publish his "Moral Inquiries on the Situation of Man and Brutes" and cofound the Society for the Prevention of Cruelty to Animals in 1824.[25] The compassion Gompertz showed equine creatures was expressed in his refusal to ride in horse-drawn carriages.[26]

Jewish concern for animals, once known as "sympathy for the brute creation," has long been evident, as we have seen, in the Jewish rejection of hunting, an activity that has always tied horses to killing in the Western imagination.[27] The unfavorable Biblical portrayals of the hunters Nimrod and Esau stand at the beginning of centuries of Jewish distaste for the "sport" of hunting, just as the ancient Hebrews saw the horse as a symbol of war.[28] As historian Israel Abrahams noted a century ago: "Now, as the Jews were frequently forbidden in the middle ages to carry arms, even in Spain, and as, moreover, Jews were never noted riders, it is obvious that the moral objection to sports in which weapons and horses were necessary accessories must have gained overwhelming strength from compulsion. Hunting in particular was resented as cruel, and therefore un-Jewish."[29] Jewish revulsion at the spectacle of animal cruelty of any kind became one aspect of a superior Jewish distinctiveness that separated civilized Jews from gentile savages. A century ago, even a Jewish laborer in England knew the crucial repertory of cultural differences that distinguished him from his "rough, coarse, and tasteless" neighbor, and tender regard for wife and children led the list. "The heart of the average British workman never throbs with any such sentiments," one "Jewish alien workman" confidently asserts; "I doubt whether it beats at all, except, perhaps, when he is engaged in rabbit-coursing, dog-fighting, or other such noble and instructive amusements."[30] Animal cruelty was associated with the all-round coarseness of *goyim* whose instincts were so deranged that they treated their own kin like animals. Conversely, the shtetl Jews of Poland distrusted the peasant who treated his animals better than his family, hence the warning to "beware a man who is good to his horse and beats his wife."[31]

Over many years, the estrangement from hunting pervaded Jewish life so thoroughly that "Jewish" versions of the hunting experience could evolve in the minds of Jews and gentiles alike, playing upon a Jewish propensity to find indirect ways to fulfill the instinct to stalk or kill. "She liked observing people closely: their hands and feet, the way they sat, rested, ate," Aharon Appelfeld says of a character in one of his novels. "It was a soundless hunt which absorbed her for hours."[32] A British merchant banker who had worked closely with enormously successful Anglo-Jewish business magnates such as Sir Isaac Wolfson described their Jewish version of hunting as follows: "Striking a good bargain is a kind of national sport with these heroes, rather like shooting and fox-hunting is with the Tory squires."[33] Such differences in male taste and self-expressive style proliferated throughout the Diaspora during the nineteenth and twentieth centuries. Jews now left the confines of the ghetto and began to work and play and compete with gentile adversaries or companions whose masculine norms had originated in the chivalric ethos that continues to shape idealized versions of male identity to this day. The classic Jewish meditation on the moral and psychological abyss that separates the Jewish temperament from that of the chivalric hero, Maurice Samuel's *The Gentleman and the Jew* (1950), will be called upon in this essay as we interpret the Jewish relationship to equestrian activities.

Racial folklore about Jews and horses focuses primarily on Jewish disabilities that manifest themselves in the equestrian sphere that includes the cavalry and the hunting venues of England and continental Europe. The fundamental theme of this folklore, however, is not that the Jew lacks equestrian skill, but that he simply does not belong in the dynamic male milieu in which man and horse enter into a partnership that can take on the world. Albert Memmi, for example, recalls a friend who, "though a superb horseman with several prizes to his credit . . . was not permitted to enter the cavalry," because "military nobility cannot be shared with a Jew."[34] In this context it is worth noting that the French army evaluations of Captain Alfred Dreyfus included the observation that he "mounts a horse quite well."[35] A generation later, the sight of a little Parisian Jew on a cavalry horse was too much for Henry de Montherlant to endure without prolonged comment. His response to this provocation was to raise the traditional questions about Jewish courage and cowardice under fire.[36] Such episodes make it clear that the equestrian failure of the Jew, when it did occur, was only a symbol of the primal exile from male fellowship that awaited him irrespective of how well or how badly he mounted a horse. As Montherlant says of the amiable little Jew in his story: "He was being as dashing as he could manage, but wasn't quite up to the mark; you can only show off properly on horseback if you have a long heredity behind you." From this perspective, life on horseback is absorbed into a racial essence that can accommodate the mystical union of man and horse.

The sheer oddity of the coupling of Jew and horse has long been acknowledged by Jews themselves. Daniel Boyarin has pointed to Rashi's response, in the early Middle Ages, to a passage that speaks of a "skill-ful knight [*Reiter*]" who is a Jew. "Rashi feels that he has to inform the reader that this man was a Jew, in spite of the fact that this is entirely obvious from the context, precisely because it is so counterintuitive to Jews that there would be a Jewish knight."[37] Maurice Samuel, growing up in England, had heard that every member of King David's elite corps "had to be so strong, and so skillful a rider, that he could at full gallop uproot a sapling without being unhorsed." But for a boy in early twen-tieth-century England, such echoes of equestrian heroism among the ancient Hebrews did not mean that modern Jews could handle horses. Samuel's point is rather that horses belong to a cultural universe where Jews do not belong. This is the virile ethos, embodied in "The Charge of the Light Brigade," that animates "that gay, magnanimous, adventur-ous and gamesome world" to which "the non-Jewish man of the western world" so naturally belongs and Jews do not.[38] "How fiercely that Gentile rides!" exclaims Isaac of York in *Ivanhoe.* Variations on this response to *goyishe* dynamism on horseback will appear over and over in Jewish texts. "A Jew who has mounted a horse has stopped being a Jew and has become a Russian," says one of Isaac Babel's characters.[39] "The supreme *goyishe* gift of all," says Philip Roth's Alex Portnoy, is "the courage and know-how to get up and ride around on a horse."[40] These timid (and envi-ous) aphorisms show how fantasies about horses have made their own contribution to Jewish feelings of inferiority when confronted with the classic male action figures of Western societies: the Crusader, the sport-ing gentleman, and the cowboy.

The fundamental dichotomy between equestrian and Jew has been expressed in a variety of ways. For example, on carnival occasions, the Hassidim of Poland would "ride on horseback, shouting and brandishing wooden swords or whips. They gallop so for miles to meet the wedding party, provoking laughter among the peasants—and scorn among some of the other Jews—who jeer at the 'Jewish Cossacks'."[41] Whereas the point of such excess was to suspend and even invert a Jewish value system, the incongruous aspect of Hassidic equestrianism could also be presented less ironically. "There was a great commotion in the small city," writes Joseph Roth in 1927. "About 200 Hassidim had gotten dressed up, cloth-ing themselves in old Russian garments, buckled on old swords and rode bareback through the city on horses. There were among them good rid-ers who put the lie to all of the bad jokes about Jewish military doctors and how Jews are afraid of horses."[42]

The legendary Jewish fear of large animals cited by Roth has helped some observers explain why Jews are not comfortable with horses. "The

Jew," according to one British anti-Semite, "does not evince deep interest in brood mares, nor would he look twice at a great Clydesdale or a
Hereford bull. He would hasten out of the way of great beasts and keep
a respectful distance."[43] In *A New Life*, Malamud's Jewish protagonist
acts out this fearfulness on several occasions. The pedigreed black bulls
he finds in a barn are "marvelous beasts, but when they bellowed at the
sight of him he quickly left." Even "a hefty, big-uddered white cow" is too
much for him. "Horrified by the immensity of the beast, he retreated, his
hat snapped off by a poplar branch."[44] And the same idea has been heard
outside of fiction. "You couldn't be Jewish," a gentile neighbor once told
one of the Jewish chicken farmers of Petaluma, California. "Jews don't
have bulls."[45]

Horses could also be invoked to define the racial essence of the Jew
against the racial essence of other men. According to Werner Sombart,
the European peoples who "had dwelt on their soil and smelt of the earth
. . . differed from the Jews as a horse of the Ardennes differs from a fiery
Arab charger."[46] Lacking vitality, the Jew resembled a domesticated horse.
Similarly, in the mind of Sir Walter Scott, Ivanhoe was a "war-horse"
while Isaac rode on a mule.[47] Comparing equine and human types produced a typology of character essences that could be judged as superior
or inferior.

Equine symbolism also lent itself to novel formulations of Jewish
self-hatred. It is not surprising, for example, that the tormented Otto
Weininger idealized horses as "aristocratic" creatures and, in contradis-
tinction to the Talmud and the Midrash, praised their sexual discipline.[48]
In *Die Juden von Zirndorf* (1906), Jakob Wassermann describes his idealized young (Jewish) male as a virtual anti-Jew whose eyes are the perfect
antithesis of fearful Jewish eyes: "His smile expressed an extraordinary
mildness. He was handsome and tall. He never ruminated, but only
dreamed. His gaze resembled the unlimited gaze of a horse of noble breed-
ing."[49] Isaac Babel's fascinated and submissive relationship to Cossacks
and their horses—an early analogue of Norman Mailer's Hemingway
complex—is a fine example of Jewish self-abnegation achieved through
the mythifying of the horse.[50] All of these cases demonstrate how pro-
foundly the chivalric tradition has shaped the image of the ideal male in
Western societies.

Eventually, the Jew's equestrian deficiency invited the intervention
of equestrian therapy. In Gustav Freytag's anti-Semitic novel *Debit and
Credit* (*Soll und Haben*, 1855), a Jewish father begs his studious son to
heed the doctor's advice and take up riding as a form of healthy exercise, promising the boy (in typical Jewish fashion) "the most expensive

horse in the city."[51] More specifically, riding might do something to counteract the Jewish nervousness that is discussed, to take one of many examples, by *The Menorah Journal* in 1924. Here we read about how the multiple traumas inflicted on Jews by European history had developed in them a "lack of mental poise" and a "cringing sense of inferiority."[52] Such timidity is wholly incompatible with horsemanship, since the nervous horse is often reacting to "an unskilled rider who, being nervous himself, conveys his own fear to the animal."[53] It thus stands to reason that both man and horse might develop a new confidence in partnership with each other. The idea of such a horse-centered therapy aimed specifically at Jewish deficiencies is coolly satirized by Aharon Appelfeld in *The Retreat* (1984), where the Jewish physical educator and horse-trader Balaban has taken upon himself the task of rehabilitating his physically deficient coreligionists as the Holocaust draws closer. "All I was trying to do," he says, "was teach you the lessons of nature, the virtues of the horse, the benefits of a healthy diet, the cunning of the hunter, the pleasures of sport, and wine. It has nothing to do with preaching. I'm not a preacher, I'm a simple horse farmer. I saw the suffering of my race and I wanted to share my experience with them."[54] Here Appelfeld addresses that complex of interrelated themes—nature, horses, hunting, sport—that once defined what was quintessentially *not* Jewish. From the standpoint of the equestrian reformer, Jewish disease required an Aryan cure. The ideological status of these themes changed, of course, when the state of Israel turned the nature-averse sensibility inside out for the purpose of cultivating the traditional military values that European Jews had spent centuries learning to distrust.

In the real world, the idea of equestrian therapy found articulate defenders among the Nazis. The horse's status as a symbol of war prompted a Nazi ideologist like Hans F. K. Günther to claim there was a special association between horses and "the Nordic race."[55] The importance of equestrian skill among the Germanic knights of the Middle Ages had already been established by Johann Gottfried von Herder, whose vocabulary constantly reiterates the fusion of horsemanship and German manhood: *Reiterei, Reiterzunft, Reitermeister, Ritterwesen, Reitergefolge, Rittergestalt.*[56] Applying this special relationship to the formation of (masculine) character was, therefore, a logical extension of Nordic racial doctrine. So it was a natural development when, along with the Nazi seizure of power, came the new slogan: "Riding—a Sport of the People!"

A pedagogical interpretation of human-equine collaboration was elaborated in a Nazi physical-education periodical in 1939. The author,

Dr. Harald Siems, looks back nostalgically to a medieval era when, as Herder had portrayed it, "equestrian (*reiterliche*) and knightly (*ritterliche*) bearing (*Haltung*)" were one and the same. The aristocratic formation of character at that time was inseparable from the intuitive communication that flowed back and forth between the rider and his mount. "The rider and the horse educate each other," Dr. Siems explained to his readers.[57] In a similar vein, Ernst Göring, a relative of Hermann Göring, joined the SA Riding Corps (*SA-Reitersturm*) and developed a psychotherapy he called "riding therapy" (*Reittherapie*), a technique he was practicing as late as the 1970s.[58]

It is impossible to contemplate the idea of therapeutic horsemanship without thinking of Franz Kafka and the search for health, so moving and so pathetic, that quietly consumed him before his early death from tuberculosis. Kafka admired all physically graceful creatures, whether human acrobats or athletic animals, and thought of them as metaphorical versions of the artist that achieved a perfect freedom from constraint.[59] Because he was an exquisitely self-conscious Jew who paid constant attention to his corporeal inadequacies, Kafka's relationship to the ideal of physical perfection could only be one of longing for an unattainable condition. Given the prominent role of the horse in the racial folklore of his time, it is not surprising that his short prose works include three scenarios involving horses that are ridden by three variations on the idea of the athlete.[60] "Reflections for Gentlemen-Jockeys" is a curiously somber meditation on a rider who has won a horse race. "Up in the Gallery" features a female circus rider who wins an ovation for her "artistic skill." "The Wish to Be a Red Indian" is a breathtaking fantasy ride on horseback experienced by Kafka himself.

These imaginative sketches represent Kafka's conflicted responses to the symbolic potency of the horse. While "Up in the Gallery" and "The Wish to Be a Red Indian" appear to confirm Mark Anderson's observation that "horses and riders often symboliz[e] literary inspiration in Kafka's work," "Reflections for Gentlemen-Jockeys" deflates the romance of horsemanship with single-minded persistence. The triumph associated with victory is not even worth the effort; win or lose, the rider is left with nothing in the way of gratification or fulfillment. Equestrian competition creates no comradeship. The preening male on horseback is simply ridiculous. All in all, the celebrated drama of thundering hoofs produces no satisfaction and is thoroughly discredited by the end of the narrative. Even "Up in the Gallery" begins ominously, as Kafka imagines "a ruthless, whip-flourishing ringmaster" forcing a "frail, consumptive equestrienne" to ride her horse to exhaustion. This nightmare, and its echo of the sadism of "In the Penal Colony," then dissolves into an audience-enchanting performance that, in wrenching contradiction to the promise of a happy ending, leaves the author-observer in a state of despondency.

"The Wish to Be a Red Indian" may be presented in its entirety: "If one were only an Indian, instantly alert, and on a racing horse, leaning against the wind, kept on quivering jerkily over the quivering ground, until one shed one's spurs, for there needed no spurs, threw away the reins, for there needed no reins, and hardly saw that the land before one was smoothly shorn heath when horse's neck and head would already be gone." As tempting as it may be to interpret this compelling fantasy as equestrian romance, it should be noted that it is the experience of being transported, not the horse, that matters here. Unlike his contemporary Weininger, with whom he shared the standard Jewish male insecurities of this era, Kafka does not identify with the aggressor by taking refuge in the "aristocratic" and Aryan myth of the horse. His longing for "the undressed freedom of the animal" (Mark Anderson) is very different from that glorification of equine vitality that symbolizes martial virtue and a masculine style long associated with anti-Semitism.[61] On the contrary, his treatment of equestrian skill, like his treatment of racial folklore in general, is indirectly rather than overtly estranged from the romantic myth of the horse and its daring rider.

The romantic Jewish alternative to Kafka's ironic treatment of the dynamic "racing horse, leaning against the wind" appears in a poem by the Yiddish writer Uri Tsvi Greenberg:

> Set me on a horse and command it to race with me to the desert.
> Yield me my sands again. Farewell to the boulevards. Let me have
>   my sands of the desert.
> There is such a people of naked bodies, bronzed youth under
>   sunbrands. . . .[62]

"In the Kingdom of the Cross" was published in Berlin in 1923, and its Zionist aspirations are evident. When Greenberg eventually did emigrate to Palestine, he found a nascent Jewish society in which the horse was already acquiring an iconic status suited to desert expanses, Jewish agriculture, and mounted soldiers. Whatever his interest in nature and physical exercise and his dabbling in nudism, Kafka could never have composed such literal paeans to swift horses and naked bodies. Nor could he have adjusted to the sheer utilitarianism of the Zionist enterprise. For how could the horses he described as "unearthly beings" have pulled the settlers' plows?[63] In later years the tough Jewish state could be thought of as the Marlboro country the Jewish founders of Hollywood had invented to promote the myth of the American frontier: "Israel: the Jewish Zorro, cowboy with calloused hands."[64] The conversion of febrile Diaspora Jews into rugged Israelis had found an equine idiom to express this dramatic metamorphosis.

The grotesque fulfillment of the blood-soaked relationship between Jews and horses—an episode that might have been invented by Kafka himself—befell a French-Jewish soldier named Gaston Bernard in 1899, as Alfred Dreyfus languished on Devil's Island. Although too sick to ride his horse, Bernard was ordered by his squadron leader, an outspoken anti-Semite, to mount the animal and perform equestrian exercises. He was apparently thrown from the horse, which inflicted a mortal wound by kicking in the chest of its Jewish rider.[65]

This terrible event was one of a thousand humiliations inflicted on Jewish soldiers in the European armies of this period. It is a primal scene in which the anti-Semite inflicts upon the Jew a punishment that fulfills the prophecy of the original stereotype—the Jew who is unfit to ride a horse is put to death by the animal he cannot master at the behest of the superior male type. In an analogous fashion, the death camps of the Nazis were places where Jews could be reduced to that state of physiological misery they already represented in the realm of racial folklore.

The symbolic power of the horse (cheval) survives to this day in the mythology of chivalry that continues to shape our thinking about war and masculinity, the value of competition, and the circumstances in which it is legitimate to kill. Mediated through the Victorian ideal of the gentleman, chivalric ideals provided Western society with a pseudo-ethical vocabulary of "fair play," honor, self-restraint, and noble competition that has always excluded the vengeful, egotistical, partisan, and ignoble Jews who were kept off horses and thus out of most European officer corps. Elements of this vocabulary are still evident in the business world, where the company that saves a firm from a hostile takeover by a Jewish "vulture" is sometimes called a "white knight."[66]

Given the enormous culture-creating power of the chivalric ideology, it is not surprising that Jews incorporated some of its essential terms into the vocabulary they used to describe the differences that marked them off from their gentile compatriots. In 1867, for example, a Jewish traveler noticed "a certain chivalric essence" (ein gewisses chevalereskes Wesen) that was peculiar to the Poland in which Jews felt like strangers. He felt aesthetically inadequate, associating his lack of style and bearing with an inability to participate in Tournüre.[67] In 1910, Binjamin Segel accused his fellow Jews of a shameful lack of the "knightly indignation" (*ritterliche Entrüsting*) that would have forbidden concessions to the gentile "enemy."[68] The chivalric idiom also makes an appearance in Kafka's *Letter to His Father* (1919), in the final section in which Franz savages himself through the imagined voice of his father, the former drill sergeant Hermann Kafka. Addressing himself like a ventriloquist through his father's voice, Franz finds himself unworthy of "chivalric struggle" (*ritterlichen Kampf*) and fit only for the "struggle waged by vermin" (*Kampf des Ungeziefers*).[69] The language of chivalry that denigrated Jews in *Ivanhoe* had now been embraced by a Jewish master of self-abnegation.

Having met a thoroughly assimilated Anglo Jewry, Chaim Weizmann remarked: "They seem to live in an entirely different world."[70] One can only wonder whether this outsider understood the subtle barriers to assimilation that persisted amid the prosperity of Anglo-Jewish horse owners, whose doomed attempts to fit into the English country life and its equestrian diversions are movingly dramatized in Somerset Maugham's famous story "The Alien Corn" (1931). At the turn of the twenty-first century, obituaries of the great Anglo-Jewish businessmen still included accounts of their attachments to horse racing. Lord Arnold Weinstock would attend the races at Longchamps and Deauville and study his company's cash flow while sitting beneath pictures of his race horses—a tableau from *The Economist* that offers a striking, and no doubt unintentional, contrast between healthy animal vitality and bloodless Jewish finance.[71] Juxtapositions of this kind serve as fair warning that the Jewish relationship to the horse remains, as we say, "problematic." Memories of murderous Crusaders and Cossacks on horseback commingle with that "sympathy for the brute creation" that can still appear as evidence of the ancient Jewish refusal to adopt the mind-set of the gentile world. One need only think of the late Louis Freedman, property developer and race horse breeder, who retired one of his champions because "the life of a race-horse is not a natural one."[72]

Notes

1. "Bloomberg's Test: Will New York Vote for a Jew Who 'Rides Horses'?" *Forward*, August 3, 2001, 6.
2. I have identified and discussed a "Jewish male predicament" in John M. Hoberman, "Otto Weininger and the Critique of Jewish Masculinity," in *Jews and Gender: Responses to Otto Weininger*, ed. Nancy A. Harrowitz and Barbara Hyams (Philadelphia: Temple University Press, 1995), 141–53.

3. Edward Rice, *Captain Sir Richard Francis Burton* (New York: Charles Scribner's Sons, 1990), 172.

4. A comic grotesque version of this deficit was enacted by Chicago gangster Samuel J. "Nails" Morton, an enthusiastic equestrian, who was killed when he was thrown from a horse. His associates retaliated for this humiliation by killing the unfortunate animal. See Rachel Rubin, "Killer Jews," *Journal of Criminal Justice and Popular Culture* 8 (2001): 145–48.

5. "Wie ein Jude aufs Pferd kommt, ist nicht unbedenklich," quoted in Rudolf Augstein, "Ein Nietzsche für Grüne und Alternative?" *Der Spiegel,* June 8, 1981, 163.

6. Quoted in Léon Poliakov, *The Aryan Myth: A History of Racist and Nationalist Ideas in Europe* (New York: Meridian Books, 1977), 275.

7. Alain Finkielkraut, *The Imaginary Jew* (Lincoln and London: University of Nebraska Press, 1994), 87.

8. Quoted in John Murray Cuddihy, *The Ordeal of Civility: Freud, Marx, Lévi-Strauss, and the Jewish Struggle with Modernity* [1974] (Boston: Beacon Press, 1987), 143.

9. Steven S. Schwarzschild, "The Unnatural Jew," *Environmental Ethics* 6 (Winter 1984): 347, 349, 356.

10. In 1949, writer Yehuda Bourla wrote about the cultivation of the soil in the following terms: "The whole Jewish people was an invalid, an abnormality, and it is therefore its greatest ambition that the major part of the people should be rooted in the soil of the Homeland, linking heart and soul with the labor of its cultivation, for there is no more marvelous a cure to restore the Jewish people to national health, homely simplicity and human naturalness, than the cultivation of the soil." Quoted in Tom Segev, *1949: The First Israelis* (New York: Henry Holt, 1998), 293. This Jewish perspective on the pathological condition of European Jewry was already well developed by the end of the nineteenth century.

11. Quoted in Mark Zborowski and Elizabeth Herzog, *Life Is with People: The Culture of the Shtetl* [1952] (New York: Schocken Books, 1965), 244.

12. Isaac Bashevis Singer, *The Slave* [1962] (New York: Fawcett Crest Books, 1980), 14.

13. Bruce Jay Friedman, *Stern* (New York: Signet Books, 1962), 19.

14. "Although he had lived little in nature Levin had always loved it, and the sense of having done the right thing in leaving New York was renewed in him. . . . Although Levin rejoiced at the unexpected weather, his pleasure was tempered by a touch of habitual sadness at the relentless rhythm of nature; change ordained by a force that produced, whether he wanted it or not, today's spring, tomorrow's frost, age, death, yet no man's accomplishment; change that wasn't change, in cycles eternal sameness, a repetition he was part of, so how win freedom in and from self?" See Bernard Malamud, *A New Life* [1961] (New York: Avon Books, 1980), 2, 171.

15. Marc A. Weiner, *Richard Wagner and the Anti-Semitic Imagination* (Lincoln and London: University of Nebraska Press, 1995), 168, 344.

16. Sir Walter Scott, *Ivanhoe* [1819] (New York: Signet Classics, 1983), 223, 218. Scott's interest in the psychology of the Jew is apparent in the following passage: "And thus it is probable that the Jews, by the very frequency of their fear on all occasions, had their minds in some degree prepared for every effort of

tyranny which could be practised upon them; so that no aggression, when it had taken place, could bring with it that surprise which is the most disabling quality of terror" (216–17).

17. Amos Oz, "Crusade," in *Unto Death* (New York and London: Harcourt, Brace, Jovanovitch, 1975), 56.

18. Shmuel Almog, "'Judentum als Krankheit': Antisemitisches Stereotyp und Selbstdarstellung," *Tel Aviver Jahrbuch für deutsche Geschichte* 20 (1991): 218, 219. The German text of Heine's comment is: ". . . der Sinn für die Jagd liegt im Blute. . . . Meine Ahnen gehörten aber nicht zu den Jagenden, viel eher zu den Gejagten, und soll ich auf die Nachkömmlinge ihrer ehemaligen Kollegen losdrücken, so empört sich dawider mein Blut." Heine's odd use of the word *Kollegen* to refer to the ancestors of the animals he might hunt would appear to be an expression of his famously ironic temperament. On Heine's concern about the pain suffered by animals, see also Barker Fairley, *Heinrich Heine: An Interpretation* (Oxford: Clarendon Press, 1954), 121.

19. "Das Leid der Tiere," *Jeschurun* 15 (May–June 1928): 454.

20. W. N. Evans, "The Passing of the Gentleman: A Psychoanalytic Commentary on the Cultural Ideal of the English," *Psychoanalytic Review* 18 (1949): 32.

21. Reinhold Lewin, "Der Krieg als jüdisches Erlebnis," *Monatsschrift für Geschichte und Wissenschaft des Judentums* (January–March 1919): 3.

22. "Dogs are associated with fights, but not with boyish games. To the people of the shtetl the dog is not a pet, but a symbol of brute strength and unpredictability. Whatever his breed, he is a bloodhound. The watchman on the estate of the absentee noble is accompanied by fierce dogs, hoping to surprise adventurous boys looking for nuts, fruits, berries or firewood. The outlying peasant houses are always guarded by dogs whose inclinations and masters prompt them to snap at the long caftans of the shtetl boys. The boys always run and the dogs always chase them. His role in the shtetl has stereotyped the dog as the dangerous beast. When melted wax is thrown into water to discover what has frightened a baby, the figure most often seen is that of a dog." See Zborowski and Herzog, *Life Is with People*, 344–45. The eponymous protagonist of Bruce Jay Friedman's novel *Stern* (1962) relives the European Jew's fear of dogs in the tranquility of an American suburbia. "Stern was able to see two thin, huge dogs vault a fence that encircled one of the houses and make for him with a whistling sound. They skimmed through the night and came to an abrupt halt at his feet, their gums drawn back, teeth white, both dogs reaching high above his waist. One took Stern's wrist between his teeth, and the two animals, hugging close to his side, walked with him between them, as though they were guards taking a man to prison." See Friedman, *Stern*, 21. In Israel, the use of dogs—even for the purpose of self-defense—remains culturally problematic to this day. See "Jews Let the Dogs Out," *Forward*, August 2, 2002.

23. "Das Leid der Tiere," 261.

24. Peter Singer, "A Professor Who Disputes Moral Absolutes on Euthanasia," *New York Times*, April 10, 1999.

25. Gompertz "was an able administrator but, as both a Jew and an eccentric, a public relations liability. He was eased out of his position in the early 1830s." See Harriet Ritvo, *The Animal Estate: The English and Other Creatures in the Victorian Age* (Cambridge, Mass.: Harvard University Press, 1987), 129.

26. Michael Landmann, *Das Tier in der jüdischen Weisung* (Heidelberg: Verlag Lambert Schneider, 1959), 127.

27. See, for example, "Sympathy with the Brute Creation," *The Jewish Quarterly Review* 8 (1896): 714–15. Here, as elsewhere, one must often distinguish between the Jewish sensibility of the Diaspora and that of the Jewish state. A 1974 report on hunting in Israel suggests that official Israeli policy at this time did not make the association between Jews and hunted animals that prompted Heinrich Heine and so many other European Jews to oppose hunting. On the contrary, Israel's game warden at this time saw his work as a contribution to the redemption of the land of Israel. See Sidney Du Broff, "Hunting in Israel," *The American Zionist* (March–April 1974): 23–25.

28. "In early Israel the horse was never included among the domesticated animals, such as the ass or ox. Indeed the ass was a symbol of peace, but the horse was a symbol of war and in the Bible the horse is always represented, with few exceptions (e.g., Isaiah 28: 28) as a fighting animal." See Shlomo Pesach Toperoff, *The Animal Kingdom in Jewish Thought* (Northvale, NJ, and London: Jason Aronson, 1995), 123.

29. Israel Abrahams, *Jewish Life in the Middle Ages* [1898] (New York: Atheneum, 1981), 375–76.

30. Quoted in Arnold White, *The Modern Jew* (London: William Heinemann, 1899), 141.

31. Zborowski and Herzog, *Life Is with People*, 252.

32. Aharon Appelfeld, *The Retreat* (New York: Penguin Books, 1985), 113–14.

33. Stephen Aris, *The Jews in Business* (Harmondsworth: Pelican Books, 1973), 103.

34. Albert Memmi, *Portrait of a Jew* [1962] (New York: Viking Compass, 1971), 42.

35. Quoted in Jean-Denis Bredin, *The Affair: The Case of Alfred Dreyfus* (New York: George Braziller, 1986), 20.

36. Henry de Montherlant, "Un petit juif à la guerre," in *Essais* (Paris: Bibliothèque de la Pléiade, 1963), 481–82. See John M. Hoberman, "Montherlant's Masculine Ideology and the Jews," presented at the Seventeenth Annual Conference of the Western Society for French History, New Orleans, Louisiana, October 19, 1989.

37. Daniel Boyarin, *Unheroic Conduct: The Rise of Heterosexuality and the Invention of the Jewish Man* (Berkeley: University of California Press, 1997), 51.

38. Maurice Samuel, *The Gentleman and the Jew* (New York: Alfred A. Knopf, 1950), 30, 34, 39. Or, as Samuel puts it: "And yet Jewish wars and Jewish heroes and Jewish songs of triumph failed to strike the right note" (30). The male type Samuel calls "the Tennyson-Kipling man" was simply incompatible with the requirements of a Jewish ethics that renounces killing as sport.

39. Quoted in James E. Falen, *Isaac Babel: Russian Master of the Short Story* (Knoxville: University of Tennessee Press, 1974), 132.

40. Philip Roth, *Portnoy's Complaint* [1969] (New York: Fawcett Crest, 1985), 171.

41. Zborowski and Herzog, *Life Is with People*, 176.

42. Joseph Roth, "Juden auf Wanderschaft," in *Werke in drei Bänden* (Köln-Berlin: Kiepenheuer & Witsch, 1956), 651.

43. H. S. Ashton, *The Jew at Bay* (London: Philip Allan, 1933), 64.

44. Malamud, *A New Life*, 58, 63.

45. Kenneth L. Kann, *Comrades and Chicken Ranchers: The Story of a California Jewish Community* (Ithaca: Cornell University Press, 1993), 162.

46. Werner Sombart, *The Jews and Modern Capitalism* [1911] (New York: Collier Books, 1962), 308.

47. Scott, *Ivanhoe*, 288, 85.

48. Otto Weininger, *Über die letzten Dinge* (Wien und Leipzig: Wilhelm Braumüller K.u.K Hof- u. Universitäts-Buchhändler, 1907), 125. On the Talmudic and Midrashic view of the horse, see Toperoff, *Animal Kingdom in Jewish Thought*, 124–25.

49. "Er hatte eine außerordentliche Milde, zu lächeln. Er war schön und groß. Nie grübelte er, sondern träumte nur. Sein Blick hatte etwas von dem unbestimmten Blick eines Pferdes edler Rasse." Quoted in Joseph Bass, "Die Darstellung der Juden im deutschen Roman des zwanzigsten Jahrhunderts," *Monatsschrift für Geschichte und Wissenschaft des Judentums* 58 (1914): 212.

50. See, for example, Isaac Babel, "Argamak," in *Isaac Babel: The Collected Stories* (New York: New American Library, 1974), 194–200.

51. Gustav Freyrag, *Soll und Haben* [1855] (Leipzig: S. Hitzel, 1909), vol. 1, 277.

52. Israel S. Wechsler, "Nervousness and the Jew: An Inquiry into Racial Psychology," *The Menorah Journal* 10 (April–May 1924): 122.

53. "Horsemanship," *Journal of the American Medical Association* 170 (July 11, 1959): 1340–41.

54. Appelfeld, *The Retreat*, 61.

55. "Erinnert man sich daran, daß das Pferd durch Stämme überwiegend nordischer Rasse nach Vorderasien und Palästina gebracht worden war. . . ." See Hans F. K. Günther, *Rassenkunde des jüdischen Volkes* (J. F. Lehmann, 1931), 163.

56. Johann Gottfried von Herder, *Herders ausgewählte Werke*, vol. 6 (Stuttgart: J. G. Gotta'sche, n.d.), 249–50.

57. Harald Siems, "Reiten als körperliche Erziehung," *Leibesübungen und körperliche Erziehung* (1939): 260–61.

58. Geoffrey Cocks, *Psychotherapy in the Third Reich: The Göring Institute* (New York: Oxford University Press, 1985), 222, 235. Riding therapy is not, of course, an exclusively Nazi idea. On the use of *Hippotherapie* for patients suffering from neurological disorders such as multiple sclerosis, see "Helfer auf vier Hufen," *Süddeutsche Zeitung*, May 7–8, 1997.

59. Here I follow Mark Anderson's persuasive interpretation in *Kafka's Clothes* (New York: Oxford University Press, 1992), 50–97. "Kafka also introduced other types of performance which, like the dance, foreground the body as an object of aesthetic interest. The gymnast, acrobat, trapeze artist, circus horse-rider, singing mouse, or hunger artist—these figures have all externalized their art into visible corporeal display. What interests Kafka in these figures is the impersonality of a body that has been subjected to constant training and exercise, a body that is 'flawless' because it has been absorbed by the artistic process itself" (70).

60. See *Kafka: The Complete Stories* (New York: Schocken Books, 1976), 389–90 ("Reflections for Gentleman-Jockeys"), 401–2 ("Up in the Gallery"), 390 "("The Wish to Be a Red Indian").

61. Anderson, *Kafka's Clothes*, 53.

62. Uri Tsvi Greenberg, "In the Kingdom of the Cross," in *The Penguin Book of Modern Yiddish Verse*, ed. Irving Howe, Ruth R. Wisse, and Khone Shmeruk (New York: Viking, 1987), 486, 488.

63. "Es ist charakteristisch, daß Kafka die Pferde als 'unirdische' Wesen bezeichnet, nicht als 'überirdische'. Sie sind die Negation des Irdischen, nicht die Position einer außer- und überirdischen Sphäre." See Wilhelm Emrich, *Franz Kafka* (Bonn: Athenäum-Verlag, 1958), 135.

64. Finkielkraut, *Imaginary Jew*, 132.

65. "L'Antisémitisme dans l'Armée," *Archives Israélites*, December 14, 1899, 407–8.

66. "Victor Posner," *The Economist*, March 9, 2002, 83.

67. I. Horowitz, "Ein Blick auf die Juden in Galizien," *Monatschrift für Geschichte und Wissenschaft des Judenthums* (1867): 127, 46.

68. Binjamin Segel, *Die Entdeckungsreise des Herrn Dr. Theodor Lessing* (Lemberg: Verlag "Hatikwa," 1910), 43.

69. Franz Kafka, *Letter to His Father/Brief an den Vater* (New York: Schocken Books, 1966), 122.

70. Quoted in Aris, *Jews in Business*, 31.

71. "Lord Arnold Weinstock," *The Economist*, July 27, 2002, 73.

72. "Louis Freedman," *The Daily Telegraph*, December 24, 1998.

STEPHEN J. WHITFIELD

3   *Unathletic Department*

Brooklyn, in the era of the Great Depression and the Good War, belied the notion that blacks were oppressed, Norman Podhoretz recalled. In the neighborhood where he was growing up, a world circumscribed by a few square blocks, "the Italians and Jews . . . feared the Negroes." They were "more ruthless, and on the whole they were better athletes." Those kids were "*tough . . .* enviably tough." As a child Podhoretz had "envied Negroes for what seemed to me their superior masculinity," and the adult editor looked at blacks and saw them "on the kind of terms with their own bodies that I should like to be on with mine." In Harlem at the same time was a Jewish enclave where the future sociologist Irving Louis Horowitz grew up, fearful of mugging. His black neighbors suspected that "even Jews without money had money," trumping physical assurance and prowess, qualities that Jews like Horowitz "viewed . . . with more fear than respect."[1] Move over to the east Bronx, in the era of World War II, when Jules Feiffer was painfully aware of how unathletic he was. The future satirist recalled his "great desire to grow up" because, "as I understood it, adults did not have to take gym."[2]

Three boroughs, three boyhoods. Is it permissible to generalize from such instances, and to describe Jewish males as defining themselves outside of the vigorous and assertive muscularity that is so widely admired in American society? If so, the subject of "Unathletic Department" collides directly with the thrust of this book. My theme is the flip side of the rationale that has animated other contributors to this volume, and is tinged with a certain wariness about "joining the club." Consider my topic as equivalent to the dissidence of Murray Sperber, who teaches English at

Indiana University. In 2000 he spearheaded a drive among his colleagues to fire another faculty member, basketball coach Bobby Knight. Outrage among Hoosier fans at Professor Sperber's effrontery was intense; bodily harm was threatened. So endangered did Sperber feel in Bloomington that his fall classes were canceled; and when he resumed teaching, his students were not informed in advance that Sperber would be their instructor—for his own protection. "Stealth courses," he called them.[3]

The Sovereignty of a Stereotype

Perhaps everyone else's chapter in this book is at least implicitly designed to repudiate a stereotype. But reinforcing it is what my essay is intended to do, and to specify the sort of evidence that might suggest why such an expectation endures. Stereotypes are often mischievous and nasty. But they persist not because of the harm they cause and not because they are false, but because they have enough truth to sustain themselves. Stereotypes exist or persist not because (or not *only* because) they satisfy irrational needs or reflect aggressiveness and bigotry, but because they roughly approximate and simplify the otherwise inchoate experience of society. What ought to intrigue scholars is to explain the enduring power of what Walter Lippmann called "the pictures inside our heads." His own explanation, advanced in 1922, is surely correct, which is that stereotypes are validated by their connection to observable reality. They harbor at least a tincture of truth. Without stereotypes, we would see the world from an utterly innocent, even childish perspective.[4] Even as we are morally obligated to treat people as individuals, we would have to pretend that groups are the same, were we to insist that stereotypes are utterly unanchored in actuality.

What this essay seeks to substantiate is therefore a distinguishing feature ascribed to one particular minority in the United States. The world of the fathers of Podhoretz, Horowitz, and Feiffer was marked in part by a "suspicion of the physical, fear of hurt, anxiety over the sheer 'pointlessness' of play," Irving Howe claimed. "All went deep into the recesses of the Jewish psyche."[5] In a sense he concurred with the most influential anti-Semite in the nation's history, Henry Ford, who once announced that "Jews are not sportsmen." The concision was admirable. Nor was he alone in underestimating or denying the Jews' athletic achievements, or even their capacity to inhabit with any assurance their own bodies. "Jews are distinctly inferior in stature and physical development . . . to any other race," Harvard president Charles W. Eliot informed the members of the University's Menorah Society in 1907.[6]

Seven years later, eminent sociologist Edward Alsworth Ross contrasted the westward-bound pioneers to the Jews, who mostly crossed the Atlantic instead of the continent. They are, Ross averred, "undersized and weak-muscled," and shun "bodily activity." He quoted an anonymous settlement house worker who called Jews "absolute babies about pain." They simply weren't "gritty."[7] In a series of nativist articles in the *Saturday Evening Post*, Kenneth Roberts reported on his visits to Europe in 1920–21. Jews were depicted as "all very fearful of pain." The mere sight of a physician could produce cries of "Oi Yoi." When given shots, Jewish patients emitted "awful wails of Yoi Yoi." Gentiles, by contrast, "don't give a damn," Roberts claimed.[8]

Such generalizations may account for the recent publication of two very different books with the same surprising, man-bites-dog title: *Tough Jews*. The claims of both Paul Breines and of Rich Cohen hint at a certain eagerness to dispel a stereotype. That is twice as many books as one that seems instead to polish the pictures inside our heads by bearing the title *Smart Jews*. The smartest Jew of all, Albert Einstein, "like so many other Jews and scholars, takes no physical exercise at all," *Time* magazine reported in its cover story on the physicist on February 18, 1929. Hence the eagerness of iconoclastic Harold U. Ribalow to let the games begin by devoting six editions to tabulating the accomplishments of *The Jew in American Sport* (from 1948 until 1985). In profiling athletes who proved that "Jews can fight," that "Jews have guts," Ribalow too may have yearned to highlight what might not otherwise be obvious: "It is a lie to call Jews cowards."[9] In betraying an awareness of the power of the myth of an historic indifference to sports, Jews and their enemies did not disagree.

Humor is a key that can unlock an ethos; and satire is amusing only when the hits are direct, when it can illumine what is special about a minority. What is a Jewish triathlon? An Internet answer, presumably of Jewish provenance, goes as follows: "gin rummy, then contract bridge, followed by a nap." (A self-taught mechanic, Ford himself had noted the Jews' "physical lethargy, their dislike of unnecessary physical action.") *Portnoy's Complaint* is, in part, a case study in the comic confusions of interfaith relations; and its narrator is almost as interested in describing how Jews and gentiles differ as he is in surmounting and impugning those differences. In awe of the winsome and healthy blondes who seem so tantalizingly out of reach, young Alex Portnoy envisions their older brothers doing what Jewish boys would not succeed in doing—starring as "swift and powerful halfbacks for the college football teams" of Northwestern, Texas Christian, and UCLA.[10] Jackie Mason, a comedian with acutely developed ethnographic interests, noticed the absence of his coreligionists on the roster of rodeo performers. Only gentiles would risk falling off broncos ("I say, *schmuck*, use the other hand!"). As for jockeys, who must weigh under a hundred pounds, "a Jew is not going to give up coffee and cake just to sit on a horse," Mason conjectured.[11]

The most important Jewish comedian of the post–World War II era—probably the most important *American* comedian of the post–World War II era—converted his unprepossessing physical traits into self-mockery. Woody Allen's stand-up act (1964–68)—and his earliest films—are replete with episodes of physical vulnerability. A neighborhood bully was so evil that in the 1944 Roosevelt-Dewey election, "his parents voted for Hitler." When the local menace taunted Allen, who was carrying a cello, by yelling at him ("Hey, Red!"), the future comedian foolishly demanded more respectful treatment, asking to be addressed henceforth as "Master Haywood Allen." He spent that winter in a cast, while a team of doctors removed splinters from his body. In the summertime, he was sent away to an interfaith camp, where he recalled having been beaten up by boys of every race, creed, and color. Indeed, Allen was so puny and defenseless that he was once even beaten up by Quakers. When he was old enough and successful enough to afford a Manhattan apartment, he preferred for security reasons to live in a building that had a doorman—until the doorman beat him up. Returning to the lobby one night, Allen found himself facing a Neanderthal man, a dangerous creature who had just learned the secret of fire. But he was mollified by bright, shining objects; and Allen was able to flee. Nor did the subways of New York offer refuge. Once a gang of young hoodlums barged onto the subway, "dribbling a social worker"; and in *Bananas* (1971) the gang that threatens him on the subway includes aspiring actor Sylvester Stallone. In *Play It Again Sam* (1972), another thug muscles in on him and his date in a nightclub; and Allan Felix (Woody Allen) tries to ward off the threatening motorcyclist: "I'd love to stay but I gotta be up early tomorrow; go to temple. It's my people's sabbath." The ploy does not work; there is a fight outside. Allan Felix later explains what happened: "Some guys were gettin' tough with Julie, I—had to teach 'em a lesson. . . . I snapped my chin down onto some guy's fist and hit another one in the knee with my nose."[12]

In James L. Brooks's satire of television journalism, *Broadcast News* (1987), the wittiest guy in the newsroom is Aaron Altman (played by Albert Brooks, the son of comedian Harry Einstein). Aaron is first shown delivering the valedictorian's speech upon graduating from high school, after which he is beaten up by bigger but stupider *goyim* (a fate to which he submits as though it were routine, like showing up for homeroom).

In his pursuit of Jane Craig (Holly Hunter), Aaron will lose out again—to the sandy-haired hunk, William Hurt. Consider also a comic moment in Elaine May's *The Heartbreak Kid* (1972), screenplay by Neil Simon, based on a story by Bruce Jay Friedman. New Yorker Lenny Cantrow (Charles Grodin) pursues the blonde Kelly Corcoran (Cybill Shepherd) all the way to a Minnesota campus. Three taller, heftier guys who seem directly descended from Vikings want to prevent him from getting any closer to Kelly. But Lenny pretends to be an agent from the "Bureau of Narcotics" of the Department of Justice and manages to throw them off stride. In physical encounters with belligerent and imposing gentiles, Jewish men are expected to be overmatched (although they may win through guile).

The Corrective of a Counter-Myth

A counter-myth can of course be summoned; it crystallized in the nineteenth century and was devised by anti-Semites. According to them, Jews are powerful rather than powerless. They make *others* victims. Their furtive domination of the world's finances and media enabled this cunning minority to be—even more than Shelley's fellow poets—"the secret legislators of mankind." An apocalyptic novel by the Populist tribune Ignatius Donnelly, *Caesar's Column* (1890), puts Prince Cabano (*né* Jacob Isaacs) at the center of the Oligarchy. Indeed the master class of financiers, "the aristocracy of the world" as of 1988, "is now altogether of Hebrew origin." Its opposing force consists of revolutionaries, known as the Brotherhood, of which "the brains" is a Russian Jew named Gabriel Weltstein. But not even Donnelly's classic of conspiracy theory can be recruited into service as a criticism of the stereotype. Neither the Jew who dominates the Oligarchy nor the Jewish strategist of the Brotherhood is an exemplar of physical prowess: Cabano is cowardly, and Weltstein is crippled. Their *modus operandi* is not intimidation but craftiness.[13] Because Jews might expect to be beaten up by bullies or bigots (unless a miracle intervened), the ethnic appeal of, say, Benny Leonard is easy to account for. "To see him climb in the ring sporting the six-pointed Jewish star on his fighting trunks," the boxing *maven* Budd Schulberg noted, "was to anticipate the sweet revenge for all the bloody noses, split lips, and mocking laughter at pale little Jewish boys who had run the neighborhood gauntlet."[14] Hence the charm of an anecdote about Hank Greenberg, whom even Henry Ford liked. The Detroit Tigers's slugger was assigned to an army unit in which another soldier demanded to know if there was "anybody here named Goldberg or Ginsberg" in the outfit.

Sensing trouble, the six-foot, four-inch athlete walked up and identified himself as Greenberg. The intimidated—and smaller—bully then denied interest in the presence of any Greenbergs and reiterated the limit of his curiosity: "I said Goldberg or Ginsberg."[15]

Nevertheless, Goldbergs and Ginsbergs have been much more common than Hank Greenberg (who denied that the incident ever happened). He "was this guy . . . doing all those wonderful things in a *physical* sense," an awestruck Tigers fan recalls in Aviva Kempner's 1999 film on his career. "And there were never any Jews doing anything in a *physical* sense." (The baseball fan had apparently never heard of Benny Leonard, or other Jewish boxing champions.) To show how rarely Jews have been sportsmen, statistics can be selectively deployed as well. Fewer Jews perform in the National Football League than currently serve on the U. S. Supreme Court—even though the highest appellate court has far fewer members than a single squad of such gladiators. "Bar mitzvah is the age," a sports agent once told law professor Alan M. Dershowitz, "when a Jewish boy realizes that his chances of playing on a major league sports team are considerably less than his chances of owning one." A Jewish Sports Hall of Fame is located at the B'nai B'rith National Jewish Museum in Washington, DC. But the exhibition space is not enormous, and the list of honorees is padded by adding coaches and sportswriters as well. Through the World Wide Web it is possible to locate a dozen local shrines as well, including the Montreal Jewish Sports Hall of Fame and the Western Pennsylvania Jewish Sports of Fame.[16] Perhaps they seek to impress visitors by also including the memorabilia of owners of teams as well.

A stereotype is not necessarily invalidated because exceptions can be cited. Some Jews, after all, *have* been sportsmen—and succeeded brilliantly at their vocations. In every year between 1910 and 1939, historian Peter Levine has observed, Jews held at least one boxing championship (except in 1913); and in seven of those years, "Jews held three titles simultaneously. . . . So prominent were Jewish boxers in certain weight divisions that nine times between 1920 and 1934, Jews fought each other in championship bouts."[17] And then there was Hall of Famer Sandy Koufax, whose excellence moved Casey Stengel to speculate: "If that young fella was running for office in Israel, they'd have a whole new government over there."[18] A special case was an escape artist born as Ehrich Weiss, whose bar mitzvah ceremony had been conducted by the famed Orthodox Rabbi Bernard Drachman and whose extraordinarily dexterous body and dazzling feats of physical daring made Harry Houdini a name to conjure with.

But a certain ethos had to be transcended or dismissed, and that sometimes happened in the New World. Born in Minsk, Hymie Auerbach worked hard enough to own a dry-cleaning business, and "never approved of all the time I spent playing games as a kid," according to his son, "Red" Auerbach, who grew up to coach the Boston Celtics.[19] Realizing that Minnie Leiner, an immigrant from Russia, had a horror of boxing as dangerous and a violation of Judaic norms, her son Benny used the surname Leonard so that she would not read about his bouts in the *Forward*. Barnet Rasofsky also became Barney Ross to spare his immigrant mother from the knowledge of his profession; despite the dishonor, no other boxer had ever held three world titles simultaneously.[20] In Robert Rossen's *Body and Soul* (1947), Charlie Davis (John Garfield) is a boxer whose mother sternly criticizes his line of work. He is a creature not of the Jewish past but of the new environment, a student not of the Torah for its own sake but of "the manly art" of bashing others for pay. His faith is in the superiority of winning over getting a one-way ticket to Palookaville. Hollywood makes Charlie Davis a hero. In the light of the pre-American history of the Diaspora, however, he's an anomaly, who contradicts the verities of decency, piety, family, and tradition.

The Patrimony of the Mouse Nation

Enjoyment of a sport like boxing could not easily blend into *yidishkeyt*— the culture to which the bulk of American Jewry had subscribed a century ago. The protagonist of Abraham Cahan's iconic novel, *The Rise of David Levinsky* (1917), cannot recall, among his fellow Talmudists in Antomir, any "such thing as athletics or outdoor sports in my world." Physical exercise, or "even a most innocent frolic," had to be suppressed, Levinsky remembered, "as an offense to good Judaism." Introducing their anthology of Yiddish literature, Irving Howe and Eliezer Greenberg claimed that at the very center of the fiction that they translated and canonized was "*the virtue of powerlessness, the power of helplessness, . . . the sanctity of the insulted and injured* [italics in original]. These," according to the two editors, "are the great themes of Yiddish literature."[21] *PM*, the progressive New York City daily of the 1940s, must have endeared itself to its pronounced Jewish readership if only because of the newspaper's motto: "We are against people who push other people around." (This was a faint echo of the Passover injunction not to gloat over the fate of the Egyptians who drowned in the Red Sea in pursuit of the Hebrews.)

Unathletic Jews must have found solace in the credo ascribed to the deity by one of the later prophets: "not by might, not by power, but by my spirit" (Zechariah 4: 6); and to exalt powerlessness is to forge links with earlier eras in Jewish history and with other sites in the Diaspora. Publicist Maurice Samuel argued, for example, that the ancient Hebrews, as well as the impoverished immigrants of his own Manchester, England, took no notice of sports. "The language that my parents and my *Rebbi* spoke," he recalled, "was altogether free from the sporting expressions that were so thickly distributed, in strategic ideological areas, throughout English." Samuel added that "if you read the Bible and . . . the Mishnah and Talmud, and ignored the references to Gentile nations and customs, you would likewise never suspect that the world of antiquity had been as addicted to sports as is the modern world." Archaeologists working on the Hellenistic and Roman periods have uncovered considerable gymnastic activity to disprove Samuel's claim. But indifference to play became the history that was socially constructed in memory and myth.[22]

Rabbinic interpretation distinguished between Jacob, the dreamer and the good provider (first for Leah, then for Rachel), and his brother Esau, the coarse hunter who is rendered mythically as the ancestor of (other) "nations," of *goyim* from Edomites to Romans. (One tenth-century work, *Jossipon*, makes Esau a direct ancestor of Romulus.)[23] Historian David Biale's overview of the politics of the Diaspora (mostly) is significantly entitled *Power and Powerlessness in Jewish History* (1986). It is as though the natural condition of this Diaspora people was not to dominate but to yield, not to win but to wait, and to operate only on the margins of worldly influence. Franz Kafka neglected to mention the word "Jew" in any of his fiction. But in "Josephine the Singer, or the Mouse Nation," the most admired Jewish writer of the previous century imagined that his own people were as weak and vulnerable as mice. (This is the anthropomorphic switch that Art Spiegelman would also adopt for *Maus*.) A different metaphor would emerge after the Holocaust, when the accusation was leveled against the victims that they meekly accepted their own extinction, that they were led to the camps and gas chambers like "sheep to the slaughter."

That resistance was very rare among others whom the Third Reich sought to murder is not a decisive rebuttal. There *was* a history of passivity and accommodation in the Diaspora politics of the mouse nation. Such tactics were indeed a function of weakness, which helps explain the extent of stereotypes of physical enfeeblement in modern Western European culture, as though an entire people were prone to impotence. The Jewish male was sometimes depicted as feminized. Such was the criticism of Western European racialists. The notorious extreme case of the acceptance of such stereotypes was the baptized Otto Weininger, who associated femininity and weakness with the people from whom he had sprung. The tortured Viennese ideologue committed suicide early in the last century, in "the age which is most Jewish and most feminine."[24] His *Sex and Character* (first published in German in 1903) was the frenzied terminus of the disassociation of Jewry from the capacity to exert a will to power, a mastery over adversity. The sense of fragility and passivity—and the disdain for the hollow victories occurring on playing fields—would be transferred to the New World, where Jewish males were commonly viewed as belonging to an unathletic department.

One pastime was nevertheless alluring as a guarantee of Americanization. A father wrote to the *Forward*, wondering about "the point of this crazy game" of baseball that bewitched his son. "I want my boy to grow up to be a *mentsh*, not a wild American runner." Worthy editor Abraham Cahan judiciously countered that "the really wild game is football . . . but baseball is not dangerous." He advised parents to "let your boys play baseball and play it well, so long as it does not interfere with their education or get them into bad company." Kids should not "grow up foreigners in their own country," Cahan sighed.[25] On the Lower East Side, Esther Kantrowitz would scold her grandson as follows: "You—you—you baseball player you!" This "was the worst name she could call me," entertainer Eddie Cantor recalled. Indifference to sport could also be indistinguishable from insularity. The principal of Milwaukee's United Hebrew Schools was an immigrant named Moshe Schwartzman. As late as 1960, a full six years after third baseman Eddie Matthews had graced the cover of the first issue of the Time, Inc., weekly, *Sports Illustrated*, Schwartzman had to ask his young daughter: "Is there a major league baseball team in this city?" When she mentioned that the Braves were indeed locally based, the father of the future historian Hasia R. Diner then posed a follow-up question: "Do they hit or pitch?" Her assurance that the Braves could and did accomplish both left him puzzled.[26]

Cornell University's Barry Strauss took up sculling in middle age, and remembered the pain of playing Little League baseball games, during which he "stood in the outfield thinking about how badly I wanted to be somewhere else . . . praying that nobody would hit the ball into whichever corner of the outfield they had put me in."[27] Jewish boys were expected to grow up to become something other than sportsmen; Strauss himself is a classicist. Wallace Shawn, the son of a famed editor of *The New Yorker*, grew up to become an actor and a playwright. He recalled: "I was brought up in that Jewish tradition where the man is a reader of books and does nothing physical." Yet even intellectuals were not immune from hero worship. Soon after immigrating from Germany, the young Henry Kissinger learned a little about America by sitting in the bleachers of Yankee Stadium, and could not remember ever seeing a ball get past the home team's center fielder, Joe DiMaggio. Kissinger later got the chance to watch a World Series game when he shared the skybox with his fellow Republican. "If you had told me in 1938 that I would be Secretary of State, and I would be friends with DiMaggio," Kissinger speculated, "I would have thought the second was less likely than the first."[28]

The stereotype that this essay addresses need not be confined to games. In *American Tough,* historian Rupert H. Wilkinson's 1984 analysis of projections of strength and power, barely any Jews are mentioned; an exception is Bella Abzug. No one projected that image on a movie screen more indelibly than John Wayne, whom a 1969 cover story in *Life* contrasted with Dustin Hoffman. As Marion Morrison, Wayne had been a star football player at USC. He "became an actor because of his looks and his size. . . . Hoffman became one in spite of his physical attributes—he's 5 feet 6–1/2 inches, 135 pounds." Hoffman's rise to fame was therefore counterintuitive, challenging the very sense of what a movie star is supposed to look like. *Life* quoted Wayne as saying, "I can only kill by the code," and Hoffman as observing that "acting is a female profession." In a cover story on Elliott Gould, *Time* reported: "In this era of the inescapable nude scene, Gould's ordinary and not especially well-cared-for proportions come as a blessed relief." In contrast to "the Mr. America chest" of a Lancaster or a Heston, the magazine added, Gould "might even persuade a few victims of anatomical insecurity to forget about jogging."[29] These particular Jewish males were helping to puncture the cinematic ideal of American Tough.

Drawing a contrast with the inner city, Jackie Mason has noted that no one fears going into a Jewish neighborhood. What should a stranger be afraid of, he asks—being beaten up by a bunch of accountants? To stroll there is to walk on the mild side. Then what is the viewer to make of a scene in *Casablanca* (1942), scripted by the Epstein brothers and Howard Koch? Why would Rick Blaine (Humphrey Bogart) tell the Gestapo's Major Strasser (Conrad Veidt), who asks him what he would think about a German occupation of New York City: "Well, there are certain sections of New York, Major, that I wouldn't advise you try to invade." But whether they would be physically threatening, or just socially uncongenial, is unspecified. It is not in suburban Jewish neighborhoods where bumper stickers boast: "My Kid Beat Up Your Honor Student." In the Southern mill town where *The Ballad of the Sad Cafe* is set, bullies enjoy harassing Morris Finestein, a "little Jew who cried if you called him Christkiller." Though he would feel compelled to eject himself from the village, Carson McCullers writes, "if a man were prissy in any way, or if a man ever wept, he was known as a Morris Finestein."[30]

Some observers believed that what had been transplanted from the *shtetl* was a culture that promoted meekness and moderation. How else to explain the popularity of a number one best seller entitled *Chutzpah?* For Dershowitz had to argue *against* a posture that he believed was much too common among his coreligionists facing threats to communal vitality in the United States and elsewhere. He had to insist that vestiges of cringing and habits of accommodation had not utterly disappeared. Dershowitz's plea ("we are not pushy or assertive enough") was a political gesture,[31] but had the inadvertent effect of sustaining a stereotype to which Leon Uris had objected four decades earlier. An ex–U.S. Marine, the author of *Exodus* (1958) wanted to discredit the negative stereotypes that he believed other Jewish novelists were reinforcing: "We Jews are not what we have been portrayed to be. In truth, we have been fighters." Uris positioned himself as an opponent of the image of the cowering, cowardly Jew, and thus echoed the opinion of Max Nordau, the physician whose fear of degeneration at the end of the nineteenth century stirred Zionists to invoke the need for a "Judaism with muscles" that might redeem a people from the physical infirmities that threatened their very existence as an historic entity. Another Zionist tribune, Vladimir Jabotinsky, also complained that the ethos of the Diaspora not only "despised physical manhood" but also dismissed "physical courage and physical force" as pointless.[32] Such concerns coursed through Jewish culture.

Israelis and Irishmen, Fighters and Writers

The establishment of Israel would of course complicate and upend this picture of passivity. The rebirth of a Jewish commonwealth in violence shattered expectations. The Christian triumphalism of Western civilization designated Jews as victims who would eventually disappear, and Islamic civilization expected Jews to be stateless rather than agents of their own collective destiny. In 1948, the stereotype of impotence was intact enough for Secretary of State George C. Marshall to advise President Truman against recognition of the Jewish commonwealth, since the former general could not foresee how the Hagganah might defeat the half-dozen Arab armies bent on strangling the new state in its cradle. The victory of the Israel Defense Forces in the War of Independence as well as all subsequent wars served to contrast with the lingering effects of "the virtue of powerlessness" in the United States, where Jewish indifference to machismo has been connected to distaste for militarism or indeed to the military. Emotionally, the Jewish ethos in the United States has been pacifistic.

Take Irving Berlin. For all of his forthright patriotism, he did not compose songs that exalted soldiering. Even "God Bless America" (1938) omits echoes of warfare, unlike "The Star-Spangled Banner," which takes note of "the rockets' red glare, the bombs bursting in air." In "Good-Bye Becky Cohen" (1910), the eponymous narrator tries to dissuade her boyfriend from taking up arms: "What, fight for nothing / Where's the percentage in that? / No, you better mind your store / Let McCarthy go to war." During World War I, his "Oh! How I Hate to Get Up in the Morning" (1918) was a satiric objection to reveille, a high-spirited expression of resentment at the rigor of military life. What Berlin admired in the bugler was not his heroism but his schedule: "A bugler in the army / Is the luckiest of men, / He wakes the boys at five and then / Goes back to bed again." The song worked as well in a revue during World War II. His Irish-American rival, George M. Cohan, had no comparable songs in his repertory. "Over There" (1917), for example, urged Johnnie to "get your gun, get your gun / Johnnie[,] show the Hun you're a son of a gun / Hoist the flag and let her fly, / Like true heroes do or die." The Lower East Side was not exactly the burned-over district of militarism. To be sure, "Alexander's Ragtime Band" (1911) had included the lyric: "They can play a bugle call / Like you never heard before, / So natural / That you want to go to war." But in the 1960s, Berlin rewrote the last line: "That you want to hear some more."[33] Those who were born on Cherry Street (or Maxwell Street in Chicago) rarely grew up to become the sorts of combatants who love the smell of napalm in the morning. When General George S. Patton slapped a couple of soldiers who were suffering from shell shock, he accused them of cowardice. Any psychiatric diagnosis of their plight, "Old Blood and Guts" sneered, could only be a fabrication, "an invention of the Jews."[34]

Because physical weakness has been so closely associated with a distinctive Jewish ethos, ink-stained wretches who wished to exalt toughness or to imagine athleticism have felt compelled to turn elsewhere. The ablest literary journalist to cover "the sweet science" of boxing was undoubtedly Abbott Joseph Liebling. He grew up in Far Rockaway, and stood out among domineering working-class Irish kids because he was pudgy, bespectacled, uncoordinated, puny, and bookish. He studied at Dartmouth when probably no Ivy League college tried more earnestly to be *Judenrein*. "Liebling's enthusiasm for Catholic toughs," his biographer conjectured, stemmed from a desire "to cut himself off from the emasculating Jewish tradition."[35] He was hardly unique in spending his life in flight from his ethnic origins. But Liebling did so through a celebration—in print, not in emulation—of toughness. Budd Schulberg was far more willing to identify himself as a Jew. His first novel, *What Makes Sammy Run?* (1941), traces the rise of a cunning and unscrupulous Jewish movie executive. But in the scenario of *On the Waterfront* (1954), Schulberg makes the protagonist a has-been boxer and a lapsed Roman Catholic named Terry Malloy; and the boxing novel Schulberg published in 1947, *The Harder They Fall*, centers on another non-Jew, Toro Molino (inspired by Primo Carnera). Boxer Joe Bonaparte, the son of an Italian-American fruit vendor, is the *Golden Boy* of Clifford Odets's 1937 play. In his earlier portrait of an impoverished Jewish family, *Awake and Sing!* (1934), the most violent moment consists of the smashing of phonograph records.

Even before publishing his first novel, Alan Lelchuk ran up against a New York Jew posing as an American tough. The plot of Lelchuk's *American Mischief* (1973) includes a murder in a Harvard Square hotel room. The victim is Norman Mailer, who is shot in the buttocks with his pants down, leaving him both naked and dead. In the fall of 1972, prior to publication, Mailer tried to dissuade the Brandeis University professor of English from keeping the offending passage in his book. The two novelists met in an attorney's office, where Mailer is reported to have predicted: "By the time this is over, Lelchuk, you ain't going to be nothin' but a hank of hair and some fillings." Very minor revisions of the passage were made, no doubt to the slight satisfaction of the future author of *Tough Guys Don't Dance* (1984), who had once even risked running afoul of the sullen Charles (Sonny) Liston at a press conference; they seemed to relish taunting one another. In 1964, Liston may have threatened one tough Jew, a five-foot-three-inch, 64–year-old mobster named Moe Dalitz, in the Beverly Rodeo Hotel restaurant in Hollywood. According to one volume of anecdotes on Jewish gangsters and gunsels, the heavy-drinking, enraged heavyweight drew back his fist; Dalitz thereupon advised the champ to kill him if he hit him at all. "Because if you don't," Dalitz added, "I'll make one telephone phone call, and you'll be dead in twenty-four hours." Liston got sober enough to back off. (A biography by Nick Tosches, *The Devil and Sonny Liston*, makes no mention of the incident, however.) What Mailer himself had been trying to prove immediately after the Liston–Floyd Paterson championship bout remains unclear. But perhaps the novelist's motive bore some resemblance to Robert Cohn's, in *The Sun Also Rises* (1926). To be sure, the middleweight boxing champion of Princeton doesn't even like boxing. Yet "he learned it painfully and thoroughly to counteract the feeling of inferiority" to which other undergraduates subjected him.[36]

Like Liebling, Mailer had an equivocal relationship to the Jewish people. The two writers also shared a fascination with pugilism as well as an empathy with Irish-Americans rogues and roustabouts. For example, in "The Time of Her Time" (1958), Sergius O'Shaugnessy is the stud who engages in sexual marathons with a young woman named Denise Gondelman. Another fictional alter ego is an intellectual named Stephen (Raw Jock) Rojack, who is brave and big enough to beat up a streetwise black named Shago Martin, stomping him perhaps twenty times before hurling him down the stairs ("I never had an idea I was this strong, exhilaration in the fact of the strength itself"), in a preposterous fantasy entitled *An American Dream* (1965). "The White Negro" (1957) had already declared Mailer's independence from "the virtue of powerlessness" by hypothesizing that two teenaged hoodlums who "beat in the brains of a candy-store keeper," "a weak fifty-year-old man," are "daring the unknown, and so no matter how brutal the act, it is not altogether cowardly."[37]

By hinting at what might be admirable about defiance of the criminal law as well as norms of decency, by withholding sympathy from the innocent and harmless merchant murdered by such thugs, Mailer separated himself from the texture of Jewish society, from the norms of the mouse nation. In 1924, Barney Ross's own father, Isidore Rasofsky, was senselessly murdered by two hoodlums trying to rob the modest grocery and dairy store he owned in the Maxwell Street neighborhood of Chicago.[38] In the year "The White Negro" appeared, Bernard Malamud's *The Assistant* made a shopkeeper named Morris Bober into a wisdom-sprouting *mentsh*, inspired by the novelist's own father. In seeming to praise the life-affirming value of violence, Mailer was in effect pitting himself against Doc in *West Side Story* (1957). The puzzled but sane store owner cannot stop the gang violence of the tough guys who dance in that musical. Incidentally, Cynthia Ozick's father was a pharmacist in the Bronx, as was Leslie Fiedler's in Newark. The father of Morris (Moe) Berg was also a Newark pharmacist, and never saw his son play baseball—not even as a major leaguer, not even when the Brooklyn Dodgers were playing at home. Bernard Berg usually spat when baseball was even mentioned, and lamented that his son "doesn't have a profession"—though Moe earned a law degree too.[39] The immigrant druggist was close enough to the traditional culture, though he was a fiercely anticlerical freethinker, to be mystified—and troubled—by his son's diamond ambitions.

Berg was not the only New Jersey Jew to display formidable athletic ability, however. The protagonist of Philip Roth's *American Pastoral*

(1997) personifies a kind of terminus of the Diaspora experience. Seymour Irving "Swede" Levov is so Americanized, so apparently emancipated from Old World neurosis—of the cringing or alienation that this particular promised land was supposed to extinguish—that narrator Nathan Zuckerman is forced to wonder: "What did he do for subjectivity?" Levov exhibits a self-assured "isomorphism to the Wasp world." He is "a blue-eyed blond" wearing a "Viking mask" for a face. He has served in the U.S. Marines (whom Lenny Bruce had called "heavy *goyim*"), prepared "to fight as one of the toughest of the tough." He marries a Roman Catholic who had been Miss New Jersey in 1949. But what distinguishes the Swede so sharply from the other kids who were attending Weequahic High School is his athletic prowess. "Physical aggression, even camouflaged by athletic uniforms and official rules and intended to do no harm to Jews, was not a traditional source of pleasure in our community," Zuckerman asserts.[40] The Swede's feats in football, basketball, and baseball make him a non-Jewish Jew, a rebuke to the stereotypes that have burdened so many others in a nation that makes idols out of sportsmen.

The implications can therefore be summarized. Because a Jew hath eyes as well as other organs, the harm that bullies and bigots can inflict upon the Jew's body is no less painful than what everyone else suffers. But neither is the Jew's body seen as akin to other nations'. The Jew's mind has been among the glories of Western civilization, a testament to soaring spiritual and intellectual grandeur. The Jew's body has long been portrayed as feeble and inferior. Overendowed with brains (according to his enemies), the Jew has not been quite virile enough. In the climactic fight that Malamud stages in *The Tenants* (1971), the blocked black writer Willie Spearmint aims at the groin of Harry Lesser with a saber, as though picking the site where the Jew is least impressive and most vulnerable. By contrast, the blocked Jewish writer puts an ax to the skull of his opponent, targeting the attribute where the Jew has long felt superior. But physical ease and assurance have not been the most celebrated attributes of the coreligionists of Harry Lesser.

Comic Compensation

If puniness has been integral to the sensibility of male American Jewry, then an account of the most striking case of overcompensation in the popular arts is a fit way to conclude this essay. Jerry Siegel, a Cleveland high school student, was earning $4 a week as a delivery boy during the Great Depression, helping to support his family. Some of his savings, however, were spent on comic books. One night in the summer of 1934, he imagined Superman. Unbidden to the sleepless Siegel came the story of the origins of a figure on a planet that would be destroyed, of the discovery of a child with exceptional strength near a midwestern village named Smallville, of his assumption of a second identity. He would be a "mild-mannered" reporter named Clark Kent. The next day, Siegel raced to the home of his classmate Joe Shuster, the impoverished son of a tailor who had moved to Cleveland from Toronto; and with Siegel doing the writing and Shuster doing the drawing, the pair was inspired to complete twelve newspaper strips that day. It then took four years for Detective Comics to accept their work. Less than a decade was needed for Superman to become one of the most familiar mythic characters on earth. But talk about projection! "Outside their worlds of fantasy," one analyst of the Man of Steel wrote, "Siegel and Shuster were classic nerds: bespectacled, unathletic, shy around girls."[41] No wonder that Siegel and Shuster envisioned an icon of *goyish* strength—the ultimate alpha male, and that they could satisfy fantasy in a nation that has itself symbolized the promise of autonomy and freedom and even of power.

This comic-book figure had special meaning for other young Jews. Larry Gelbart, for example, would later write television shows, plays, and films. But he claimed that the most decisive literary influence on his Chicago childhood began—and virtually ended—with "Superman, Action Comics, first issue, June 1, 1938. Ten cents then, thousands now, but the memories are priceless." The only other text in Gelbart's home was the *Haggadah*, and he imagined as "the ideal book" one that had "Superman helping the Hebrews during the Exodus." Only slightly later, Jules Feiffer knew exactly what Siegel and Shuster were feeling: "We were aliens. We didn't choose to be mild-mannered, bespectacled and self-effacing. We chose to be bigger, stronger, blue-eyed and sought-after by blond cheerleaders. *Their* cheerleaders. We chose to be *them*." Superman thus represented "the ultimate assimilationist fantasy," Feiffer realized. "The mild manners and glasses that signified a class of nerdy Clark Kents was, in no way, our real truth. Underneath that schmucky façade there lived Men of Steel!"[42]

Lois Lane was based on Lois Amster, a high school queen of the hop who had barely noticed Siegel or Shuster. Interviewed half a century after her graduation from Glenville High School, Mrs. Robert Rothschild expressed doubt, had either Siegel or Shuster asked her for a date, that she would ever have accepted.[43] Snubbed by Lois Lane, Clark Kent is also bullied by editor Perry White, and comes across so unglamorously in his business suit that the term *schlemiel* might have been invented to categorize this weakling who does not fight back. Clark Kent is humiliated, unauthentic, and impotent, merely the self-effacing masquerade deployed by Superman, who *is* authentic. Even as the protagonist in Arthur Miller's novel *Focus* (1945) puts on the eyeglasses that cause him to be mistaken for a Jew, the disguise of Clark Kent hints at the actual identity of his creators. In the representations of the 1930s, whether in comic books or in Hollywood movies, the Jew was too timid to be overt, and had to be presented furtively, implicitly, encoded.

Is it accidental that Superman is a foreigner, in a populace composed of so many foreigners, in a nation of nations? And how apt that a couple of Jews concocted an icon who is, in the clever phrase of one literary critic, a "Krypto-American immigrant."[44] On Krypton his name was Kal-El, the Hebrew phrase for a "god that is light" in weight; that is, a deity that does not oppress. His lightness of being is bearable to the decent citizens of Metropolis, and enables him to scoff at the laws of gravity. Omnipotent and beneficent, Superman is like a god. In America, the man of steel is an outsider who succeeds in a new world. He does so by applying his superhuman powers in a way that Jews typically wished others to behave—by helping the weak. Superman is an idealized gentile who honors his elderly foster parents' pleas to use his awesome potentiality "to assist humanity," to rescue the beleaguered rather than to dominate them. Superman is no Nietzschean *Übermensch*, but is instead episodically and heroically engaged in the repair of the world.

In *Action Comics*, number 3, in 1938, Superman is so outraged that the owners of a mine are indifferent to the dangers it poses to workers that the Man of Steel exposes one boss to the horridly unsafe conditions, forcing him to see the blessings of occupational safety. A later story has Superman smashing an automobile plant because its products are so dangerous, its owner so greedy. Superman also demolishes a slum so that "the authorities" might provide "splendid housing conditions" instead. No wonder that in *Action Comics*, number 6, also in 1938, Superman is said to display his "dedication to assisting the helpless and oppressed." This messianic New Dealer was conceived during the presidency of Franklin D. Roosevelt, to whom Jews showed deeper loyalty than did any other bloc of Democrats. Superman signified the yearning to protect the vulnerable and to stimulate the confidence-building efforts at nationalist recovery. He reliably fights for "truth, justice and the American way." But by the early 1940s, when the state was struggling not only against massive poverty but also against Axis aggressiveness, Superman's radical opposition to social injustice was abandoned. This superhero continued to embody the virtues of democracy, and was especially part of its arsenal in crushing America's enemies during World War II. By then, his political activism had disappeared. But, as Umberto Eco noted, Superman does continue to have a conscience. Though he is no longer a very energetic citizen,[45] he is still a humanitarian, and happens to be more effective than the golem who protects the Jews of Prague. The benefactor whom Siegel and Shuster imagined is less parochial and thus more inclusive as well.

So much so that another form of compensation has emerged. Superman now has a body double, named Shaloman, brandishing a *shin* instead of an *s* on his chest. He springs from the second culture that has coexisted with the larger national culture. Shaloman battles Palestinian terrorists as well as an arch-fiend named Dr. Traif, and is the creation of Al Wiesner, a Philadelphian who first imagined an ur-Shaloman in 1939, when he was nine years old. "I often wished there was something Jewish I could put on there for a Jewish superhero," Wiesner recalled. "But none existed. I yearned for this kind of thing, of being able to pick up a comic book and find some relationship to my heritage."[46] But *The Legend of Shaloman*, it seems fair to say, is freakishly dependent on the fame of Superman, with whom Wiesner's protagonist enjoys a parodistic or parasitic relationship. Shaloman lacks mythic resonance of his own. Superman makes cultural sense when gentiles can be idealized for their power and strength, and thus he fits within the dream-life of the nation. Shaloman is like the poster sold immediately after the Six-Day War, showing a Hasid in a telephone booth wearing a rather familiar cape as well as black garb. Superman's Jewish parodists play off common knowledge of the unathletic department to which their coreligionists have tended to belong, and inject him into the field of Jewish humor. Superman himself may be a creature of the comic books, but there is nothing "comic" about him. He is instead a projection of ethnic hopes and psychic needs, grounded in an evident awareness of the weakness of the Jew's body.

Notes

1. Norman Podhoretz, "My Negro Problem—and Ours" [1963], in *Doings and Undoing: The Fifties and After in American Writing* (New York: Farrar, Straus, 1964), 355, 364, 367; Irving Louis Horowitz, *Daydreams and Nightmares: Reflections of a Harlem Childhood* (Jackson: University Press of Mississippi, 1990), 3.

2. Quoted in Julius Novick, "Jules Feiffer and the Almost-In-Group," *Harper's*, September 1961, 60.

3. Steve Lopez, "Verbal Judo for Beginners," *Time*, December 11, 2000, 6.

4. Walter Lippmann, *Public Opinion* (New York: Free Press, 1965), 53–66.

5. Irving Howe, with Kenneth Libo, *World of Our Fathers* (New York: Harcourt Brace Jovanovich, 1976), 182.

6. Quoted in Elliott Horowitz, "'They Fought Because They Were Fighters and They Fought Because They Were Jews': Violence and the Construction of Modern Jewish Identity," in *Jews and Violence: Images, Ideologies, Realities*, ed. Peter Y. Medding (New York: Oxford University Press, 2002), 32.

7. Henry Ford, *The International Jew: The World's Foremost Problem* (n. p., n. d.), vol. 3, ch. 45, 38; Peter Levine, *Ellis Island to Ebbets Field: Sport and the American Jewish Experience* (New York: Oxford University Press, 1992), 4; Edward Alsworth Ross, *The Old World in the New: The Significance of Past and Present Immigration to the American People* (New York: Century, 1914), 289–90.

8. Quoted in Joseph W. Bendersky, *The "Jewish Threat": Anti-Semitic Politics of the U.S. Army* (New York: Basic Books, 2000), 160–61.

9. Harold U. Ribalow, *The Jew in American Sports* (New York: Bloch, 1949), 3; Steven A. Riess, ed., "Sports and the American Jew: An Introduction," in *Sports and the American Jew* (Syracuse, N.Y.: Syracuse University Press, 1998), 15.

10. Ford, *International Jew*, 38; Philip Roth, *Portnoy's Complaint* (New York: Random House, 1969), 144.

11. Quoted in Robert Brustein, *Cultural Calisthenics: Writings on Race, Politics, and Theatre* (Chicago: Ivan R. Dee, 1998), 85.

12. Richard J. Anobile, ed., *Woody Allen's Play It Again, Sam* (New York: Grosset and Dunlap, 1972), 104–5, 107–10.

13. Frederic Cople Jaher, *Doubters and Dissenters: Cataclysmic Thought in America, 1885–1918* (Glencoe, Ill.: Free Press, 1964), 131–32; Richard Hofstadter, *The Age of Reform: From Bryan to F. D. R.* (New York: Alfred A. Knopf, 1955), 67–70, 79.

14. Quoted in Levine, *Ellis Island to Ebbets Field*, 155; Horowitz, "They Fought Because They Were Fighters," in *Jews and Violence*, 25–26, 32–35.

15. Leo P. Ribuffo, *Right Center Left: Essays in American History* (New Brunswick, NJ: Rutgers University Press, 1992), 101; Hank Greenberg, *The Story of My Life*, ed. Ira Berkow (New York: Times Books, 1989), 282–83.

16. Alan M. Dershowitz, *Chutzpah* (Boston: Little, Brown, 1991), 100; Donald Altschiller to author, January 23, 2001.

17. Levine, *Ellis Island to Ebbets Field*, 145.

18. Quoted in Mordecai Richler, *Hunting Tigers Under Glass: Essays and Reports* (London: Weidenfeld and Nicolson, 1969), 60.

19. Quoted in Levine, *Ellis Island to Ebbets Field*, 44.

20. Levine, *Ellis Island to Ebbets Field*, 152, 174, 178.

21. Abraham Cahan, *The Rise of David Levinsky* [1917] (New York: Harper Torchbook, 1960), 43; Irving Howe and Eliezer Greenberg, eds., Introduction to *A Treasury of Yiddish Stories* (New York: Meridian, 1958), 38.

22. Quoted in Paul Milkman, *PM: A New Deal in Journalism, 1940–1948* (New Brunswick, NJ: Rutgers University Press, 1997), 37–38; Maurice Samuel, *The Gentleman and the Jew* (New York: Alfred A. Knopf, 1950), 103–5; Uriel Simri, "Jews in the World of Sport," *Jerusalem Post Magazine*, June 28, 1985, 8.

23. Gerson D. Cohen, "Esau as Symbol in Early Medieval Thought," in *Studies in the Variety of Rabbinic Cultures* (Philadelphia: Jewish Publication Society, 1991), 257.

24. Quoted in Sander Gilman, *The Jew's Body* (New York: Routledge, 1991), 137.

25. Quoted in Howe, *World of Our Fathers*, 182; Irving Howe and Kenneth Libo, eds., *How We Lived, 1880–1930* (New York: R. Marek, 1979), 51–52; Riess, "Sports and the American Jew," 38.

26. Eddie Cantor, with David Freedman, *My Life Is in Your Hands* (New York: Harper and Brothers, 1928), 50; Hasia R. Diner to author, January 6, 2001.

27. Barry Strauss, *Rowing Against the Current: On Learning to Scull at Forty* (New York: Scribner, 1999), 39–40.

28. Quoted in John Lahr, *Show and Tell: New Yorker Profiles* (New York: Overlook Press, 2000), 167, and in Richard Ben Cramer, *Joe DiMaggio: The Hero's Life* (New York: Simon and Schuster, 2000), 479.

29. "Dusty and the Duke: A Choice of Heroes," *Life*, July 11, 1969, 42; Esther Romeyn and Jack Kugelmass, *Let There Be Laughter! Jewish Humor in America* (Chicago: Spertus Press, 1997), 66–68; "Elliott Gould: The Urban Don Quixote," *Time*, September 7, 1970, 36.

30. Richard J. Anobile, ed., *Casablanca* (New York: Darien House, 1974), 74; Carson McCullers, *The Ballad of the Sad Cafe* (Boston: Houghton Mifflin, 1951), 8, 65.

31. Dershowitz, *Chutzpah*, 3.

32. Quoted in Philip Roth, "Some New Jewish Stereotypes" (1961), in *Reading Myself and Others* (New York: Farrar, Straus and Giroux, 1975), 138, and in David Biale, *Power and Powerlessness in Jewish History* (New York: Schocken, 1986), 137; David Biale, *Eros and the Jews: From Biblical Israel to Contemporary America* (New York: Basic Books, 1992), 178–79.

33. Quoted in Howe, *World of Our Fathers*, 562, and in Robert Gottlieb and Robert Kimball, eds., *Reading Lyrics* (New York: Pantheon, 2000), 17, 82; Laurence Bergreen, *As Thousands Cheer: The Life of Irving Berlin* (New York: Viking, 1990), 152–53, 156, 158–59, 423, 429, 433; Philip Furia, *The Poets of Tin Pan Alley: A History of America's Great Lyricists* (New York: Oxford University Press, 1992), 50.

34. Phillip Knightley, *The First Casualty* (New York: Harcourt Brace Jovanovich, 1975), 320.

35. Raymond Sokolov, *Wayward Reporter: The Life of A. J. Liebling* (New York: Harper and Row, 1980), 24–25, 28, 30, 40, 42.

36. Eric Pace, "Mailer Finds Book Not an Advertisement for Himself," *New York Times*, October 18, 1972, 49; Norman Mailer, *The Presidential Papers* (New York: Bantam, 1964), 264–66; Carl Sifakis, *The Mafia Encyclopedia* (New York: Facts on File, 1999), 107; Robert A. Rockaway, *But He Was Good to His Mother: The Lives and Crimes of Jewish Gangsters* (New York: Gefen, 2000), 47–48; Ernest Hemingway, *The Sun Also Rises* (New York: Charles Scribner's Sons, 1954), 3.

37. Norman Mailer, *An American Dream* (New York: Dell, 1970), 181, and "The White Negro" (1957), in *Advertisements for Myself* (New York: G. P. Putnam's Sons, 1959), 347; Philip Roth, "Imagining Jews" (1974), in *Reading Myself*, 232–33.

38. Levine, *Ellis Island to Ebbets Field*, 173.

39. Nicolas Dawidoff, *The Catcher Was a Spy: The Mysterious Life of Moe Berg* (New York: Random House, 1994), 345–49.

40. Roth, *American Pastoral*, 3, 14, 20, 89; John Cohen, ed., *The Essential Lenny Bruce* (New York: Ballantine, 1967), 42.

41. Otto Friedrich, "Up, Up and Awaaay!!!," *Time*, March 14, 1988, 66; Les Daniels, *Superman: The Complete History* (San Francisco: Chronicle Books, 1998), 12, 18.

42. Larry Gelbart in "Books That Influenced Me," *New York Times Book Review*, December 7, 1986, 46; Jules Feiffer, "The Minsk Theory of Krypton: Jerry Siegel (1914–1996)," *New York Times Magazine*, December 29, 1996, 14–15.

43. Friedrich, "Up, Up and Awaaay!!!," 69.

44. Werner Sollors, *Beyond Ethnicity: Consent and Descent in American Culture* (New York: Oxford University Press, 1986), 100.

45. Quoted in Thomas Andrae, "From Menace to Messiah: The History and Historicity of Superman," in *American Media and Mass Culture: Left Perspectives*, ed. Donald Lazere (Berkeley: University of California Press, 1987), 130; Ian Gordon, *Comic Strips and Consumer Culture, 1890–1945* (Washington: Smithsonian Institution Press, 1998), 134; Umberto Eco, "The Myth of the Superman," *Diacritics* 2 (Spring 1972): 21–22; Neil Harris, *Cultural Excursions: Marketing Appetites and Cultural Taste in Modern America* (Chicago: University of Chicago Press, 1990), 234–38, 245.

46. Andrew Kardon, "The Kosher Crusader," *Moment* 24 (August 1999): 22.

PART II

Sound Bodies, Healthy Nations

4 National Regeneration in the Ghetto: The Jewish Turnbewegung in Galicia

> Why don't you hurry in Galicia to universalize these gymnastics associations, to popularize them and to make the people understand? Exactly there they are most needed. There . . . where there is a blooming Jewish culture that would be better protected by strong people. There, where so much Jewish strength lies, just waiting for organization.
>
> —Matthias Acher (Nathan Birnbaum) (1907)

Much of the scholarship on the history of European Jewry in the modern period has tended to have a Central European, especially German, focus.[1] This is especially ironic in regard to the Jewish gymnastic movement, the so-called *Turnbewegung*, whose intense propaganda against physical degeneracy focused overwhelmingly on the Jewish "ghettos" of Eastern Europe. To be sure, the Jewish Turnbewegung did rotate to a considerable extent around a Berlin-Vienna axis. The university students who formed Bar-Kochba Berlin in 1898, the first Jewish *Turnverein* (gymnastics association) in Europe, also organized the international Jewish Turnbewegung itself, and published the movement's official organ, the *Jüdische Turnzeitung*.[2]

East European Jews were not merely an abstract population against whom Western Jewish *Turner* propagandized, however. They formed real and dynamic communities, which were not at all monolithic. Galician

Jewry, in particular, challenged common assumptions about "Eastern" Jews. Galician Jews (numbering over 800,000 in 1900) sat on the frontier between East and West, religiously and economically similar to Russian and Romanian Jewry, but since their emancipation in 1867 enjoying wide-ranging civil and political rights more like their Western brethren.

This paradoxical situation would have important ramifications for the Jewish gymnastics movement in Austria's distant province. On the one hand, the vast majority of Galician Jewry, devoutly religious and opposed to pedagogical innovation, typified the "degenerate mold" that the Turn-bewegung hoped to transform, and would present formidable opposition to the movement. At the same time, however, Galicia was a part of the Habsburg Empire, thus situating it favorably both in terms of language (i.e., German) and geography (i.e., open travel to Vienna) to access and adapt easily "Western" Jewish movements like the Turnbewegung.

The nature of this adaptation, of course, was a result of the particular conditions of that population. Ideologically, the Jewish Turnbewegung in Galicia differed from its Central European counterparts in that it was much more influenced by its confrontation with religious Jewry on the one hand and its Slavic setting on the other. Organizationally, the Gali-cian movement reflected the unusual nature of Jewish nationalism in Galicia. Whereas the Jewish Turnbewegung was everywhere a product of Zionists, Jewish nationalism in Galicia, as a largely Diaspora-oriented movement interested primarily in cultivating Jewish national culture and identity in Galicia, was in a better position to take command of the Jew-ish Turnbewegung and to exploit its nationalist potential. Likewise, the nationalist struggle then raging between Poles and Ruthenians in Gali-cia, and its impact on Galician Zionism, would also affect the nature of the Turnbewegung there. Ultimately, the history of the Jewish Turnbe-wegung in Galicia highlights the critical role of local, external stimuli in shaping modern Jewish society and identity.

The Beginnings of the Movement

In October 1898, forty-eight university students formed "Bar-Kochba Berlin," the first Jewish gymnastic society in Europe. Although modeled after German athletic fraternities, from which Jews were increasingly excluded, Bar-Kochba reflected an intense, internally motivated need by many Jewish nationalists at the time to remake the Jewish body, and thereby to transform the Jewish people.[3] Theodor Herzl's leading officer Max Nordau (1849–1923), a physician by training, blasted the "degenera-tion" of "coffee-house" Jews in Central and especially Eastern Europe at

the second Zionist Congress in Basel in 1898, and called for the formation in their place of "muscle Jews."[4] Such rhetoric struck a strong chord
among Central European Jewry, and from Berlin the movement spread
quickly, so that within two years all-Jewish Turnvereine had been established in dozens of cities throughout central Europe, a sufficient mass
to support Bar-Kochba Berlin's official organ, the *Jüdische Turnzeitung*,
later the organ of the world Jewish gymnastics union, the Jüdische Turnerschaft, formed in 1903.[5]

Galician Jewry, as a part of the Habsburg Empire, seemed well positioned, both linguistically and geographically, to be strongly influenced by
the German and Austrian movements. And, to be sure, as early as 1901,
students in both Galician capitals, Cracow (in the West) and Lemberg (in
the East), had formed gymnastic societies. But these quickly dissolved,
meriting only one brief mention in the *Turnzeitung* (December 1901), and
then only Cracow. The statutes of the "Jewish-Nationalist Youth Gymnastic Club," the paper reported optimistically, once denied approval because
of irregularities, were finally approved by state authorities, and the group
would be starting its activities in the coming days. Unfortunately, neither the Cracower nor the Lemberger Turner would hold any meetings for
several years. The Lemberg group remained dormant until 1903, while in
Cracow, the association was not reactivated until the fall of 1907.[6]

Moreover, the Lemberg association, although reestablished in 1903,
remained extremely small. As late as 1906, it could boast only thirty
members, twenty on average taking part in exercises, as well as eighteen
so-called supporting members. This was still an organization fighting
for its existence. Thus its January 1906 press release, for example, mentioned an upcoming show tournament, "on which all hopes were tied."
The Jewish university students still kept away from the organization, it
lamented, and a dance planned for December was ultimately canceled in
response to news of the Russian pogroms.[7] To be sure, the movement had
begun to spread outside the capital. Jewish students in Stanislau began
to organize a Turnverein in 1905 and in Przemyśl in early 1906. But considering the enormous Jewish population of Galicia, and the scores of
Zionist associations already established throughout the province, this
was surely disappointing.[8]

Why did the movement develop so slowly in comparison with Central Europe? After all, to many, Galicia epitomized the problem of Jewish
degeneracy that the Turner movement hoped to correct. Indeed, calls for
pedagogical modernization, including at times the partitioning of physical and temporal space in schools for physical exercise, had been at the
heart of *maskilic* discourse in Galicia for decades. Besides, living in the

eastern outpost of the Habsburg Empire, Galician Jews enjoyed free access to Central European publications, as well as the civil rights to organize their own independent associations and produce their own literature.

But Jewish Turner in Galicia suffered from two obstacles largely absent farther west: strong resistance from religious leaders, who opposed pedagogical innovation, and widespread impoverishment, which engulfed the entire province, limiting the ability of local organizers to advance their cause. The critical obstacle to Turn expansion in Galicia, emphasized by nearly every report from the province, was the fledgling movement's inability to afford equipment and hall space. Thus, the grave economic situation was at once the cause of the Jews' physical degeneracy, as Turner saw it, as well as the basis of their inability to overcome it. The president of the group "Betar" in Tarnopol, Israel Waldmann, described the terrible irony. "Nowhere are gymnastic clubs so necessary as here in East Galicia. Nowhere is our nation physically so degenerate as here in the great ghetto of Galicia. Nowhere, however, are the difficulties so enormous that stand in the way of the founding of gymnastic societies."[9]

Partly this was because of opposition from the Jewish community councils, controlled often by Polonized Jewish elites who refused to let the aspiring gymnasts use Jewish community facilities.[10] Often this successfully blocked the formation of a Jewish *Turnverein*.[11] Indeed, Galician Turner, like their Western counterparts, faced a formidable obstacle in the "assimilationist" community leadership. The Galician Turn leader Josef Katz complained in 1908 that this compounded the material problems of Galician Turner because community board members very rarely supported "purely Jewish" projects; the Lemberg Turner association received just fifty Kronen annually, for example.[12] Several years earlier, the president of the Lemberg Turnverein, Israel Zinn, reported how the local community council twice denied them the use of the orphanage for meetings. After one lone member of the board finally helped them find a space, they went ahead and bought all of the necessary equipment, but were then closed down because other councilmen feared that the Poles would suspect Jewish "separatism." "The gentlemen of the Community Executive Board probably came to be convinced that the support of an association with 'separatist' tendencies could threaten their position with the Polish nobility."[13]

The Heder Campaign

If assimilationist "*kahalniks*" proved to be an annoying obstacle to the movement, the Turner ideology was shaped much more by its religious opponents. Turn leaders were very aware of the tremendous ideological hurdle that joining the gymnastics movement entailed for Galicia's still very traditional Jewish population. They often felt themselves to be unappreciated harbingers of progress or even redemption, and as a result often described themselves as under siege from traditional elements. Israel Zinn's 1905 report, for example, bemoaned "the martyr history of the association, which is a crass proof of how little understanding the Jews of Galicia have for physical exercise. Gymnastics is called by them 'making yourself crazy' and overall it is a matter [more] 'for a *shaygetz'* (Aryan youth [*arischer Junge*]) than for a Jew."[14]

Although Jewish community boards rested often in secular hands, both assimilationist and (increasingly) Zionist religious leadership remained a formidable force in Galicia. Hasidic rebbes and other rabbinical leaders were extremely influential among Galicia's largely traditional population. Indeed, Galicia can boast Europe's first Orthodox political party, "Machzike Hadath," formed as early as 1878. Religious leaders strongly opposed pedagogical innovation, at least in boys' instruction, or the introduction of Western subjects into the Jewish curriculum. And, to be fair, their hostility toward the Turnbewegung was not unjustified; the Turner targeted their most virulent attacks against the traditional form of Jewish education that still dominated in the region, namely the heder.

Rare was the Turner report from Galicia that did not emphasize the backwardness and immoral character of the traditional heder. Already in 1904, before the gymnastics movement had even taken root in Galicia, the *Jüdische Turnzeitung* published an article on the province that focused on this issue. Its author complained that although the public primary schools, which did offer physical education, were theoretically opened to Jews, they were scarcely used, partly because of the difficulties of the Ruthenian language, but mostly because of the Jews' "religious exceptionalism." He then described at length the conditions of a traditional heder, which represented to him the precise antithesis of the Turn ideal.

> So are the Jewish children in the heders raised—cramped, dark and dusty rooms, in which one finds a place for a table with a bench next to the enormous oven and the family bed of the teacher. On this bench the students crouch crooked, in ages from 5, 4 even 3 years old until ages of 12 years old. . . . So are the *hedarim* a source of physical and mental depravation.[15]

More bluntly stated, wrote Josef Katz several years later, "When a child does not visit the heder, his education is the better for it."[16]

As the Turner hardly commanded the resources to offer real alternatives to the heders, such assertions might have remained mere rhetoric. Fortuitously, however, the Turner did have an important pedagogical ally in their campaign against the heders; this was the Baron Hirsch School Fund. Established by the famous Parisian-Jewish philanthropist Baron de Hirsch and his wife in 1888 (although not approved by the authorities until February 1891), the fund was designed to improve the lot of Galician Jewry through modern primary and vocational education, geared especially toward artisan crafts and agriculture. The foundation at its height ran as many as fifty schools for boys throughout Galicia and Bukowina, which specifically redressed the faults of the heder system. Physically, the schools were housed in proper facilities; school buildings were properly constructed with sufficient air and light, and sometimes included playgrounds. In terms of curricula, the schools were to provide children with an elementary education, in the local language (i.e., Polish), of sufficient caliber to guarantee state recognition.[17]

Besides addressing the pedagogical complaints of the Jewish intelligentsia against the heder (lack of secular education, overcrowding, etc.), the Hirsch schools increasingly and deliberately included sport and gymnastic activities in their curricula, although such activity was not delineated in the foundation's statutes. Already in 1894–95—that is, four years before the founding of the first Jewish Turnverein anywhere — some schools had begun to introduce a program of physical education. Those schools that lacked proper facilities for gymnastics or sports substituted those hours with outdoor excursions. By 1900–1901, physical education became a regular feature of the fund's annual reports.[18] The reports emphasized that the Hirsch schools were not just for traditional classroom instruction, but must also be "*Erziehungsinstitute,*" complete educational institutions, including physical education, sports activities, and outdoor excursions. In 1900–1901, 5,902 boys (about two-thirds of the total system's enrollment) received Turn instruction, 3,667 played in sport games, and 5,545 took part in 277 organized excursions. "If you consider," the report adds, "that these are almost without exception children who live mostly in cramped, closed rooms without cheer and amusement, so it certainly cannot be disputed that through such endeavors a fresher and freer character will be awakened."[19] Participation in these activities grew during the course of the decade and was repeatedly emphasized throughout the annual reports. By 1906–7, at the latest, physical education had become an official subject in the curriculum, receiving two hours weekly instruction. Even this activity was not sufficient for all Turner, but it certainly reflected the growing influence of the Turn idea on the Liberal Jewish establishment.[20]

Relationship with Zionists

The relationship of the Turnbewegung to the Zionist movement was complex.[21] On the one hand, as mentioned above, Herzl's leading officer Max Nordau had consistently championed such efforts. But the World Zionist Organization did not directly fund or otherwise support the movement at its first congresses. Moreover, the founders of Bar-Kochba Berlin, fearing that they would alienate much of their potential clientele (i.e., Liberal and patriotic German Jews), carefully avoided any direct affiliation with the Zionist movement. Richard Blum, a founding member, later recalled: "We wanted to nurture in our circles a love of the Jewish People and its culture, not however at the cost of our devotion to our Fatherland, in which we were raised and to which we owe much despite all of the hostilities."[22]

Nevertheless, Bar-Kochba's purpose was clearly and explicitly nationalist. It carefully constructed a Jewish national identity that, in the words of Blum, "had the same platform as Zionism but without its political conclusions." In other words, it promoted Jewish unity and national cultural development, without any specific political objectives, namely the Zionist project to establish a Jewish home in Palestine. Thus, after rancorous debate, its platform declared "that the Jews constitute a community based on common descent and history, in no way merely religious foundations, which, endowed with its particularly spiritual as well as psychological characteristics, has defended a strong awareness of togetherness until this very day."[23]

This distinction between Jewish cultural nationalism on the one hand and Zionism on the other becomes extremely blurred in Galicia because of the particular nature of Galician Zionism. To be sure, the Basle Program, the founding platform of the World Zionist Organization, did call for the "strengthening of Jewish national feeling and consciousness."[24] The organization's principal objective, however, still remained the establishment of an independent Jewish state. Zionist leadership in Galicia, on the other hand, in defiance of Viennese pressure, had already set an agenda of national cultural development in the Diaspora as its principal activity at the founding convention of the Jewish National Party of Galicia in 1893.[25] At that time, Galician Zionists adopted their so-called double program, which acknowledged the establishment of a

Jewish national home in Palestine as a long-term dream, but set their work agenda toward spreading "Jewish national consciousness" among the masses and securing national minority rights from the Austrian government.

This would have significant implications for the Jewish Turnbewegung in Galicia. Even more than in the West, the Galician Turnbewegung was largely a Zionist project. The province's very first Jewish Turn association in Cracow, after all, called itself the "Jewish Nationalist Youth Gymnastic Club." If the group's name did not announce its orientation clearly enough, the Zionist student organization "Hashachar" voted to dedicate its revenue from the Maccabee celebration that year to the new Turnverein. In Lemberg, the Zionist leader Alexander Waldmann lectured as early as 1901 about the necessity of the physical regeneration of the Jewish people, and founded in that year the short-lived "Jewish Gymnastics Association," headed by Heinrich Gabel, chairman of the East Galician district of the Zionist movement, and later a Zionist delegate to the Austrian parliament. It was also Zionist agitation, a short while later, that built the Jewish youth center (*Studentenheim*) in Lemberg, designed to serve as a gymnastics and tournament hall as well. It thus comes as no surprise that when the "First Jewish Turnverein of Galicia" was finally (re)founded on November 1, 1903, its postal address was the East Galician district committee of the Zionist movement! Similarly, in Cracow it was Sam Wahrhaftig, a member of the West Galician district committee, who led the agitation for a Jewish *Volkshaus* with a gymnasium.

That Galician Zionist leadership built the foundations of the Turnbewegung is not in and of itself unusual. After all, Bar-Kochba itself was also founded almost entirely by Zionists. But in Galicia the overlap was more complete, to the extent that the movement's clubs could even share a postal address. Why this was so points to the distinctive position of Galician Jewry.

First and foremost, Galician Jews did not live in a nation-state but in the multinational Habsburg Empire, where ethnic nationalism not only did not contradict Habsburg loyalty, but also was actually embedded in the Habsburg constitution itself.[26] Unlike in Germany, or even Vienna, Galician Jews by and large did not aspire to integrate into a different national group. As a result, Galician Turner did not have to fear that they would alienate acculturated Jews who would have joined the movement but for its connection to Zionism.[27] Galicia was a province divided between two nationalities, Poles and Ruthenians, with the Jews awkwardly holding the demographic balance between them.[28] At a time when many previously politically disinterested Jews felt increasing pressure to choose a national identity, growing numbers considered Jews themselves to constitute a nationality, despite their continued opposition to political Zionism. Thus the so-called "Zionist" movement in Galicia became extraordinarily concerned with the cultivation of a Jewish national identity and Jewish national culture, that is, precisely those goals which the Turner anyway advanced. As one Turner emphasized in a 1909 report, "We are neither Germans nor Poles nor Ruthenians, we are Jews from *shaytel* to sole."[29] Similarly, a 1910 report from the flagship Lemberg association "Dror" clarified, "We established Dror as a national institution, which has not only the physical, but also the moral strength of our nation as an ideal."[30]

At the same time, Jewish nationalists in Galicia recognized immediately the usefulness of the Turner in their campaign; even Austrian Zionists realized its particular value in the eastern province. Nathan Birnbaum, for example, the pioneering Viennese Zionist leader who by now had left the Zionist camp in favor of Jewish autonomism, saw the Turnbewegung as a great contributor to the Jewish national *volk*. "The Jewish Turner recognized already instinctively what we most need: our own, so to speak *heimische* organization power, with which we will again become a creative People, with which we will again be able to create strong men and new cultural productivity."[31] Indeed, as the quote that begins this article indicates, Birnbaum felt that the potential of the Turnbewegung was especially strong in Galicia, where a growing number of Jews felt alienated from traditional Jewish society and sought a secular substitute that maintained their Jewish identities. A Graz Turn leader expressed similar sentiments.

> We don't believe that the [Turn] advocate will soon have luck with his proposal in the West. . . . The idea has prospects of more rapid realization in the East, thus especially in Galicia, where it is not new. And the sooner it will be realized there, the greater its direct usefulness for those Jews. Specifically in Galicia, where the Polish *Sokols* find such great attention, it is important to demonstrate the independence of the Jewish People [*Volkselementes*] through their own particular *Turnertracht ad oculos*.[32]

Galician Turner did in fact form a critical part of the Jewish nationalist movement, and they drew on much of the same rhetoric as the Zionists. Galician Zionists, for example, sought to portray themselves as the great builders of *akhdes*, unity, among Jews, and Galician Turner tapped into the same language. Israel Zinn, speaking to a packed house

at Lemberg's March 1908 show tournament, described the great importance of physical education for the regeneration of the Jewish people. It
unified "the entire Jewish youth without consideration of class and occupation." Turner were especially interested in bannering their Orthodox
membership, which signaled both their victory over religious opponents
and their role as Jewish unifiers.

> One Turner received especially hearty applause due to his appearance.
> It was a young man from the Orthodox circles of the city. The curly,
> dark black *peyes*, proud and self-aware, muscular and full of energy, he
> marched in the rows of athletes. Our association has succeeded in win-
> ning over a great number of Orthodox youth and their number grows
> from day to day. In our associations, where the student youth forms the
> overwhelming majority, they feel themselves very much at home.[33]

Opposition to the Jewish gymnastics associations from "assimilationist *kahalniks*" who controlled Jewish community funds also invited
Zionists to bring their struggle against these "Poles of the Mosaic Con-
fession" to the Jewish Turnbewegung. The Turn and Zionist leader Israel
Waldmann, for example, viciously attacked the "*Moszkos*"[34] in his letter quoted above regarding Betar Tarnopol's grave financial situation.
Repeating Zionist mantra, he described how the Poles and Ruthenians
respect those Jews who show Jewish pride, and blamed anti-Semitism
on the assimilationist sycophants who disgust the Christian nations.
"The Poles and Ruthenians approve of these ideas, only Mauschel, here
called Moszko, appear to us unfriendly. And with right. Moszko knows:
strengthen the hand of a Jewish Turner—so it goes above all on the Moszko's throat!"[35]

To be sure, not always was there such open cooperation between
Zionist and Turn activists. HaKoah in Stanislau, for one, complained of
the opposite problem. The members found so little interest among the
local Zionist associations that the organization nearly folded, and was
saved only by support from Lemberg.[36] The very fact, however, that the
indifference of Stanislau Zionists merited special notice by the *Turnzeitung* serves to highlight the prevalent assumption that Zionists would
support the *Turner*. Overall, this was certainly an exception that proved
the rule.

External Factors

Despite the heavy investment of the Zionists in the gymnastics movement, ultimately the turning point in the growth of the Galician Turn-

bewegung would not come from any internal Jewish momentum as such, but from broader political events, specifically the 1907 parliamentary elections. These were the first in Austria with universal manhood suffrage and they sparked a huge campaign by the Zionists whose Diaspora-oriented nationalism was now totally dominant.[37] Past overtures from the Ruthenians, whose leader Iulian Romanczuk had become the first member of parliament to raise the issue of Jewish national rights in parliamentary debate, led to an electoral alliance that helped to secure a Zionist victory in three Galician districts. Together with Bukowiner incumbent Benno Straucher they formed the first Jewish Club, or faction, in Austrian history. The result of this highly charged campaign and the Zionist victory was a sudden surge of Jewish national pride in Galicia, seen, for example, in the rapid expansion of Galician Zionist associations; the sudden growth of the Jewish Turnbewegung there can only be understood in this context.

The elections also intensified the nationalist significance of the Turn associations. The most obvious example of this is the friendly relationship of the Jewish and Ruthenian gymnastics movements, which reflected the alliance forged between the groups' national leadership.[38] Indeed, the Jews' reliance on Ruthenian support for electoral victory closely mirrored the Turner's dependence on Ruthenian material assistance. Most Jewish gymnastics associations could still not afford their own equipment, much less facilities, and relied on their Slavic brothers for help. Josef Katz noted in a report at the fourth international Jewish tournament in Berlin, for example, that Betar (in Tarnopol) existed only out of Ruthenian generosity. Although other associations were slightly better off (Betar could not even afford an instructor), financial hardship plagued them all.

> Jewish Turn associations cannot at all think about building their own halls. Either they rent the hall of a Ruthenian Turn association, including its equipment, or else [they] buy a hall on monthly interest payments, purchasing the equipment through gradual installments, while the association must at all times reckon with the possibility of being thrown out the door.[39]

As late as 1913, a report from the field admitted that every single association in Galicia, with the exception of Dror in Lemberg, relied on significant support from the Ruthenian or Polish Sokols. This dependence on non-Jewish resources certainly suggests a far different picture than that in Central Europe where, despite substantial technical assistance between the movements, the anti-Semitic exclusion of Jews from German clubs and facilities was an important impetus to the Jewish movement.[40]

Of course, the most obvious external mark of the Jewish Turnbe-wegung in Galicia is the non-Jewish movement against whose image it formed. In Galicia, it was the Poles and especially the Ruthenians of East Galicia, where 75 percent of Galician Jews lived, with whom the Jewish Turner interacted, and decidedly not the Germans, whose influence was more indirect, filtered through the Jewish movement in Germany or else through the Slavic movements themselves. The deep influence of the Sokol system was especially impressive during the earliest years of the Jewish movement, when Jewish associations, lacking their own instructors, relied on Polish and Ruthenian teachers from the local Sokol groups.[41]

In short, Galician Turner, despite joining the Jüdische Turnerschaft, were more influenced by the Slavic Sokol movement than its German counterpart.[42] Thus, whereas Jewish national pride in Germany entailed recreating German associational life and athletic forms, but in a Jewish context, in Galicia it specifically implied a rejection of that model as foreign. Fencing, for example, was rejected early on by Galician Zionists (and Turner) as a "symbol of an assimilationist, foreign [fremdtümeln-den] disposition."[43] On the other hand, whereas German Jewish Turner tended to oppose sport as a symbol of decadence and English individual-ism, Galician Jews readily embraced it, and even came to criticize Berlin's failure to do so as well (see below).

In other ways, Galician Jews did resemble their German counterparts, but in a Galician context. Just as the German Jewish Turner worried about their image among their non-Jewish neighbors, Jewish Turner in Galicia were extraordinarily concerned about their image vis-à-vis their Polish and Ruthenian counterparts. They took great pride, for example, in Polish or Ruthenian praise of their activities. "After the close of the [Lemberg show] tournament," one report exclaimed, "the government inspector of all Polish Sokol associations in Galicia, and a member of the state examination commission for physical education instructors, expressed his fullest recognition of our chairman for his great accom-plishment." The movement mentioned above to build a Volkshaus in Cracow was largely motivated by "national pride," according to one of its leaders, because the Polish students in Cracow had already built their own home. Similarly, the Lemberg association proudly boasted of its growth vis-à-vis the non-Jewish groups in its April 1908 report. "The 'Jahn and Pfuel' are building a new building with a pool, but we already have a play area on the outskirts of the forest, while they don't even yet have their dusty halls."[44]

Naturally, there was also direct competition with the Sokol groups, and these carried strong nationalist significance. In the summer of 1908, for example, the Lemberg Turner sent a football team to challenge the Polish club "Pogon III" to a game on the bicycle racecourse. The conditions of play, the report ominously begins, were very unlucky, with rainstorms the entire second half. "Our team valiantly stood firm. The players showed great courage, verve, energy and talent." He finally admits that they lost 4–3, but national pride compels him to conclude the opposite: "In offense our players were always the stronger." A rematch was scheduled for two weeks later.[45]

A similar story took place the following year, when Jewish Turner in Cracow finally formed an independent sports club, "Makkabi." Naturally, they too scheduled competitions with foreign teams, and managed to play six games against the Polish clubs Cracovia II and Wisla II. The Jews, unfortunately, lost five and tied one. "We were," admitted a report in the Viennese-Zionist paper the *Jüdische Zeitung*, "as one can see, not winners [note how he carefully avoids calling them "losers"], but . . ." he continues, and here one can already predict the conclusion, "taking into account our being in existence [only] three months, we won a colossal moral victory."[46]

This theme of moral victory over the Poles and Ruthenians unfortunately did not end in 1909 either. How long Jewish Turner felt that they could excuse themselves by claiming that they were still in their infancy is not entirely clear. That year, a report was still forced to repeat the already rehearsed interpretation of the Jewish Turners' defeat. "Although the successes were varied, the fact itself that a Jewish club at all dared openly to appear, this fact was so tremendous that also the non-Jews began to respect the Jews as sportsmen."[47]

Galician Autonomy and the Formation of the Galician Kreis

By 1909, the Turnbewegung in Galicia had matured considerably. At the tenth anniversary of Bar-Kochba Berlin, and the fourth international tournament of the Jüdische Turnerschaft, Galician Jews could boast active gymnastics and sports clubs in at least four major cities (Lemberg, Tarnopol, Stanislau, and Cracow) and Josef Katz was building a club in Brody. Thus, the Viennese *Jüdische Zeitung* could finally report of the province, "The nurturing of a young, strong, and proud muscular Jewry has thus, after many struggles, finally won steady ground in Galicia, where it is most needed."[48]

As Galician Turner began to achieve a certain critical mass, they increasingly began to call for autonomy from their Western counterparts.

Not surprisingly, this directly paralleled a similar movement among Galician Zionists who had demanded (and, in 1907, reclaimed) autonomy from Vienna, stressing the unique socioeconomic conditions in the province that local agitators felt better equipped to address. "The Jewish population of Galicia lives in completely different cultural, political, [and] economic conditions than the Jews of the West," wrote Josef Katz in a *Jüdische Turnzeitung* report. "What the Western Jew sees as useful, necessary and thus as something self-evident, this is foreign, unknown and incomprehensible to Galician Jews." Galician Jews have absolutely no conception of the benefits of physical exercise, Katz complained, and only through a unified Galician gymnastics organization can they hope to succeed.[49]

Already in March 1908, at a show tournament in Lemberg between five of Galicia's seven gymnastics associations (Tarnopol, Tarnow, Cracow, Stanislau, and Lemberg itself), Israel Waldmann, the leader of the Tarnopol association, had called for the amalgamation of all Jewish gymnastics associations in Galicia into a single federation, in order to facilitate a more intensive propaganda campaign. Following a stormy debate, the following resolution was unanimously adopted: "The executive board of the Jewish gymnastics association in Lemberg is instructed to get into close contact with [all of] the Jewish gymnastics associations of Galicia in order to found a union; to locate trustworthy men in all the large cities, and in this manner to prepare the convocation of a tournament day, together with a large show tournament."[50]

Over the next several years, Josef Katz then wrote a series of articles in the *Jüdische Turnzeitung* clarifying the need for a united, autonomous Galician federation of Jewish gymnastics associations. These calls did not go unheeded. When the Jüdische Turnerschaft decided to decentralize its activities at its fifth general meeting in 1912, Galicia (together with Bukowina) was constituted as one of five districts, or *Kreise*. At the district's first conference held December 29, 1912, Galician Turn leaders imposed unity on all its member associations. Delegates elected a single tournament system for all Galician clubs, based mainly on the Swedish model, to be conducted in Hebrew.[51] The system would be published in Hebrew with Polish explanations, and clubs with Polish or Ruthenian instructors would be offered special courses in the Hebrew language.[52] Finally, all clubs were required to take the name "Gymnastic and Sport Association."

Delegates at the conference were frustrated by Berlin's inability to support the Galician organizations sufficiently, largely as a result of the Germans' unfamiliarity with local conditions. Members of the sports associations were especially disappointed, complaining that the Berlin-controlled *Turnzeitung* did not sufficiently address sport in its articles. The executive committee adopted resolutions declaring themselves an independent district and establishing a committee to draft preliminary statutes to be discussed at the second district conference set for 1913.

The district accepted responsibility to found new associations, with particular support directed toward acquiring equipment and hall space. Dror in Lemberg sponsored traveling show tournaments to inaugurate new associations throughout the province. In addition, painfully cognizant of the Jews' deep reliance on Polish and Ruthenian instructors, the group also ran a teacher-training program in July 1913 that instructed the participants in "medical questions, gymnastics, sport and national-Jewish education." The impact of these activities was considerable. By the second district conference in March 1914, twenty-seven associations could be counted in twenty cities. Ten of these, it should be noted, were exclusively self-defense organizations, while thirteen others included self-defense activities.[53] Total membership stood at about 2,500.[54] By now the Galician district was effectively an independent organization. It changed its name to "Makkabi" and voted to publish its own organ in Polish, plans that were interrupted by the outbreak of World War I.

Conclusion

In his monumental history of Cisleithian Zionism, Adolf Gaisbauer argued that the Galician Jewish Turnbewegung was from its beginnings more Zionist than its western counterpart. Whereas in the West, he writes, the Jewish gymnastics movement formed as a result of anti-Semitic exclusion and the aping of German associational models, only later allowing its nationalist leaders to attach the groups to the Zionist movement, in Galicia the movement from its outset was, in his words, "a child of Zionism." The groups were consciously created by Zionists as Zionist institutions. According to Gaisbauer, neither anti-Semitism, which he argues arose earlier and more aggressively in the West, nor the desire to copy foreign models, because the German Turnbewegung developed much earlier than its Eastern counterparts, were critical to its development.[55]

Gaisbauer is correct in identifying the strong connection between Galician Zionists and the Galician Turnbewegung, but the Turnbewegung was as much the child of external circumstance as internal momentum. Political anti-Semitism as such did not play as important a role in Galicia as in Germany, but a nationalist conflict strongly charged with anti-Semitic rhetoric did. Moreover, the Zionist movement that gave birth to the Jewish Turnbewegung in Galicia must be carefully defined. The ideology of Galicia's so-called Zionists was far closer to Bar-Kochba Berlin's "National-Jewish" formulation than that of Herzl's *Der Judenstaat*.[56] Zionist leaders did run the Turnvereine in Galicia, often out of the same offices, but their rhetoric continued to be one of national unity and strength, parity with the province's other nationalities, and Jewish autonomy. Whereas visits to Palestine and colonization rhetoric became an increasingly prominent feature of the Western Turner experience, Galician Turner reports almost never discussed the Turn ideal as a preparation for the settlement of Palestine, and there was no agrarian sentimentalism.[57] Instead, one finds nationalist Jews, charged by their growing political strength, advancing the goal of Jewish national rights in the Diaspora.

In sum, the Galician Turner movement, like the nationalist movement of which it was a part, adopted a great deal of rhetoric from Western intellectuals, but the particular conditions of the Austrian province (severe economic impoverishment, strong resistance from a religiously entrenched population, and the difficult Jewish position between the competing Polish and Ruthenian nationalities) led it to develop characteristics that differed from their Western brethren. Galician Turner fought a more targeted attack on the heder system, unnecessary in the West, and they enjoyed a much closer working relationship with the non-Jewish Turner movement as a result of economic dependency on their facilities, and especially because of the broader national links that the Jewish nationalists had made with the Ruthenian leadership. The Galician Turnbewegung thus reflects the unique position of Jewish nationalism itself in Galicia.

Notes

1. A series of conferences began to reassess this bias in the 1980s. See Jacob Katz, ed., *Towards Modernity: The European Jewish Model* (New Brunswick and Oxford: Transaction Books, 1987).

2. For a general history of the Jewish Turnbewegung, see Richard Blum, *Geschichte der jüdische Turn- und Sportbewegung 1895–1914*, M.A. thesis draft, Maccabi World Union Archives, Ramat Gan.

3. Of course, as Daniel Boyarin, George Mosse, and others have pointed out, the origins of this "need" to remake the Jewish body, indeed the entire image of the Jewish body as being in need of remaking, lie in European culture and reflect an assimilationist absorption of an anti-Semitic stereotype (i.e., Jews as nervous, weak, feminine, etc.). See George Mosse, *Nationalism and Sexuality* (Madison:

University of Wisconsin Press, 1985), and Daniel Boyarin, *Unheroic Conduct: the Rise of Heterosexuality and the Invention of the Jewish Man* (Berkeley: University of California Press, 1997).

4. Nordau's most important article on this subject appeared two years later. Max Nordau, "Muskeljudentum," *Jüdische Turnzeitung*, June 1900, 10–11. The term "degeneration," coined in 1857 to characterize those whose nerves had been shattered either by physical or social toxins, was popularized by Nordau in his best-selling tome *Degeneration*, first published in 1892, just before his conversion to Zionism. George Mosse, *Confronting the Nation: Jewish and Western Nationalism* (Hanover and London: Brandeis University Press, 1993), 161–75. For a critical revision of Mosse's analysis, especially his portrayal of Nordau as a Liberal, see Michael Stanislawski, *Zionism and the Fin de Siècle: Cosmopolitanism and Nationalism from Nordau to Jabotinsky* (Berkeley: University of California Press, 2001). Nordau clearly singled out East European Jewry as the epitome of physical degeneracy, comparing the "robust bodies" of Western Jewry to the "emaciated and cough-racked frames of the Eastern Ghetto," however he blamed this situation on financial hardship and not cultural or racial inferiority. See his speech to the fifth Zionist Congress, translated in Max Nordau, *Max Nordau to His People* (New York, Nordau Zionist Society/Scopus, 1941), 137–38.

5. In 1913, the paper changed its name to the *Jüdische Monatshefte für Turnen und Sport*, and in 1919 to the *Jüdische Turn- und Sportzeitung*.

6. E. M. Zweig, "Einige Notizen über die körperliche Lage der Juden in Galizien," *Jüdische Turnzeitung*, March 1904, 45–49.

7. *Jüdische Turnzeitung*, January–February 1906, 19.

8. A 1907 review of the movement by the Zionist *Selbstwehr* in Prague commented on Galicia only that it sadly contained just two of Austria's eighteen Jewish Turnvereine, despite its disproportionately large Jewish population (about two-thirds of Austrian Jewry). *Selbstwehr*, June 14, 1907.

9. *Jüdische Turnzeitung*, March 1908, 40.

10. Likewise, Polish bureaucrats often refused to allow Jews the use of municipal buildings. In 1908, for example, Lemberg Turner complained that their bid to use public school facilities was denied after the school inspector, Herr Nowosiekski, stated that no group whatsoever could use school grounds. One week later, a Polish *Sokol* association held a tournament in the school. *Jüdische Turnzeitung*, August–September 1908, 178.

11. Other times it led to cooperation with non-Jewish Turner. See below.

12. Josef Katz, "Agitation in Galizien," *Jüdische Turnzeitung*, October–November 1908, 192.

13. *Jüdische Turnzeitung*, April 1905, 62.

14. *Jüdische Turnzeitung*, April 1905, 62.

15. Zweig, "Einige Notizen über die körperliche Lage der Juden in Galizien," 45.

16. Josef Katz, "Bericht über die Turnbewegung in Galizien," *Jüdische Turnzeitung*, August 1909, 128.

17. On the Hirsch schools, see Kurt Greenwald, "A Note on the Baron Hirsch Stiftung Vienna 1888–1914," *Leo Baeck Institute Yearbook* 17 (1972): 227–36.

18. These reports are available at the Jewish National Library in Jerusalem as well as in the Hirsch files at the Österreichischer Staatsarchiv in Vienna. The

principal reports are entitled *Bericht des Curatoriums der Baron Hirsch Stiftung zur Beförderung des Volksschulunterrichtes im Königreich Galizien und Lodomerien mit dem Grossherzogthume Krakau und Herzogthume Bukowina* (Vienna).

19. *Bericht über die Stiftungsthätigkeit im Schuljahr 1900/1901* (Vienna, 1902), 9.

20. Dr. Zweig was for one not enthralled with the Hirsch schools. "But physical education is also poor here, partly for lack of 'Turnerish' qualified teachers—[although] in national respects they deserve every praise—and for the most part because physical education is fundamentally neglected." Zweig, "Einige Notizen über die körperliche Lage der Juden in Galizien," 46. Note that the Kolomea association "Dror" was not allowed to use the local Hirsch facilities because of its "separatist" leanings. See Blum, *Geschichte der jüdische Turn- und Sportbewegung*, 88.

21. On the connection of Turner to the Zionists in Germany, see George Eisen, "Zionism, Nationalism and the Emergence of the Jüdische Turnerschaft," *Leo Baeck Institute Yearbook* (1983): 247–62. For an ideological analysis of the role of physical regeneration in Zionism, see Shmuel Almog, *Zionism and History: The Rise of a New Jewish Consciousness* (Jerusalem: Magnes Press, 1987), 108–18.

22. Blum, *Geschichte der jüdische Turn- und Sportbewegung*, 3.

23. Blum, *Geschichte der jüdische Turn- und Sportbewegung*, 4.

24. Stenographisches Protokoll der Verhandlungen des I. Zionisten-Kongresses in Basle (Vienna, 1897).

25. See Adolf Gaisbauer, *Davidstern und Doppeladler* (Vienna: Böhlau, 1988), 63–68, and Nathan Gelber, *Toldot HaTenuah HaZionut B'Galitsia* (Jerusalem: Rubin Mass, 1958), 166–91.

26. Article 19 of Austria's basic laws guaranteed certain national minority rights, including the "inalienable" right of every people (*Volkstamm*) to "preserve and cultivate its nationality and language," and the equal rights of all languages in schools, government administration, and public life. Jews did not constitute a Volkstamm according to Austrian law, and in fact winning such recognition became a major goal of Galician Zionists.

27. Thus, in a 1906 summary of all Jewish Turnvereine, although the German and Austrian associations tended to identify their orientation simply as "members of the Jüdische Turnerschaft federation," the Galician groups (except Lemberg, which had joined the Turnerschaft) identified themselves more openly as "Jewish nationalist." (Interestingly, the Bulgarian associations—13 in all!—without exception openly identified themselves as Zionist.)

28. In 1900, Poles constituted about 44 percent of the Galician population, Ruthenians about 43 percent, and Jews just under 12 percent. Jacob Thon, *Die Juden in Österreich* (Berlin: Bureau für Statistik der Juden, 1908), 110.

29. *Jüdische Turnzeitung*, January 1909, 23.

30. *Jüdische Turnzeitung*, March–April 1910, 59.

31. Nathan Birnbaum, "Die Autonomiebestrebungen der Juden in Österreich," *Jüdische Turnzeitung*, January–February 1906, 6.

32. *Jüdische Turnzeitung*, June 1906 (quoted in *Neue Zeitung*, September 14, 1906).

33. *Jüdische Turnzeitung*, April 1908, p. 67. Of course, despite such rhetoric, the fact remained that the student (i.e., secular) youth did form the "overwhelm-

ing majority" of the Turnbewegung, as it did of the Zionist movement itself. The vicious rhetoric against the heders, after all, was not likely to win over a large number of traditional Jews to the movement.

34. "Moszko," Polish for Moses, is the slang pejorative with which national-ists dismissed so-called assimilationists. Poles regularly called all Jews Moszek or Moszko, much as many white Americans used to call all African Americans "Rufus." (My thanks to Michael Steinlauf for that point.)

35. *Jüdische Turnzeitung*, March 1908, 40. "Mauschel," a corruption of Moses, was a common anti-Semitic pejorative, similar to "Moszko." Waldmann signs the letter with the traditional Zionist signature, "*Mit Zionsgruss.*"

36. See *Jüdische Turnzeitung*, April 1908, 68, and Blum, *Geschichte der jüdische Turn- und Sportbewegung*, 91.

37. As a result of the suffrage reform, the Austrian Zionist Federation also switched its position on *gegenwartsarbeit*, or "work in the present," and orga-nized the Jewish National Party to run candidates in parliamentary elections. (Similarly, as a result of political reforms in Russia following the 1905 revolu-tion, the Russian Zionists also committed themselves to political activism in the Diaspora at their Helsingfors conference in 1906.)

38. Political meaning had been infused into the two gymnastics movements as early as 1903, at which time Zionist leaders visited at least two Ruthenian Turn associations. A Ruthenian report on the opening celebrations of a new Sicz association in Waszkiwci, Bukowina, wrote of this visit quite warmly. "At the Ruthenian celebration there also appeared a delegation of the Jewish Zionist asso-ciation, whose speaker emphasized the necessity of national reconciliation and was energetically applauded by those present. Similarly we also see [such recon-ciliation] in many areas of East Galicia, where until now the majority of the Jews went hand-in-hand with the Polish authorities. Thus a few days ago the Zionist association 'Veritas' in Stryj also sent its delegates to the festival meeting of the Ruthenian Sokol-association. The representative of 'Veritas' spoke as well of the necessity of cooperation between the Ruthenians and the Jews and drew general applause." *Ruthenische Revue*, November 30, 1903, 327.

39. Katz, "Agitation in Galizien," 193. A short while later, Betar reported that, thanks to a 2,000-Kronen subvention from the community council, they had actu-ally rented their own building and equipment. Unfortunately, it was a building controlled by the Galician provincial administration, who canceled the lease, forcing the Jews to return to Ruthenian facilities. *Jüdische Turnzeitung*, Janu-ary–February 1909, 21.

40. This is not to say that such exclusion did not take place in Galicia. It most certainly did, particularly by the Polish clubs. Joachim Schoenfeld, for example, recalled in his memoirs how the Sokol club in his hometown of Sniatyn, a mag-nificent building and one of the only ones with electricity, did not "as a rule" rent its auditorium to Jews. Joachim Schoenfeld, *Jewish Life in Galicia under the Austro-Hungarian Empire and in the Reborn Poland 1898–1939* (Hoboken, N.J.: Ktav, 1990), 108.

41. As the Jewish movement matured, they would also reject this model as foreign, eventually settling on the Swedish gymnastic system. Max Geyer, "Die jüdische Turnbewegung in Galizien," *Jüdische Monatshefte für Turnen und Sport*, June 1913, 191.

42. This directly contrasts the experience of Jewish Turner in Bohemia, where

their adoption of German models led to an anti-Semitic backlash by the Czech Sokol associations. See Eisen, "Zionism, Nationalism and the Emergence of the Jüdische Turnerschaft," 256.

43. Zweig, "Einige Notizen über die körperliche Lage der Juden in Galizien," 47.

44. *Jüdische Turnzeitung*, April 1908, 73.

45. *Jüdische Turnzeitung*, June 1908, 119.

46. *Jüdische Zeitung*, January 28, 1910, 9.

47. *Jüdische Turnzeitung*, July–August 1910, 114.

48. *Jüdische Zeitung*, January 29, 1909, 4.

49. Josef Katz, "Die Frage einer Landesorganisation in Galizien," *Jüdische Turnzeitung*, January–February 1909, 8. Katz despised the reliance on Polish-language gymnastic instructions [kommandos], and called for their replacement with Hebrew. Like the Zionists, he also emphasized the dominance of the Jewish "jargon" among the masses and the need in Galicia for Yiddish language propaganda, largely ignored by the *Jüdische Turnerschaft*. Josef Katz, "Bericht über die Turnbewegung in Galizien," 158, 160.

50. *Jüdische Turnzeitung*, April 1908, 66.

51. Only those German exercises "which did not have harmful effects on the heart and lungs" were permitted. *Jüdische Monatshefte für Turnen und Sport*, January 1913, 20. See also Blum, *Geschichte der jüdische Turn- und Sportbewegung*, 84.

52. Dror had already begun to introduce Hebrew "*Kommandos*" and offered free Hebrew courses to its members. *Jüdische Monatshefte für Turnen und Sport*, January 1913, 20.

53. Rising nationalist tensions between the Poles and Ruthenians led to a sharp increase in anti-Jewish violence, and self-defense training experienced a corresponding rise in popularity. When the Polish-Ukrainian war broke out in 1918, the Zionists' claim to Jewish national leadership was probably strengthened by their network of armed self-defense forces throughout Galicia. See N. M. Gelber, "The National Autonomy of Eastern-Galician Jewry in the West-Ukrainian Republic, 1918–1919," in *A History of Polish Jewry During the Revival of Poland*, ed. Isaac Lewin (New York: Shengold Publishers, 1990), 221–326.

54. Blum, *Geschichte der jüdische Turn- und Sportbewegung*, 87.

55. Gaisbauer, *Davidstern und Doppeladler*, 432.

56. Indeed, this distinction constitutes a central theme of Gaisbauer's thesis.

57. I found just one report that concluded by referring to the nationalization of Galician Jewry through the Turnbewegung as a preparation for the return to Israel. "Jewish gymnastics in Galicia has found, on its long suffering road, the right way and has achieved today with strength and energy the return to Judaism [*Judentum*], which must precede the return to the Jewish land." Geyer, "Die jüdische Turnbewegung in Galizien," 191.

ANAT HELMAN

5 Zionism, Politics, Hedonism: Sports in Interwar Tel Aviv

Sports in "the First Hebrew City"

The film *This Is the Land*, produced in Tel Aviv in the mid 1930s, shows healthy children running into the sea, husky men boxing on a flat rooftop, and men and women racing. A proud father boasts of the strength and dexterity of his three-year-old daughter, while the narrator describes the new generation of Palestine-born Jews, unfamiliar with the Diaspora and its suffering, nurturing their mental and physical well-being.[1] This cinematic presentation portrays the prominent place of sport in Mandate-era Tel Aviv. In the following pages, I discuss three functions of sport in the city's culture: the first was to enhance and demonstrate national power; the second was to express political affiliation; the third was indicative of a modern hedonistic lifestyle.

Zionism, aimed not just at a geographic transfer of the Jewish people from the Diaspora into an ancient homeland, but also at their cultural and mental transformation. The "new" Jew was supposed to become a "Hebrew," the antithesis of the "old" Diaspora Jew. He was to be productive, active, brave, and strong. Max Nordau promoted the idea of "muscular Judaism" at the Zionist congresses, arguing that Jews already possess sufficient spiritual virtues, and should now develop their muscles as well. Sport was important to mainstream Zionists, as it was in many other national movements. And in some ways more so among Zionists, given the negative assessment they had of the Diaspora and the stereo-typical "old" Jew.[2]

How was the Zionist attitude toward sport expressed in the culture of "the first Hebrew city"? Tel Aviv was founded in 1909 by a group of Jewish families as a garden suburb of predominantly Arab Jaffa. After World War I, the neighborhood grew rapidly into a bustling city. In 1921, Tel Aviv was granted an autonomous status of "township" by the Man-datory government and was run by a locally elected municipality. By the late 1930s, the city had some 160,000 residents and had become the demographic, economic, and cultural center of Jewish Palestine.[3]

Urbanization influenced the organization of modern sports in twenti-eth-century Palestine as it did in Western countries since the nineteenth century.[4] As Tel Aviv grew, it supplied a population base for sport facili-ties and associations. Organized sport activities were conducted mainly within official clubs, most prominent of which were Maccabi—named after the national Hebrew heroes of Hellenistic times—and Hapoel ("the worker"). Hundreds of adults and children took part in swimming, bicy-cling, boxing, and other sports. In 1933, there were about 2,300 active members in Maccabi and Hapoel, composing about 3 percent of the city's population. Other sport clubs were dedicated to specific activities or were associated with various ethnic organizations, and the city's Hebrew schools included gymnastics and other forms of physical education as part of the curriculum.[5]

In the early 1920s, a group of city dignitaries founded an urban sport association that raised funds for building stadia and other sport facilities. Members came from the city's elite, including the mayor himself.[6] When Maccabi asked for financial help from the municipality, it justified its request by emphasizing the club's positive impact on Tel Aviv's culture.[7] And, indeed, the municipality aided sport activities by special subsidies and direct grants out of its annual budget. The city taxed entertainment such as movies and balls through an 8 to 22 percent surcharge to the ticket price. By contrast, the city added only 0.02 to 5 percent of the ticket's price for sport events and other forms of entertainment, which were considered educational and valuable to the national cause, such as Hebrew concerts, theater performances, and opera.[8] Maccabi, however, claimed that the municipality should try harder: "Municipalities all over the world support sport organizations, help them financially and build stadia for them; what about us? How can we develop strong sports for the benefit of the people and the country under such conditions?"[9]

Although Tel Aviv's political elite were favorably disposed to sport, some of the city's artists and writers viewed athletic activities as just an unworthy popular form of entertainment. One writer explained that in Palestine's hot climate, the serious art of literature has no chance of competing with sport and other lighter outdoor activities.[10] Bialik, the Hebrew national poet and an honorary citizen of Tel Aviv, established special Friday evening gatherings in the hope that they would attract youngsters as an alternative to football (British football; i.e., soccer) matches, which he viewed as unworthy.[11]

Sports had a positive economic impact on the city, not just by creating employment for professional trainers and other sport functionaries, but also by the demand for locally produced sport outfits and equipment.[12] Big tournaments created an opportunity for commercial advertising. In one such event, two competing cigarette manufactures in Tel Aviv suggested advertising their products by offering free cigarettes during the opening ceremony.[13] A nicotine-filled stadium for a sport event did not seem paradoxical in the 1930s, when alongside some awareness of nicotine's negative effects, advertisers still used the doctor's image to recommend new cigarette brands.[14]

Growing interest in sport was reflected in the media. Since the early 1920s, the local Hebrew newspapers—most of which were published in Tel Aviv—included brief sport news. Gradually, such columns became more detailed. By the early 1930s, magazines were dedicating more and more space to sports, both local and international, and a magazine devoted exclusively to sports began publication in 1936.[15]

As in England and many other countries, football was the most popular sport in Palestine. The game arrived at the beginning of the century, but only after the British occupation during World War I did the game's form and rules become standardized. The British army football teams set the model for the local teams and helped turn the game into a popular spectator's sport. The first local football league was established in 1920 and by the end of the decade, the Palestine Football Association was founded.[16] Well into the late 1930s, English was still used for the game's technical terms. Developed during these very same decades, modern Hebrew couldn't catch up with the growing demand for everyday words and expressions.[17]

When on occasion Jewish local teams defeated British police and military squads, the Hebrew newspapers proudly announced these victories. One Tel Aviv resident wrote worriedly to the mayor, claiming that football matches against the British were awakening British hatred toward the Jews. In the heat of the game, he had heard very hostile comments emanating from the British side.[18] The remarks were probably mutual, since Tel Aviv residents were notorious for the ferocity of their fandom.[19] The same could be said of the football players themselves. In 1927, a match between Hapoel Tel Aviv and Maccabi Petah-Tikvah had to be stopped: The referee ordered a penalty kick against Hapoel Tel Aviv, and the team's captain, convinced the decision was unfair, answered back rudely. The referee ordered the captain off the field. The team refused to comply and the game was cut short.[20]

Football was the favorite game among amateur sportsmen as well. In the early 1920s, schoolboys used to play on Maccabi's temporary field, located on the city's edge, near the citrus orchard of the neighboring Arab villages. The children would sneak into the orchards to pick some fruit. The head of the municipal police wrote to all the Hebrew schools in the city, warning against such activity because it might stir up Arab animosity. During Maccabi's football matches, the police had to make sure that none of the spectators—children and adults alike—entered the nearby orchards.[21]

Men and boys played football in Tel Aviv's empty lots and on the seashore, sometimes endangering pedestrian strollers. The municipality ordered the policemen to prevent people from playing football on the seashore and on central streets. But some of these very policemen were caught using fake sick leaves to play football themselves.[22]

Zionist Nationalism

Much has been written about the function of sport as a vehicle for national identity.[23] Following Norbert Elias, sociologist Eric Dunning mentions a correlative—though not causal—relationship between modern sport and modern state formation, as both went through a similar "civilizing process" at the same time.[24] This relationship was expressed and consolidated by increasing state intervention in sport: control and regulations, political ritual in sport, state-funded facilities, and the use of international sport as a medium for diplomacy.[25] Marxist scholars approach sports as a mechanism for ensuring state domination by providing distracting spectacles, enlisting and militarizing young people, enhancing hierarchic and authoritative values, stabilizing society, and pacifying the working classes.[26]

Other scholars have also examined how sport effectively draws and channels nationalistic fervor. Nations are enshrined in sport through flags, anthems, and national colors in sports clothes, but even more so, as sport historian Martin Polley writes, in popular imagination, where a national team can take on the guise of the nation itself, presenting an image of unity and strength.[27] Writing on interwar Norway, Matti Goksøyr describes how witnessing matches between "us" and "them" created a new "experienced community." Sport became a compelling part of nationalistic popular culture and "gave the sometimes elusive concept of National identity a new dimension."[28]

Still, the significance of sport in national identity varies from case to case. Comparing France and England, sport historian Richard Holt illustrates that the use of sport as a nationalizing and militarizing tool was applied differently according to history, circumstances, and agenda.[29] Sport historian Pierre Arnaud notes how gymnastics in the European continent served as a pedagogic and political instrument for constructing national identity, whereas in England, the country that gave birth to modern sport, gymnastics did not have the same impact.[30] Although Palestine was under a British mandate, English culture had only limited impact on local society, football being a rare exception.[31] To consolidate its *new* national entity, those who shaped Zionist sport ideology followed Central and East European nationalizing tendencies.

A Hebrew newspaper article from 1919 mentioned that although the "normal and natural" life revived in the land of Israel had somewhat improved Jewish attitudes toward sport, still the great importance of gymnastics—as imparting discipline and training for future military service—was not fully recognized.[32] The Maccabi club in Tel Aviv described its mission as "the difficult task of curing the Jewish body, educating the young generation into national discipline and preparing it for any national calling." Sport was described as an inseparable facet of the new Jew developing in the land and as an important preparation for national independence.[33]

The Maccabiah games, organized by Maccabi, were officially an international Jewish Olympics but were also used for smuggling into Palestine more Jewish immigrants than allowed by the Mandatory quota. The first and second Maccabiahs took place in Tel Aviv in 1932 and 1935. Their initiator wrote to Tel Aviv's mayor that the first Jewish Olympics should be "more demonstrative than technical"[34] and Zionist leaders agreed as to "the great national and public value of a big Zionist sport event."[35] Maccabi convinced the Tel Aviv municipality to host the "Jewish Olympics" both as a way of demonstrating to the world Tel Aviv's centrality in the national revival and as an unprecedented opportunity to boost the city's growth. The city's mayor agreed that Tel Aviv and the Maccabiah both had the same goal: national pride and independence.[36]

The opening and closing ceremonies of the first Maccabiah included parades from central Tel Aviv to the stadium (newly built at the city's northern edge) and back. The ceremonies were infused with national symbols such as twelve riders representing the twelve tribes of Israel, the Zionist flag and anthem, and speeches by Zionist and local leaders.[37] In the opening speech, Tel Aviv's mayor described the first Maccabiah as a gathering of Diaspora Jews to marvel over the achievements made in Palestine during fifty years of Jewish settlement. "And when you return to your countries and homes, please tell all our brothers around the world, that here in our country and in Tel Aviv the pioneers are preparing the land for immigrants from the Diaspora. We are waiting for our brothers to join us here and take part in the national creation."[38]

The Maccabiah's national message was clear not only to Jewish spectators, but also to Palestine's Arabs, who complained about its militant character and about its being used to smuggle illegal Jewish immigrants. The Maccabiah as a demonstration of Jewish national power angered the Arabs to such a degree that the Zionist institutions—afraid of violent eruptions—asked all Jewish cinema houses in Palestine to refrain from screening the recently shot newsreels of the event.[39] By 1935, the Mandatory government, trying to cool down Arab-Jewish hostility, prohibited a grand opening parade along the city's streets; participants in the second Maccabiah arrived at the stadium by two different routes.[40]

In 1924, the famous Jewish sport club from Vienna, HaKoah (Strength), visited Palestine. The group was well received. The visit encouraged local sport activists and boosted public interest in sports.[41] The Tel Aviv municipality arranged a public welcome, including games with local teams, exclusive dinners, concerts, and balls.[42] One citizen criticized the grandiose welcome held by the municipality as exaggerated, wondering whether this visit was more important than Albert Einstein's, who was greeted in Tel Aviv much more modestly when he visited the year before. The writer described "sports and circuses" as a sign of Western decadence and suggested that the pioneers who arrive in Palestine to build the land are much more worthy of an official welcome than a Viennese sport club that hasn't even mastered Hebrew. Another reader sent the daily paper a satirical song he wrote about the extravagant welcome.[43]

Still, many others viewed HaKoah and its visit as having great national significance. The editor of a religious-national weekly congratulated HaKoah, stating that even those "who have not been educated into appreciating and liking sports" should value its modern and fashionable importance as a new Jewish attraction.[44] Tel Aviv's leading rabbis greeted "the heroes of Israel," wishing them all the strength of youth, hoping that the spirit of old Israel will be fortified alongside the revived body.[45]

Sometimes, however, the spiritual and the physical clashed. A national-religious problem posed by modern sport was the desecration of the Jewish Sabbath by scheduling football matches on Saturdays. Numerous forms of Sabbath desecration came about with the event: Tickets were sold, people drove to the game's location, vendors sold soft drinks and fruit during the game, and spectators smoked in public. Consequently, the city's rabbis, religious parties, and organizations tried to prevent Saturday football matches.[46]

Although the municipality leased the stadium to Maccabi only on condition that no public matches take place on Saturday, this condition was never fully observed.[47] The municipality wished to preserve public peace and to prevent violent clashes between Sabbath observers and the nonobservant. Yet, while asking sport clubs to refrain from displaying Sabbath desecration, the municipality viewed gymnastics and drilling exercises as valuable national activities for Jewish youths and refused to prohibit their practice on Saturdays.[48] Even the Jewish national institutions discussed the Sabbath games conflict: While religious representatives claimed that Jewish tradition is more important than mere pleasure, Socialist representatives described Saturday as the only free day for recreation and leisure activities.[49] The debate over Saturday football matches expressed wider ideological disagreements about the national character of the future Zionist polity, whether it should be a religious or a secular Jewish state.

Factional Politics

Sport in Tel Aviv not only reflected national beliefs and ideology, but also exacerbated existing internal political affiliations and conflicts. When Maccabi was founded in Europe at the beginning of the twentieth century, it had no specific political tendency, which allowed it to become the unofficial sport organization of the whole Zionist movement. But when Hapoel was founded in Palestine in the mid-1920s, it declared its task as developing sport for the working masses and educating young Jews into Socialist Zionism.[50]

Like other Socialist sport clubs, Hapoel aspired to "strengthen and erect the worker's body; instill discipline, order and punctuality in the worker's life; revive the worker's body and spirit" and thus prepare him for defending the honor of the working class.[51] Hapoel presented itself as Maccabi's opposite: Maccabi was described as a typical "bourgeois" organization, promoting professional victories, individualistic records and personal achievement. Hapoel was supposed to be indifferent to all of these, aiming solely to improve the lot of the workers and achieve collective solidarity. In the 1930s, Hapoel even accused Maccabi of neglecting its original national role and of training Hebrew youths toward fascism.[52]

Hapoel was affiliated and sponsored by the General Worker's Organization (Histadrut) while Maccabi received most of its support from the Tel Aviv municipality. Every now and then, Hapoel demanded similar attention. In 1928, three ships from the British fleet harbored in Jaffa and the Tel Aviv municipality arranged football matches between the British sailors and Maccabi. Hapoel protested: Its football team had just won the Palestine championship, so surely they too were entitled to play the sailors! The municipality conceded and arranged a match between Hapoel and the British team.[53] Six years later, when Maccabi leased the new municipal stadium and swimming pool, Hapoel wrote to the municipality that "we do not envy Maccabi and do not contest their right to have municipal sport facilities," but claimed that their organization too must occasionally enjoy these city-funded facilities.[54]

As to Maccabi, it didn't view the founding of a Socialist sport club favorably. In 1926 it wrote to the municipality that unlike Maccabi, the new club is trying to encourage "class sports."[55] Disagreements were not only practical, but also ideological. Maccabi opposed Hapoel's insistence on playing and singing the Socialist anthem after the Zionist anthem at the opening ceremonies of joint competitions. It called on national institutions to enforce the exclusive use of the national anthem and flag in such events.[56]

Although beginning as a nonpolitical club, Maccabi was influenced by Hapoel's political character and its role as a symbol of the Socialist party. In reaction, Maccabi indeed became more closely associated with the local middle class and with those who did not belong to, and did not support, the Socialist party. Hapoel's separatism reached a peak with its decision not to take part in the Maccabiah. The games were supposed to be a unifying event and Maccabi invited Hapoel and all the other Jewish sport organizations to join in. After much deliberation, Hapoel decided not to take part, since members would not be allowed to compete with separate uniforms, symbols, flags, and slogans.[57] Instead, Hapoel held its own national and international events, where it could freely express its political identity.[58]

The Revisionist right-wing party criticized the sponsorship of the Maccabiah by the British head commissioner as typical Diasporic submissiveness. Still, the Revisionists took part in the Maccabiah through their youth movements' sports club Betar and described Hapoel's separatist demands as absurd. In their polemical view, Hapoel never really wanted to take part in the event because its only goal was to "break the united front of Hebrew sports."[59]

The politicized character of sport was extremely prominent in Palestine. Hapoel was formally affiliated with the Socialist Zionist party and the party's various political and cultural activities. It held an annual Labor Day celebration, combining the political event with sport competitions and artistic programs. Maccabi too was involved in various non-sporting concerns, such as fighting for Hebrew labor and the dominance of the Hebrew language.[60] Interestingly, as Jacobs notes in his essay in this volume, Jewish workers' sport movements in Poland also took an active part in reviving and promoting a Jewish national language—in that case Yiddish rather than Hebrew. Still, in both countries, Jewish sport organizations obviously aimed at comprehensive cultural-educational and political goals in addition to their sport-related activities.

The youth branches of the sport clubs in Tel Aviv were openly hostile to one another. One citizen wrote that they behave like "sworn enemies instead of one depressed and weak people, reviving itself in its fatherland with utmost efforts and with a dire need for healthy, unified and strong youngsters."[61] Even the fans themselves usually chose their teams according to political convictions.[62] The competition between Maccabi and Hapoel was intense, and the bitter animosity between Hapoel and Betar echoed the growing political tensions of the 1930s between the Socialists and the Revisionists.[63] Thus, although promoting broad-based collective identity, political sports clubs in Tel Aviv also fostered significant partisan fragmentation within the unifying nation-building project.

Formal declarations aside, Hapoel—while maintaining a strong partisan tendency—did not fully achieve its formal Socialist goals. An internal left-wing faction blamed the club for intentionally blurring its Socialist orientation and failed to convince the club's management to ostracize all the local "bourgeois" sport organizations.[64] Paradoxically, Hapoel's very success as a sport organization turned it into Maccabi's main opponent, which meant that the two constantly competed for the same achievements and records.

As discussed earlier, Marxist scholars note the state's use of sports to distract and pacify the working classes; they also look at sports as a window onto complex economic and cultural class consolidation and conflicts. Probably the best known theoretician from this perspective was eminent sociologist Pierre Bourdieu, who suggested that sporting practices are determined not only by factors such as spare time and economic and cultural capital, but also by the varying functions of sports among different social classes. Class habitus defines the meaning conferred on athletic activities and the intrinsic and social profits expected from it.[65] The approach offers important insights into European sports. Indeed, Bourdieu portrays different patterns of sport activity among privileged and dominated classes in France, while the historian Ross McKibbin depicts interwar British sport as class-stratified and undemocratic.[66] Similar approaches have also been applied to the United States. Tying American sport primarily to national ideals, sport researcher Alan Bairner argues that sport legitimizes social inequalities by supporting the nation's dominant value system and promoting the notion of mobility based on effort.[67]

Despite the elegance of these models, they cannot fully explain sport in immigrant societies, where class divisions and their respective habitus are not congealed. Tel Aviv, for example, was not a clear-cut class society in the European sense. Jewish Palestine's society was structured around many subcenters and by a coalition of various elites. It was an immigrant society lacking definite political sovereignty and a traditional aristocratic-feudal structure. The unifying Zionist goal softened class divisions and definitions. Economic inequality was not taken for granted, and Tel Aviv's society was described by visitors as extremely democratic. In a bustling immigrant city, where many had to find new livelihoods, the association between means of employment and social background was not that clear.[68]

Many organized workers in Tel Aviv originally came from middle-class backgrounds. Aspiring to turn the unproductive Diaspora Jew into a productive laborer, thousands of young Zionists forsook their middle-class lifestyles in Europe to become manual laborers in Palestine. This self-fashioned working class constituted a novel local "nobility," its members' level of educational, social status, and self-esteem much higher than their income.[69] Bourdieu attributes an ascetic ethos to the upwardly mobile French middle classes, training their bodies as an end in itself, counting on deferred satisfactions as rewards for present sacrifice.[70] In Tel Aviv, it was the working-class pioneers who were most associated with asceticism. However, their deferred satisfaction was not for the sake of personal well-being but rather in the service of national revival—a dedication that won them immediate rewards in the form of social status.[71] Moreover, if habitus defines the meaning and function of sport, Tel Aviv's blue-collar laborers, although short on spare time and economic capital, nevertheless held considerable cultural capital. Not surprisingly, therefore, some of their cultural preferences and values, including sports, were very similar to those of Tel Aviv's middle classes.[72]

Although in Europe different fields of sport enhanced class divisions and identities, in Tel Aviv, all clubs included the very same activities. British officers and some of the Jewish yeomen in the countryside practiced elite sports such as cricket and horse riding, but in Tel Aviv, more common sports reigned among spectators, the most popular after football being boxing.[73] In Palestine, no sport organization objected to pugilism, as did Morgnshtern in Poland. Its masculine and aggressive physicality fit a central Zionist topos, that of reviving ancient Hebrew heroism in the old-new land.[74]

Realizing the diversionary value of sport, the British head of police had an idea. "The Jew is very fond of politics," he wrote, "but since this delicate subject should be avoided in the Holy Land, the best way to distract people from politics is to keep them busy with sports, entertainment and other local matters." Toward that end, he agreed to serve as Maccabi football team's president and as chairman of the local sailing club.[75] The officer was mistakenly transferring his British background into a totally different social context: In Tel Aviv, sport did not move people from politics, but rather it reflected and even increased political involvement and convictions. Although Hapoel claimed to represent the working class, it actually represented a political party, as did Betar. Moreover, while Maccabi and Hapoel were founded originally as sport clubs, Betar was first and foremost a political youth movement that later also founded its own sports club.[76] Sport, like many other social arenas in Jewish Palestine, had more to do with politics than with class affiliations.[77]

Hedonistic Individualism

Sport played another role in Tel Aviv's culture alongside national and political ones. The development of modern sport in the West went hand in hand with gradual changes in the way people conceived of health and diet, as a part of the emerging body culture.[78] During the first decades of the twentieth century, the traditional values of citizenship, obligation, honor, and order were gradually discarded in favor of alternative values such as dominance, creativity, personal magnetism, and impression. An ethos championing moral virtues was being replaced by an ethos encouraging narcissism. Keeping the body healthful and fit became a means to the ultimate end of achieving an *appearance* of beauty, grace, and youth.[79]

Tel Aviv's leaders and many of its residents aspired to create and run a modern Western city consisting of civilized gentlemen with aspirations toward elegance, wealth, and hedonism. This conflicted with the dominant pioneering ethos of Zionist Palestine, which encouraged self-sacrifice and total devotion to the national goal. It demanded that the individual give up material comforts for the sake of building the future Jewish state, even to the extent of self-denial and asceticism. In practice, only a small minority of immigrants adhered to this, yet it remained a powerful ideal in Zionist thought and rhetoric.[80]

Because hedonism was considered a contradiction and even a betrayal of the collectivist and ascetic pioneering ideal, it was usually expressed in Mandate-era Tel Aviv only implicitly, apologetically, and subversively. Sport's role in tending the body, its beauty and presentation, was therefore never formally established as a doctrine or flaunted, but expressed indirectly in daily social practices. One could legitimate sport activity by emphasizing its national importance, but to use sport as an egotistic nurturing of one's personal pleasure and looks might be condemned as improper. So what was often practiced was rarely discussed.

Fashion can serve as an example for the informal yet practical influence that sport had on Tel Aviv's culture. The city was Palestine's fashion capital, strongly influenced by Western modes. Unlike the loose dresses of the 1920s, the tighter dresses of the 1930s demanded a slimmer figure, coinciding with the growing influence of Hollywood movie stars, new notions about diet, and the emergence of sport as a popular leisure activity. As women gradually warmed up to athletic activities, fashion incorporated more sport elements. Comfortable sandals—seen as unfit for elegant urban women during the 1920s—became fashionable footwear in Tel Aviv's streets during the 1930s. Sport also influenced the city's fashion of extremely short pants for women; although this garment was used in the West only for sport and leisure activities, in Tel Aviv, many women wore it for daily use, thereby shocking some men.[81]

The seaside culture that developed in Tel Aviv serves as another example of the place of sport in the city's culture; young men and women spent their free time playing beach games, swimming, and performing gymnastic exercises. They wore daring modern swimsuits, revealing suntanned, muscular bodies. A tourist described them as "Hebrew" as far as the language they used but "Hellenistic" in their appearance and in the manner they dedicated themselves to physical pleasure.[82] A local firm advertised its sunscreen by using a photograph of Emil, a young handsome lifeguard. Emil, who supposedly touted the virtues of the lotion, was described as "the famous lifeguard of Tel Aviv's seashore, the devoted sportsman and boxing champion."[83] Here sport is used to promote a product by tying it to other sexy attributes—youth, beauty, and health.

Nationalism was good for parades, but the individualistic and hedonistic facets of sport could sell products.

In a city often blamed for its "unpioneering" capitalism and hedonism, sport could play a part in promoting modern lifestyles, as is evident in the advertising sphere. Horse-riding lessons, offered in Tel Aviv in the early 1930s, were seductively described as "An Institute for Body Culture." A Tel Aviv merchant who wanted to sell a type of bicycle created a poster with the words: "Welcome to Hapoel bicycle riders returning from the Vienna Olympics!"[84]

Then again, one man's pleasure. . . . Sport not only promoted the lifestyles of some, it sometimes disrupted the preferred lifestyles of others. Maccabi's clubhouse was located in a central residential street. The neighbors wrote to the municipality that notwithstanding their support of the club, they must complain about the horrid noise stemming from the building that was disturbing their sleep after a long day of hard work. In addition to sport activities, the club members practiced dancing and singing well into the "scandalous" hours of the night, shouting, screaming, and boisterously driving their motorcycles. The municipality saw the complaint as "just" and asked Maccabi to keep the noise down.[85] A few years later, the neighbors complained again: Maccabi's wind band was turning their life into hell, especially in summertime when all the windows in the hot and humid city were left open. Maccabi pleaded not guilty, described the complaint as exaggerated, and claimed that all the club's activities are held under the supervision of responsible trainers, including a professional band conductor![86]

Thus, sport functioned in Tel Aviv during its formative decades on various mutually contradictory levels, reflecting the city's complex social character. Mandatory Tel Aviv exhibited both a collectivist ideology along with clearly individualistic tendencies. The city's society had a strong sense of public awareness and residents eagerly participated in various activities for the sake of city and country. At the same time, the many middle-class immigrants who settled in the city and contributed a great deal to its development aspired to personal success and the kind of lifestyle that went with it.[87] Tel Aviv's individualism was often seen as antithetical to the collective task of nation building. Consequently, the hedonistic component of sport—the focus on the body shape as an object for exhibition and source of pleasure, which did not fit well with the country's pioneering ethos—was pursued with a certain degree of discretion.

A final note; the national function of sport is still clearly noticeable in grand urban celebrations whenever Tel Aviv basketball or football teams manage to win internationally. Within the national scene, many Israeli fans still pick their teams according to political convictions, although most of the sports clubs themselves have become less politicized. The hedonistic function of sport, hushed during the 1920s and 1930s as improper, nowadays clashes with no ascetic pioneering ideal. It can and it does flourish openly.

Notes

1. "Zot hi ha-aretz," directed by Baruch Agadati, Tel Aviv, 1935, Steven Spilberg Jewish Film Archive, VT DA 018.

2. Max Nordau, "Yahadut ha-sheririm" in *Max Nordau el amo: ktavim mediniim, II* (Tel Aviv: Hoza'ah Medinit, 1936), 169–78. See also Moshe Zimmerman, "Yahadut ha-sheririm—ha-terufah le-yahadut ha-azabim," *Zmanim* 21, no. 83 (2003): 56–65; Yehiam Shorek, "Tarbut ha-guf be-mishnatam shel avot ha-tenu'ah ha-ziyonit," in *Tarbut ha-guf ve-ha-sport be-yisrael ba-me'ah ha-essrim*, ed. Haim Kaufman and Hagai Harif (Jerusalem and Netanyah: Yad Ben-Zvi/Wingate Institute, 2002), 10–24; John M. Efron, *Medicine and German Jews: A History* (New Haven, Conn.: Yale University Press, 2001), 8–9.

3. See Arieh Yodfat, *Shishim shnot hitpathutah shel Tel Aviv* (Tel Aviv: Tel Aviv Jaffa Municipality, 1969), 15–43; S. Ilan Troen, "Establishing a Zionist Metropolis: Alternative Approaches to Building Tel Aviv," *Journal of Urban History* 18, no. 1 (1991): 24; Michael Roman, "Ma'avaro shel ha-merkaz ha-demografi ve-ha-kalkali mi-yerushalaim le-tel aviv," in *Yerushalaim ba-toda'ah u-va-assiyah ha-ziyonit*, ed. Hagit Lavsky (Jerusalem: Merkaz Zalman Shazar, 1989), 222; *Yedi'ot iriyat Tel-Aviv, sefer ha-shanah Tarzat* (Tel Aviv, 1939), 5.

4. See Steven A. Reiss, *City Games: The Evolution of American Urban Societies and the Rise of Sports* (Urbana: University of Illinois Press, 1991), 252, 256–59; John Gulick, *The Humanity of Cities: An Introduction to Urban Societies* (New York: Bergin and Garvey, 1989), 210; Mike Savage, "Urban History and Social Class: Two Paradigms," *Urban History* 20, no. 1 (1993): 74. Also see Andrew Mason, "City Life and Community: Complementary or Incompatible Ideals?" in *The Culture of Toleration in Diverse Societies*, ed. Catriona McKinnon and Dario Castiglione (Manchester: Manchester University Press, 2003), 141.

5. Walter Proyss, "Pirkei statistikah shel Tel Aviv," in *Sefer Tel Aviv*, ed. Alter Droyanov (Tel Aviv: Va'adat Sefer Tel Aviv, 1936), 410; *Tesha ba-erev*, December 22, 1938, 12–13; "Moledet" newsreels from the 1930s, Jerusalem Cinematheque, V70/71; photograph of high school gymnastics, 1926, in Batia Carmiel, *Korbman: tzalam Tel Avivi aher, 1919–1936* (Tel Aviv: Eretz Israel Museum/Yad Ben-Zvi, 2004), 214.

6. Correspondence between "Sports Club" and Tel Aviv municipality, 1924–1925, Tel Aviv Jaffa Municipal Historical Archive (hereafter TAA), 3/157a.

7. Letter from Maccabi Tel Aviv to the municipality, December 21, 1926, TAA, 4/3828.

8. Letter from Mayor Bloch to Maccabi, December 27, 1926, TAA, 4/3828; "Entertainment Tax" list, summer 1937, TAA, 4/3457. The municipality also granted Maccabi fifty pounds for its twentieth anniversary celebration in 1926,

TAA, 3/157b. See, for comparison, Jeffrey Hill, *Sport, Leisure and Culture in Twentieth-Century Britain* (Basingstoke, U.K.: Palgrave, 2002), 167.

9. Letter from Maccabi to the municipality, December 12, 1937,TAA, 4/3830.

10. Ya'acov Rabinowitz, "Sefarim ve-ruach ha-zman," *Hassagot* (Tel Aviv: Mizpeh, 1935), 251–52.

11. *Haaretz*, January 23, 1927, 1; *Ha-hed*, Winter 1927, 8–10; also see Shin Shalom, *Im Hayim Bialik ve Max Brod* (Tel Aviv: Akad, 1984), 44. However, Bialik himself was very proud of his own physical prowess—see Dan Almagor, "Bein shir ha-shirim le-shir ha-sheririm," in Kaufman and Harif, *Tarbut ha-guf*, 476. On the anti-intellectual nature of sport, see Pierre Bourdieu, "How Can One Be a Sports Fan?" in *The Cultural Studies Reader*, ed. Simon During (London: Routledge, 1993), 344. In spite of its wide popular appeal, sport was not considered a worthy topic for canonical high Hebrew literature until the 1980s; see Amos Noy, "Ha-sport ba-safrut ha-ivrit," in Kaufman and Harif, *Tarbut ha-guf*, 496.

12. Maccabiah newsletter, no.16, February 24, 1932, TAA, 4/3828.

13. Letters from cigarette manufacturers to the deputy mayor, May 1935, TAA, 4/3829.

14. Advertisement posters from the early 1930s, the Poster Collection in the National Library Manuscript Collection (hereafter the Poster Collection), V2750.

15. For instance, a new permanent sport column in *Haaretz* since January 1927; articles and photos in *Kalnoa*, October 9, 1930, 4, and August 26, 1932, 10–11; *Yedi'ot iriyat Tel Aviv, sefer ha-shanah Tarzat* (1939): 146. Also see Israel Paz, "Ha-sport ba-itonut ha-ketuvah be-eretz-yisrael u-vi-medinat yisrael," in Kaufman and Harif, *Tarbut ha-guf*, 344–46.

16. Hit'ahdut eretz yisraelit le-mishak kadur ha-regel, *Sefer shimushi li-shnat 1930/1* (Jerusalem: Azriel, 1931), 4–6; Also see Ya'acov Shavit and Gideon Biger, *Ha-historyah shel tel aviv: mi-shekhunot le-ir, 1909–1936* (Tel Aviv: Ramot/Tel Aviv University, 2001), 338; Amir Ben-Porat, "'Linesmen, Referees and Arbitrators': Politics, Modernization and Soccer in Palestine," in *Europe, Sport, World: Shaping Global Societies*, ed. J. A. Mangan (London: Frank Cass, 2001), 147–49; Yehuda Gabai, "Hitpathut ha-kaduregel be-yisrael," in Kaufman and Harif, *Tarbut ha-guf*, 190–208.

17. *Iton meyuhad*, winter 1938, 4; *Tesha ba-erev*, July 8, 1937, 11. On the "Anglization" of the world's sports, see Ross McKibbin, *Classes and Culture: England 1918–1951* (Oxford: Oxford University Press, 1998), 339, 385; Eric Dunning, *Sport Matters: Sociological Studies of Sport, Violence and Civilization* (London: Routledge, 1999), 102–5.

18. Letter to the mayor, spring 1930, TAA, 3828.

19. Photographs of Maccabi versus the British "Lancers" team, 1925, in Carmiel, *Korbman*, 160–65. See also George Eisen, *The Maccabiah Games: A History of the Jewish Olympics* (unpublished Ph.D. dissertation, University of Maryland, 1979), 252.

20. *Davar*, July 31, 1927, 4.

21. Letter from the head of police to schools, December 9, 1921, TAA, 2/62a; police daily orders, December 14, 1921, TAA, 2/90a.

22. Police daily orders, May 18, 1923, TAA, 2/90c; letter from the head of police to the mayor, January 3, 1924, TAA, 2/61a.

23. See, for example, Eric Hobsbawm, "Mass-Producing Traditions: Europe,

1870–1914," in *The Invention of Tradition*, ed. Eric Hobsbawm (Cambridge: Cambridge University Press, 1989), 300–301; S. W. Pope, *Patriotic Games: Sporting Traditions in the American Imagination, 1876–1926* (New York: Oxford University Press, 1997), 3; J. A. Mangan, ed., *Tribal Identities: Nationalism, Europe, Sport* (London: Frank Cass, 1996).

24. See Dunning, *Sport Matters*, 43, 74. Also see Norbert Elias and Eric Dunning, *Quest for Excitement: Sport and Leisure in the Civilizing Process* (Oxford: Basil Blackwell, 1986); Roger Chartier, *On the Edge of the Cliff: History, Language, Practices* (Baltimore: John Hopkins University Press, 1997), 135–43. The brilliant "civilizing process" theory of sport sheds interesting light on Zionist sport, its modernizing yet paradoxically *de*-civilizing missions, and deserves detailed treatment elsewhere.

25. See Martin Polley, *Moving the Goalposts: A History of Sport and Society since 1945* (London: Routledge, 1998), 20, 29.

26. See Grant Jarvie and Joseph Maguire, *Sport and Leisure in Social Thought* (London and New York: Routledge, 1994), 96–98; Ellis Cashmore, *Making Sense of Sports* (London: Routledge, 1998), 94.

27. See Polley, *Moving the Goalposts*, 35.

28. Matti Goksøyr, "The Popular Sounding Board: Nationalism, 'The People' and Sport in Norway in the Inter-war Years," *The International Journal of the History of Sport* 14, no. 3 (1997): 112.

29. Richard Holt, "Contrasting Nationalisms: Sport, Militarism and the Unitary State in Britain and France before 1914," in Mangan, *Tribal Identities*, 39–54.

30. See Pierre Arnaud, "Sport—a means of national representation," in *Sport and International Politics: The Impact of Fascism and Communism on Sport*, ed. Pierre Arnaud and James Riordan (London: E & FN Spon, 1998), 4.

31. See Marcella Simoni, "'The Only Little Corner of the Great British Empire in Which No One Ever Played Cricket': Reciprocal Relations in British Palestine Health and Education (1930–39)," in *Jewish Studies at the Turn of the Century*, ed. J. T. Argarona Borras and A. Saenz-Badillos (Leiden: Brill, 1999), 383.

32. *Doar hayom*, December 7, 1919. On similar notions in the Soviet Union and Germany, see David L. Hoffmann, "Bodies of Knowledge: Physical Culture and the New Soviet Man," in *Language and Revolution: Making Modern Political Identities*, ed. Igal Halfin (London: Frank Cass, 2002), 280–83; George L. Mosse, *Nationalism and Sexuality: Respectability and Abnormal Sexuality in Modern Europe* (New York: Howard Fertig, 1985), 50, 101.

33. Letter from Maccabi to the municipality, December 21, 1926, TAA, 4/3828.

34. Memorandum on the first Maccabiah program, 1931, TAA, 4/3828.

35. Letter from Arlozoroff to the mayor, October 6, 1931, TAA, 4/3828.

36. Correspondence between Maccabi and the municipality, February 1929 and November 1931, TAA, 4/3828. The national cause and Tel Aviv's role are visually depicted in the second Maccabiah poster, TAA, 6/7—11d.

37. See Eisen, *Maccabiah Games*, 17, 152–56, 161–63; Shavit and Biger, *Ha-historyah shel tel aviv*, 139; Fred Worms, "Muscular Judaism," *Ariel* 113 (2002): 35; photographs from the 1932 Maccabiah, Central Zionist Archive, Oron Collection 558 (27); letter from the municipality to the Jewish Agency, March 25, 1935, Central Zionist Archive, S25/3690.

38. Mayor Dizengoff's speech, March 1932, TAA, 4/3828; photographs of the first Maccabiah, 1932, in Carmiel, *Korbman*, 175–79.

39. *Hazit ha-am*, April 3, 1932, 4; see also Eisen, *Maccabiah Games*, 175–76.

40. See Shavit and Biger, *Ha-historyah shel tel aviv*, 140.

41. "Program for HaKoah visit," 1924, TAA, 2/56a. See also Ben-Porat, "Linesmen, Referees and Arbitrators," 143–44.

42. HaKoah municipal welcome committee's meeting protocol, October 1923, TAA, 2/52b; letter from the Zionist Institutions to the municipality, January 2, 1924, TAA, 2/56a; *Haaretz*, January 8, 1924, 2–3; photographs of HaKoah reception and football match, 1924, in Carmiel, *Korbman*, 158–59.

43. *Haaretz*, January 9, 1924, 2; *Haaretz*, January 18, 1924, 4.

44. *Ha-yishuv*, January 15, 1925, 3.

45. The head rabbis' greetings to HaKoah, January 1924, TAA, 2/56a. On radical and conscious transformation of traditional Jewish attitudes toward the body in general and sport in particular, see Yoni Garb, "Rabbi Kook: Working Out as Divine Work," in *Sport and Physical Education in Jewish History*, ed. George Eisen, Haim Kaufman, and Manfred Lammer (Netanyah: Wingate Institute, 2003), 7–14.

46. Complaint letters to the municipality, summer 1930 and fall 1934, TAA, 4/23R; public notice from the municipal rabbinate, 1927, TAA, 8/209; correspondence between the head rabbi, the Jewish Agency and the Palestine police, June 1931, Central Zionist Archive, S25/9955. On Rabbi Kook's controversial 1926 ruling that football *can* be played on the Sabbath as long as no specific violation is committed, see Aharon Arnd, "Tarbut ha-guf ba-safrut ha-rabanit ba-dorot ha-aharonim," in Kaufman and Harif, *Tarbut ha-guf*, 43.

47. Correspondence between the municipality and "The Sabbath Guard," 1935, TAA, 8/779, 8/780.

48. The municipality's response to a complaint letter, July 21, 1938, TAA, 4/23R; letter from the municipality to Maccabi, November 7, 1932, TAA, 4/3828.

49. Protocol from June 12, 1932, Central Zionist Archive, Jewish Agency protocol book, Tarzab, 3456–57.

50. See Haim Kaufman, "Agudot ha-sport ha-ziyoniot—mi-sport leumi le-sport politi," *Zmanim* 63 (1998): 81–91.

51. *Hashomer ha-za'ir*, March 15, 1936, 5.

52. *Hashomer ha-za'ir*, March 15, 1936, 5–6; and April 15, 1935, 3.

53. Correspondence between Hapoel and the municipality, September 1928, TAA, 4/3203.

54. Letter from Hapoel to the municipality, March 6, 1934, TAA, 4/3828. More such letters from the 1930s, TAA, 4/3829.

55. Letter from Maccabi to the municipality, June 1926, TAA, 4/3828.

56. Letter from Maccabi to the Zionist national institutions, April 25, 1939, TAA, 4/3830.

57. *Hashomer ha-za'ir*, April 1, 1936, 17; see also Eisen, *Maccabiah Games*, 142, 148, 152.

58. In 1936, for instance, Hapoel sent its delegation to the Socialist counter-Berlin Olympics in Barcelona. Photographs of Hapoel gathering, 1928, in Carmiel, *Korbman*, 180. See also Shavit and Biger, *Ha-historyah shel tel aviv*, 140.

59. *Hazit ha-am*, February 23, 1932, 4; March 11, 1932, 5; April 1, 1932, 1.

60. Posters announcing Hapoel and Maccabi dancing balls, 1933, the Poster Collection, V1970/12; May 1st celebration announcement, April 1937, Lavon Institute, IV-250-72-1-275.

61. Letter to the mayor, August 1929, TAA, 4/3452.

62. *Tesha ba-erev*, June 2, 1938, 7.

63. Correspondence about the Levant Fair guards, 1934, TAA, 4/3177c; the Hapoel guards regulations, 1938, Lavon Institute, IV-250-72-1-276.

64. *Hashomer ha-za'ir*, May 1, 1936, 5; March 15, 1936, 2; April 1, 1936, 16–18. On internal debates over the essence and purpose of Hapoel, see Yaakov Goldstein, "Sports Association and Politics: The Case of Igud Hasadran," in Eisen et al., *Sport and Physical Education in Jewish History*, 96–98.

65. See Bourdieu, "How Can One Be a Sports Fan?" in During, *Cultural Studies Reader*, 351–52.

66. Ibid., 345–46, 349, 353–56. McKibbin, *Classes and Culture*, 357–70, 384–85. Also see Hobsbawm, "Mass-Producing Traditions," in Hobsbawm, *Invention of Tradition*, 288–99.

67. See Alan Bairner, *Sport, Nationalism and Globalization: European and North American Perspectives* (Albany: SUNY Press, 2001), 111.

68. See Moshe Lissak, *Ha-elitot shel ha-yishuv ha-yehudi bi-tekufat ha-mandat* (Tel Aviv: Am Oved, 1981), 19, 119; Marsha Gitlin on Tel Aviv, 1933, TAA, 4/3563a; Federation of British Industry's report on the Levant Fair, 1934, TAA, 4/3177.

69. Hayim Arlozoroff, "Ha-soziyaliyut u-milhemet ha-ma'amadot be-mezi'ut eretz yisrael," in *Ve'idat ha-essrim shel ha-poel ha-za'ir be-petah tikvah* (Tel Aviv: Ha-Poel Ha-za'ir Central Committee, 1927), 133–40. See also Israel Bartal, "The Ingathering of Traditions: Zionism's Anthology Projects," *Prooftexts* 17 (1997): 87–88.

70. See Bourdieu, "How Can One Be a Sports Fan?" in During, *Cultural Studies Reader*, 354–55.

71. In this, as in other respects, Zionist pioneers are sometimes compared to religious monastic elites; for example, see Oz Almog, *Ha-zabar—dyokan* (Tel Aviv: Am Oved, 1997), 40–45.

72. See Anat Helman, *Hitgabshutan shel tarbut ironit ve-hevrah ezrahit be-tel aviv bishnot ha-essrim ve-ha-sheloshim* (unpublished Ph.D. thesis, the Hebrew University, 2000), 292–98.

73. *Haaretz*, April 12, 1923, 4; "Entertainment of fleet," June 1924, TAA, 2/56b; letter to Petah-Tikvah municipality from the Tel Aviv riding club branch, April 14, 1932, Petah Tikvah Municipal Archive, 6/16-sh.

74. See Bartal, "Ingathering of Traditions," 85–87.

75. *Yedi'ot iriyat tel aviv* (1938), 116.

76. See Shlomo Reznik, "Agudat ha-sport Betar: sport o politikah be-hevrah mefuleget," in Kaufman and Harif, *Tarbut haguf*, 160, 162.

77. On the national element overcoming the socialist one in the Zionist labor movement, see Zeev Sternhell, *Binyan uma o tikun hevrah?* (Tel Aviv: Am Oved, 1986).

78. See Jarvie and Maguire, *Sport and Leisure*, 55.

79. See Mike Featherstone, "The Body in Consumer Culture," *The Body: Social Process and Cultural Theory*, ed. M. Featherstone, M. Hepworth and B. S. Turner (London: Sage, 1991), 171–89; Stuart Ewen, *Captains of Consciousness: Advertis-*

ing and the Social Roots of Consumer Culture (New York: McGraw-Hill, 1976), 187–93. On sport's contrasting ascetic/hedonistic roles, see Bourdieu, "How Can One Be a Sports Fan?" in During, *Cultural Studies Reader,* 346.

80. See Helman, *Hitgabshutan,* 187–88.

81. See Ayala Raz, *Halifot ha-itim: meah shnot ofnah be-eretz yisrael* (Tel Aviv: Yedi'ot Aharonot, 1996), 69–81.

82. Myer Jack Landa, *Palestine as It Is* (London: E. Goldston, 1932), 22; Anat Helman, "European Jews in the Levant Heat: Climate and Culture in 1920s and 1930s Tel Aviv," *Journal of Israeli History* 22, no. 1 (2003): 81–83. For a comparison to the increasingly entertainment purposes of physical activities in French seaside games areas and sports clubs since the 1960s, see Michael Rainis, "French Beach Sports Culture in the Twentieth Century," *International Journal of the History of Sport* 17, no. 2–3 (2000): 146–58.

83. "Shemen" advertisement, *Tesha ba-erev,* July 21, 1938, 21; photographs of seaside gymnastics and exercise, 1923, 1927, in Carmiel, *Korbman,* 116–17.

84. Advertisement from 1931, the Poster Collection, V2750.

85. Complaint letter to the municipality, June 30, 1930, TAA, 4/3828; letter from the municipality to Maccabi, July 9, 1930, TAA, 4/334c.

86. Municipal correspondence, July 1937, TAA, 4/3642; complaint letters, July 1938, TAA, 4/3642.

87. See Helman, *Hitgabshutan,* 346–52.

6 Jewish Workers' Sports Movements in Interwar Poland: Shtern and Morgnshtern in Comparative Perspective

> The position that an epoch occupies in the historical pro-
> cess can be determined more strikingly from an analysis
> of its inconspicuous surface-level expressions than from
> that epoch's judgements about itself.
> —Siegfried Kracauer, "The Mass Ornament" (1927)

Moyshe Kligsberg, a veteran leader of the Bundist youth movement,[1] once asserted that Jewish youth movements in interwar Poland
were remarkably similar to each other, and that all of these movements
tended to promote the same, new, lifestyle.[2] Kligsberg was well aware
that the youth movements active among Polish Jews between the two
world wars differed sharply from one another in their ideological orienta-
tions, and that they engaged in bitter polemics with one another. From
Kligsberg's perspective, however, the similarities among these movements—including promotion of hiking, summer camps, and distinctive
clothing—were far more significant than were the ideological battles
among them. The youth movements of Polish Jewry, Kligsberg insisted,
can best be understood as a unified sector in Polish Jewish life.

The divisions among Polish Jews, which led to the emergence of
a rainbow of Jewish youth movements, also led many Jewish parties
to foster their own sports movements.[3] The workers sports movement

known as Shtern, for example, founded in 1923, was affiliated with the Poalei Zion-Left.[4] Morgnshtern, officially established at the end of 1926, was a Bundist-oriented association for the promotion of physical education among Jewish workers and their children.[5] Hapoel was linked to the Poalei Zion-Right.[6] The Kadima club in Vilna was sympathetic to the Revisionists.[7] The Samson sports club, which operated in Warsaw, considered itself to be Folkist oriented.[8] Thus, the question arises: Can Kligsberg's assertion as to the similarities among Jewish youth movements also be made as to the movements for sports and physical education that operated within the Jewish population of Poland? A comparison of the trajectories and ideologies of Shtern and Morgnshtern suggests that although there were initially significant differences between these two movements, the differences diminished markedly over time.

To be sure, the spirit of Morgnshtern had always been closer to that of the Shtern than to those of other Jewish sports movements. Though the Bund was staunchly anti-Zionist, both the Bund and the Poalei Zion-Left were Marxist, secularist, and Yiddishist.[9] Bundists and Left Labor Zionists cooperated in the context of the Tsysho (the Central Jewish School Organization), and, at times, even entered into electoral agreements.

Shtern insisted that "the worker-sportsman struggles for the liberation of the working class; sport is for him not a goal in itself, but a means by which to educate a physically developed and class conscious member of the international family of workers . . . the chief goal of the worker-sportsman is socialism. An individual victory has value only if it brings something useful to humanity. Private interests must yield to second place; the collective is the essential thing."[10] It is all but certainly the case that the leadership of Morgnshtern would have agreed wholeheartedly. Thus, the fact that Morgnshtern and Shtern had similar emblems[11] as well as similar names and goals should come as no great surprise, nor should the fact that Shtern, like Morgnshtern, had a positive attitude toward Yiddish.[12] The similarities between these two movements is also suggested by the fact that on more than one occasion individuals who had been affiliated with Morgnshtern dropped out and became members of Morgnshtern's Left Labor Zionist rival.[13]

However, the objective similarities between Morgnshtern and Shtern notwithstanding, there were, initially, subtle differences between Shtern and Morgnshtern. Moreover, these differences were underscored by both organizations in their attempts to gain influence among potential constituents. Morgnshtern placed particular emphasis on activities that large numbers of individuals could engage in simultaneously (such as gymnastics, hiking, and cycling), and soft-pedaled such widely popular sports as soccer and boxing.[14] Morgnshtern differed in this respect even from Shtern, let alone those Jewish movements that were further to the right. Morgnshtern explicitly fought against the formation of individual "masters" or "sport acrobats" at the expense of other members.[15]

Although there were dissenting voices within the Poalei-Zion Left, Shtern promoted soccer from the time of its founding.[16] In 1928, at which time the Warsaw Shtern claimed to be the single strongest Jewish workers' sports club in Poland, it proudly listed its soccer section first in a public description of its activities and accomplishments, announced that 70 of the 300 members in the Warsaw Shtern were in its soccer section, and also stressed that its soccer team had had numerous matches not only in Warsaw but also elsewhere.[17]

The leadership of Morgnshtern, on the other hand, feared that soccer (at least as played by Shtern and by bourgeois sports movements) placed too much emphasis on individual accomplishment and on the glorification of "champions." "Sports-business, commerce in football and with . . . convictions," an organ of the Bundist youth movement sneered in 1929, "our sportsmen leave for the 'experts' in the field of political and societal commerce—for the 'Left' Poalei-Zion with its 'stars' [Shtern], *mishtayns gezogt* [of whom some think so highly]."[18] There were soccer teams affiliated with Morgnshtern even in the 1920s. Soccer, however, was not as important to Morgnshtern as it was to other sports associations.

The differences between Shtern's position on boxing and that of Morgnshtern were somewhat deeper and longer lasting. The Warsaw local of the Left Labor Zionist sports movement is known to have had twenty-five members in its boxing section in the late 1920s, and to have competed with Polish boxers from the Polish workers' clubs.[19] By 1933, Shepsl Rotholts, a member of the Warsaw Shtern, was the best boxer in his weight class in all of Poland.[20] The supporters of boxing within Shtern's ranks argued that it was not true that boxing per se fostered brutality, bloodthirstiness, chauvinism, or egoism (as their socialist opponents claimed). Labor Zionists who made such a claim, one supporter of the pugilists alleged, erred because of the way that bourgeois sports were conducted. Shtern, a part of the proletarian movement, had a Marxist perspective, this supporter insisted, and a "socialist proletarian ethic." One simply did not find among Shtern's boxers, imbued with this ethic, the attitudes that boxing's opponents had feared. "Every comrade in Warsaw knows that it is precisely the boxing section which has the best comrades and which is most closely tied to our slogans and tasks." Boxing made the youth stronger, ready for struggle, and prepared it to undertake successfully the task it ought to perform: to aid in the victory of the international proletariat over the bourgeoisie. Thus, the misgivings of certain labor Zionists notwithstanding, if boxing could help to create healthy, conscious working-fighters, it should be supported.[21]

For a number of years, Bundists were among the sharpest opponents of boxing within the Workers Sports International (SWSI).[22] However, by 1937, the Warsaw branch of Morgnshtern—which was by far the largest branch of Morgnshtern in all of Poland—had an official, active section devoted to boxing and was competing not only with Shtern and with Polish clubs but even with Maccabi (which was generally despised in Morgnshtern circles as a bourgeois, chauvinistic, and linguistically Polonized movement). The spokesmen for the boxers affiliated with Morgnshtern insisted that health concerns that had earlier been raised by opponents of boxing had proven to be unfounded. They also pointed out—in what may have been a political analogy—that boxing was first and foremost a defensive sport, but that it teaches an "important truth about life, that one can best defend oneself if one attacks."[23]

Morgnshtern and Shtern flung charges at one another throughout the late 1920s and 1930s. Early in January 1929, for example, there were struggles between supporters of the bourgeois parties and supporters of the workers' parties within the Football Association of Warsaw. *Nasz Przegląd*—an "influential pro-Zionist Jewish daily"[24]—apparently criticized the role that had been played by the representatives of Shtern in this struggle, and the Bundist *Folks-tsaytung* allegedly endorsed *Nasz Przegląd*'s criticism. A report in the *Arbeter-tsaytung* (an organ of the Poalei Zion-Left) shortly thereafter claimed that one delegate to the Football Association, who it described as an adherent of the right-wing National Democratic Party and an anti-Semite, had credentials authorizing him to represent the Morgnshtern affiliate in Włosławek. This, *Arbeter-tsaytung* claimed, was why the *Folkstsaytung* endorsed the critique of *Nasz Przegląd*—the Bundists needed to support those with whom they were (purportedly) newly connected: "the Polish anti-Semitic and Jewish bourgeois sports clubs."[25]

In 1930, the *Folkstsaytung* criticized the soccer team of the Warsaw local of Shtern for taking part in a trophy competition sponsored by *Nasz Przegląd* for the title of "best Jewish sports club in Warsaw" in which the other participants were Maccabi, Bar-Kochba, and the Jewish Academic Union (ZASS).[26] The Bundists publicized Shtern's participation in activities sponsored by the bourgeois and by the "yellow" press, and questioned Shtern's leftist credentials.[27] Shtern suggested in reply that Morgnshtern would also have competed for such a trophy—but that it lacked sufficient ability to do so. Moreover "the *Folks-tsaytung* knows that Gwiazda [Shtern] has won a great deal of sympathy among labor and hundreds of workers for the thought of proletarian sport through its participation and its victories in the struggle over trophies."[28]

When, in 1931, *Nasz Przegląd* organized a competition for the title of best Jewish basketball team in Warsaw, Maccabi, Shtern, and the Jewish Academic Union competed—but so did Morgnshtern.[29] *Arbeyter-tsaytung* took pains to point this out to its readership.

Did Morgnshtern cave in to bourgeois values in making a place for soccer and boxing within its organization? Did it do so by competing for trophies against bourgeois clubs? Possibly. One alternative explanation is that its leadership responded to the desires of its membership. Just as the national program of the Bund in czarist Russia was allegedly influenced by pressure from below, so too, it would appear, was the program of Morgnshtern in interwar Poland. These changes, however, also made Morgnshtern far more similar to Shtern than had earlier been the case.

In certain respects, on the other hand, Morgnshtern continued to be notably different than its Left Labor Zionist equivalent. Unlike Shtern, which had a women's section (at least in its Warsaw local),[30] Morgnshtern deliberately chose not to create a special commission for women, and stressed that such a commission was not necessary because women already played a prominent role in the organization. Approximately half of the members of the Warsaw branch's gymnastics section were female, and so were half of those in the handball group, among others. Moreover, according to a report on its activities in 1938 issued by the Warsaw branch, "women participate actively not only among the 'sports consumers,' that is, the members, but also among the 'producers,' that is, among the instructors . . . and activists of the society."[31]

Morgnshtern's choice of affiliations is also worth a closer examination, and hints at another continuing difference between it and the Shtern. The Left Labor Zionist sports movement was instrumental in the formation of the Polish Workers' Sport Federation (ZRSS), which was dominated by members of the Polish Socialist Party.[32] Although Shtern disagreed with the relatively positive relationships that the ZRSS maintained with bourgeois Polish sports movements and with the governmental authorities concerned with physical education, and although it also disagreed with the decision of the ZRSS to expel certain left-oriented clubs from the federation, Shtern continued to be active within the Polish Workers' Sports Federation even after losing critical votes on these issues.[33] Shtern believed in principle in "unified class organizations," and thus believed that it ought to remain in the ZRSS for so long as it continued to have the right to express its opinion within that organization, and for so long as the possibility existed that it could have an impact on that organization's policies, rather than form a new federation with a political complexion closer to its own.[34]

Unlike Shtern, Morgnstern, by and large, was not involved with the ZRSS.[35] The Bund had a complex and not altogether smooth relationship with the Polish Socialist Party—which was, from the Bundist perspective, too reformist in orientation, too nationalistic, and insufficiently decisive in combating anti-Semitism.[36] In the late 1920s, the possibility of having the Morgnshtern and certain other movements promoting physical education and athletics affiliate with the ZRSS was explored. In the course of these exploratory talks, the ZRSS, in the wake of discussions reminiscent of debates on the so-called organization and national questions, which had rocked the Russian Social Democratic Workers' Party before the First World War, agreed to reorganize itself as a federal organization, which would, presumably, have contained Polish, Jewish, German, and Ukrainian sections.[37] However, Shtern declared that it would only form a Jewish section with Morgnshtern within the ZRSS under certain very specific conditions—which it knew the Bund would not accept—and negotiations faltered.

At the next congress of the SWSI, held in Prague in 1929, Morgnshtern demanded that it be seated as an independent delegation representing Jewish workers, and not as part of the Polish delegation (as was Shtern).[38] Although the representatives of the ZRSS vigorously objected, the SWSI ultimately acceded to Morgnshtern's perspective. Throughout the remaining years of its existence, Morgnshtern proudly broadcast that it was "the Jewish section of the Workers Sports International"[39] and, as such, fielded its own delegation to the second International Workers Olympics, which was held in Red Vienna in July of 1931.[40]

Shtern, on the other hand, pointedly declined to take part in this Workers Olympics. Shtern had been represented at earlier events of the Workers Sports International, such as the Fifth International Socialist Sports Congress, by the ZRSS.[41] However, Shtern refused to participate in the second Workers Olympics, purportedly because it did not want to be associated with sports groups indirectly affiliated with the Labour and Socialist International (which the Poalei Zion-Left considered to be opportunistic and conservative, and which the Bund joined in 1930, after sustained debate).[42] In this area as well, however, the distinctions between Morgnshtern and Shtern diminished over time. In 1937, Shtern sent a sizable delegation to the third Workers Sports Olympics, which were held in Antwerp.[43] Morgnshtern intended to participate, but the

Polish government refused to grant the members of Morgnshtern the visas that they would have needed in order to travel to Belgium.

Both Morgnshtern and Shtern were subjected to political repression. Between 1929 and 1934, divisions of Morgnshtern in thirty-two different Polish cities were closed, for varying lengths of time, by order of the government.[44] In 1933, when Shtern was organizing its first nationwide gathering, train discounts usually granted to participants in such events were denied at the last moment—an apparent attempt to diminish the size of Shtern's gathering, seemingly motivated by Shtern's radical socialist ideology.[45] A report from Brisk indicates that the quarters of the Shtern in that city were searched and sealed in 1937.[46]

The Jewish workers sports movements were also affected by anti-Semitism. In the wake of an incident that took place at a soccer game in 1930, a number of Polish papers—*Kurier Warszawski, Gazeta Warszawska*, and *Przegląd Sportowy*—published attacks on Shtern that the *Arbeter-tsaytung* described as inciting to a pogrom.[47] There were, similarly, systematic anti-Semitic attacks on Shtern in Prushkov, in which, *Arbeter-tsaytung* sadly admitted, Polish workers participated.[48]

Neither membership in Morgnshtern nor membership in Shtern was stabile. Large numbers of individuals moved in and out of both organizations, as a result of internal migration, illness, entry into military service, and other reasons.[49] In addition to the factors that had an impact on membership in Morgnshtern, membership in Shtern may well have been affected, to a limited degree, by *aliya*. A small number of Shtern's activists emigrated from Poland to Palestine before the beginning of the Second World War.[50]

It is clear, however, that individual branches of Morgnshtern—for example, in Warsaw—continued to attract substantial numbers of new members in the years leading up to the Second World War. In its formal report on activities for the year ending February 1, 1937, at which time the Warsaw branch of Shtern claimed to have over 700 active members,[51] the Warsaw branch of Morgnshtern alleged that it had 1,500 active members, and thus was the single largest local sports organization—Jewish or Polish, socialist or not—in all of Poland.[52] A year later, the total membership of Morgnshtern's Warsaw branch had grown yet again, to 1,855.[53] The number of activists in the Warsaw Shtern, on the other hand, dropped by more than 50 percent in the years immediately preceding the beginning of the war.[54] During this same period, the Bund itself (but not the Poalei Zion-Left) was increasingly successful in *kehila* and city council elections.[55] It is at least plausible—although admittedly not demonstrable—that some individuals who had previously not had ties to the Bund became more likely to vote for it as a result of participation in Morgnshtern's activities. It is also plausible that the successes of the Bund attracted some to Morgnshtern who might otherwise have joined Shtern or another movement.[56]

Whether or not Morgnshtern attracted new voters for the Bund, it is clear that Morgnshtern, operating in a hostile environment, was rather successful in the late 1930s—but its life was brought to an end only months after its third conference took place in 1939. Morgnshtern—like the Bund—was not defeated in the prewar Jewish arena. It *was* annihilated during the Second World War by the same forces that brutally tore out the heart of European Jewry.

Like their Austrian socialist comrades in Vienna, the leaders of Morgnshtern had hoped to help create and implant a counterhegemonic culture, with proletarian values, within a portion of the working class. But Red Vienna—immeasurably stronger than the Polish Bund and with far greater resources at its disposal—was swamped and drowned in 1934, and the Bund suffered a similar fate half a decade later.

This brief comparative history of Morgnshtern and Shtern, I conclude, may well shed light not only on the history of workers sports, and on the complexities of Polish Jewish life, but also on the viability of Gramscian proposals. Morgnshtern was relatively successful in attracting members. But Morgnshtern did not succeed in wooing Jewish workers away from (certain) tastes and trends popular in the larger society, and became objectively (though not subjectively) closer to Shtern over the course of its existence. Moreover, neither Morgnshtern nor Shtern accomplished their primary goals of creating a socialist society. Power within the world of Polish Jewry had considerable symbolic and psychological benefits and mattered a great deal to those who were active in Shtern and Morgnshtern, but it did not compensate in the long run for relative lack of power in the political and economic arenas of the world at large.

Notes

My thanks to Samuel Kassow for providing me with access to materials in his possession and for discussing the history of the Poalei Zion-Left with me, and to Diethelm Blecking for providing me with a copy of his unpublished paper "Der jüdische Sport in Polen zwischen den Weltkriegen." Portions of this chapter were adapted from "Creating a Bundist Counter-Culture: Morgnshtern and the Significance of Cultural Hegemony," in *Jewish Politics in Eastern Europe:*

The Bund at 100. Edited by Jack Jacobs. (New York: New York University Press, 2000), 59–68.

1. Kligsberg participated in the third convention of the Social-Democratic Youth Organization Tsukunft in 1922. J. S. Hertz (I. Sh. Herts), *Di geshikhte fun a yugnt. der klayner bund—yugnt-bund tsukunft in poyln* (New York: Farlag "unzer tsayt," 1946), 445.

2. Moshe Kligsberg, "Di yidishe yugnt-bavegung in poyln tsvishn beyde velt milkhomes (a sotsiologishe shtudie)," in *Shtudies vegn yidn in poyln 1919–1939. Di tsvishnshpil fun sotsiale, ekonomishe un politishe faktorn inem kamf fun a minoritet far ir kiem,* ed. Shikl Fishman (New York: Yidisher visnshaftlekher institut—YIVO, 1974), 174.

3. Szyja Bronsztejn, "Polish-Jewish Relations as Reflected in Memoirs of the Interwar Period," *Polin* 8 (1994): 73; Diethelm Blecking, "Jüdischer Sport in Polen," *Sozial- und Zeitgeschichte des Sports* 13, no. 1 (March, 1999): 20–27.

4. Shtern traced its ancestry back to a group known as Spartakus, which was established in Warsaw by the Labor Zionist youth organization Yugt in 1920. P. Frim, "Fun varshever arbeter sport-klub 'shtern,'" *Di fraye yugnt* 5, no. 2 (February, 1928): 18. The name Spartakus was all but certainly meant to invoke the memory of the German Marxist group with which Rosa Luxemburg had been closely identified during the First World War and that, in 1918, had founded the Communist Party of Germany. In 1923, the Polish Jewish sports group Spartakus united with a sports group made up of middle school students that called itself Gwiazda—the Polish word for "star"—and this union began to refer to itself as the Shtern [Star] Workers' Sport Club. The creation of the Shtern club in Warsaw gave an impetus to the establishment of similar groups in other areas of Poland. The Shtern group in Lodz—Poland's second largest city, and a city with a particularly large number of Jewish workers—was organized about 1925 and began to operate sometime in 1926. By 1928, it had a gymnastics section, a soccer section that had fifty active members, and a table tennis section. The bulk of the leadership of the Lodz group at that time was made up of individuals who were members either of the Poalei Zion-Left or of the youth movement of that party. B. R., "Fun lodzsher sport-klub 'shtern,'" *Di fraye yugnt* 5, no. 5 (May, 1928): 17; cf. "Rirevdike tetikayt fun lodzsher sport-klub 'shtern,'" *Arbeter-tsaytung* 5, no. 8 (February 21, 1930): 10. In the mid-1930s, however, a political dispute within the ranks of the labor Zionist movement led to the dismantling of the Shtern branch in Lodz. A new sports club, Typhoon, acted as a de facto replacement for the earlier club. A. Lagerist, "Prekhtiker derfolg funm sport-lager funm lodzsher 'tyfun,'" *Arbeter-tsaytung* 10, no. 24 (June 14, 1935): 8; B. Sh., "Unzer sport-bavegung in lodzsher reyon," *Arbeter-tsaytung* 10, no. 35 (August 30, 1935): 6; M. "Opklangen fun der 'aktivistisher' provokatsie kegn lodzsher 'shtern,'" *Arbeter-tsaytung* 10, no. 40 (October 11, 1935): 7; "Erev dem turn-yontef fun lodzsher 'tyfun,'" *Arbeter-tsaytung* 11, no. 6 (February 7, 1936): 6. Reports by local Shtern groups were regularly printed in the labor Zionist press.

5. I have described the history and ideology of Morgnshtern in "Creating a Bundist Counter-Culture: Morgnshtern and the Significance of Cultural Hegemony," in *Jewish Politics in Eastern Europe: The Bund at 100,* ed. Jack Jacobs (New York: New York University Press, 2001), 59–68, and have adapted portions of that article for use in this piece.

6. N. Kantorowicz [Kantorovitsh], *Die tsienistishe arbeter-bavegung in poyln* (n.p., n.d.), 32. The relevant article by Kantorowicz reproduced in this work first appeared in the *Yorbukh* of the Velt-federatsie fun poylishe yidn, New York, 1964. The leaders of Hapoel were Meyer Peker, Dov and Mietek Zilberman, and Khayim Glavinski.

7. Dovid Rogoff, "Sport in vilne," *Forverts*, September 8, 2000, 20.

8. "An onfrage tsum varshever sport-klub 'samson,'" *Arbeter-sportler* 5 (November 1, 1929): 7.

9. The single best study of the Bund in interwar Poland is that of Gertrud Pickhan, *"Gegen den Strom." Der Allgemeine Jüdische Arbeiterbund "Bund" in Polen 1918–1939*. Schriften des Simon-Dubnow Instituts Leipzig, I (Stuttgart, Munich: Deutsche Verlags-Anstalt: 2001). On the Poalei Zion-Left see, above all, Bine Garntsarska-Kadari, *Di linke poyle-tsien in poyln biz der tsveyter velt-milkhome* (Tel Aviv: Farlag I. L. Peretz, 1995) and the excellent article by Samuel Kassow, "The Left Poalei Tsiyon in Inter-War Poland," in *Yiddish and the Left*, ed. Gennady Estraikh and Mikhail Krutikov. European Humanities Research Center Studies in Yiddish, vol. 3 (Legenda: Oxford, 2001), 109–28.

10. Shtern membership book of Bolek Lemberger, RG-28, folder 60, YIVO Institute for Jewish Research, New York. The membership book also contains a selection of edifying quotes from Karl Marx and Ber Borochov. For additional insight into the relevant views of Left Labor Zionists toward the goals and tasks of a workers sports movement, see I. A-tsh, "Arbeter-sport," *Arbeter kultur* (September 28, 1928): 4; "Di oyfgabn fun arbeter-sport," *Arbeter-tsaytung* 5, no. 23 (July 11, 1930): 6.

11. The emblems of both the Arbeter gezelshaft far fizisher dertsiung "morgnshtern" in poyln (Robotnicze Stowarzyszenie Wychowania Fizycznego "Jutrznia" w Polsce) and that of the Arbeter-gezelshaft far fizisher dertsiung "shtern" (Robotnicze Stowarzyszenie Wychowania Fizycznego "Gwiazda") featured a line drawing of a naked male figure reminiscent of a Greek statue and engaged in athletic activity. The discus-throwing figure in the Shtern emblem appears in front of belching smokestacks—as does the javelin-throwing figure in Morgnshtern's emblem. Both the Morgnshtern emblem and the Shtern emblem contained the organization's name in Yiddish and in Polish.

12. In 1931, Shtern leaders agreed to demand that all affiliated local sports clubs produce posters and notices in Yiddish (as well as Polish). *Arbeter-tsaytung* 6, no. 43 (November 6, 1931): 7. Precisely because Morgnshtern was ideologically committed to Yiddish, it was concerned, in the late 1920s, that there was not a universally accepted set of terms in Yiddish used by its table tennis players, and it took steps to create a list of acceptable terms. "Yidishe terminologie far pingpong," *Arbeter-sportler* 5 (November 1, 1929): 7.

13. One case led Morgnshtern to accuse Shtern of using money and promises of posts to lure members. A commission of the Warsaw Workers Sports Association investigated the actions of Shtern in this matter, and recommended that Shtern be strongly reprimanded. "'Linker poyle-tsienizm' un sport," *Naye folkstsaytung* 5, no. 255 (November 3, 1930): 5); cf. "Bundisher onfal oyf unzer sport-bavegung," *Arbeter-tsaytung* 5, no. 7 (November 7, 1930): 6. Another case involved onetime members of the Warsaw Morgnshtern table tennis section, which apparently had leadership and organizational difficulties in 1937–38. Arbeter-gez. far fizisher

dertsiung "morgnshtern" in poyln. varshever optaylung. *A yor arbet. tetikayts-berikht far der tsayt fun II.1 1937 bizn II.1 1938*, 23 (Bund Archives, MG 9–158, YIVO Institute for Jewish Research, New York). Other former members of Morgn-shtern's table tennis section joined the Hashmoneans during this same period.

Table tennis was taken quite seriously during this era. All of the champion table tennis players in Poland of the interwar period came from Jewish clubs [Diethelm Blecking, "Der jüdische Sport in Polen zwischen den Weltkriegen," unpublished paper]. The widespread popularity of table tennis among members of Shtern provoked at least some dissent from within Labor Zionist ranks. "Our pious grandfathers" were better swimmers than the table tennis players of today, a Left Labor Zionist griped (M. Koyavski, "Shotn-zaytn funm arbeter-sport," *Arbeter-kultur. Eynmolike oysgabe tsum 2tn kultur-kongres. 30, 31 oktober un 1ter november 1931*, 45). The table tennis devotees don't get enough fresh air, he continued. They ought to skate, or to sled, instead of devoting so much time to an indoor game. Moreover, he noted, the rise of the so-called sport of table tennis had been accompanied by a widespread decline in educational and cultural work, by the virtual disappearance of comrades versed in sociology and labor history, and the rise of the "intellectual cripple." "This is not an exceptional occurrence in one city or shtetl. Entire regions of the movement are poisoned by this and similar sport-plagues." Koyavski, "Shotn-zaytn funm arbeter-sport," 44.

14. Mass activities were stressed because they could be easily engaged in by amateurs and beginners, they promoted health, and they did not require a great deal of practice. The individuals who were part of Morgnshtern, it was presumed, did not have a great deal of time at their disposal and could not afford sports requiring large amounts of expensive equipment. These were not, however, the only activities—or types of activities—conducted under Morgnshtern's auspices. Chess, for example, also attracted some support.

15. "Vi azoy darf oyszen a sotsialistishe sport organizatsie?" *Arbeter-sportler* 9–10 (November 15, 1930): 7.

16. Kligsberg, "Di yidishe yugnt-bavegung in poyln," 221–22. There were Poa-lei Zionists who argued that soccer and boxing were not proletarian sports. The leadership of Shtern, however, replied that there was no such thing as a proletar-ian sport. "The bourgeois or proletarian character [of a sports movement] depends only on who leads the sport organization and on its goals." *Arbeter-tsaytung* 6, no. 43 (November 6, 1931): 70.

17. Frim, "Fun varshever arbeter sport-klub 'shtern,'" 18.

18. Sh. Tshernetski, "Unzere sportler marshirn faroys (der ershter tsuzamenfor fun unzere sport-organizatsies)," *Yugnt-veker* 10 (May 15, 1929): 4.

19. Frim, "Fun varshever arbeter sport-klub 'shtern,'" 18.

20. Natan, "Kh. sh. rotholts boks-mayster fun poyln," *Arbeter-tsaytung* 8, no. 17 (April 28, 1933): 5. Rotholts went on to win widely noticed victories over three German boxers; as a result, the Nazis removed these boxers from the German national boxing team. Letter to the editor by Ben Tsheisin, *Forverts*, March 9, 2001, 21.

21. Nekhamia, "Boks un der arbeter-sport (diskusie artikl)," *Arbeter-tsaytung* 8, no. 17 (April 28, 1933): 5.

22. Arbeter-gez. far fizisher dertsiung "morgnshtern" in poyln. varshever optay-lung. *A yor arbet. tetikayts-berikht far der tsayt fun II.1 1937 bizn II.1 1938*, 21.

23. Ibid. Cf. Mik, "Boks derobert birger-rekht," *Der nayer arbeter-sportler* (June, 1937): 7.

24. Celia S. Heller, *On the Edge of Destruction: Jews of Poland between the Two World Wars* (New York: Columbia University Press, 1977), 208.

25. "An endek, an antisemit iz a bafulmekhtiker fartreter fun bundishn sport-klub in vlotslovek," *Arbeter-tsaytung* 4, no. 8 (February 22, 1929): 7.

26. "Fun arbeter-sport," *Arbeter-tsaytung* 5, 43 (October 24, 1930): 8; "Bundisher onfal oyf unzer sport-bavegung," *Arbeter-tsaytung* 5, 45 (November 7, 1930): 6.

27. "Linker poyle-tsienizm un sport," 5.

28. "Bundisher onfal oyf unzer sport-bavegung," 6.

29. "Fun arbeter-sport in varshe," *Arbeter-tsaytung* 6, 11 (March 13, 1931): 8.

30. Frim, "Fun varshever arbeter sport-klub 'shtern,'" 18. In 1933, the women's section of the Warsaw Shtern conducted a recruitment campaign. "Verbir-aktsie fun arb. froyen-sportlerins," *Arbeter vort* 11 (May 10, 1935): 5. Shtern urged women to enter the workers sports movement because women suffer from "capitalist oppression and exploitation." It encouraged women to "become healthy free people" in part through "the collective creation of the workers sports movement." "Di arbeter-froy in di reyen fun der arb. sport-bavegung," *Arbeter vort* 11 (May 10, 1935): 5.

31. *Arbeter-gezelshaft far fizisher dertsiung "Morgnshtern" in poyln. varshever optaylung. 1938. yor barikht,* 7 (Bund Archives, MG 9–158).

32. A. V. "Di proletarishe sport-bavegung," *Di fraye yugnt* 5, no. 1 (January, 1928): 17. Titlman and Yitskhok Gotlib (1902–73) were elected as representatives of Shtern to the managing committee of ZRSS in October, 1927. In 1929, Dr. Ber Opnhaym (born in 1892) of the Shtern was elected to the presidium of the third congress of the ZRSS, and served as vice chairman in the presidium. "Arbeter-sport-kongres," *Arbeter-tsaytung* 4, no. 6 (February 8, 1929): 7; "Driter kongres fun arbeter-sport-farband in poyln," *Arbeter-tsaytung* 4, no. 7 (February 15, 1929): 6. For biographical information on Gotlib, Opnhaym, and other Shtern activists (i.e., Dr. Hersh Liberman), see Shlomo Schweizer (Shloyme Svaytser), ed., *Shures poyle-tsien. portretn* (Tel Aviv: I. L. Peretz, 1981).

33. The governmental agency responsible for physical education also had responsibility for military education and preparation. The leadership of Shtern worried that the influence of this agency, therefore, might lead to the militarization of the workers sports movement, and to the "Fascistification" of young workers. "Der aroystrit fun 'shtern' forshteyer in z.r.s.s. kegn der militarizirung fun di sport-klubn," *Arbeter-tsaytung* 4, no. 35 (August 23, 1929): 7.

34. *Arbeter-tsaytung* 6, no. 43 (November 6, 1931): 7. Cf. A. V-s, "Finf yor arbeter-sport-farband," *Arbeter-tsaytung* 5, no. 10 (March 7, 1930): 6. Relations between the ZRSS and the Shtern deteriorated in the late 1930s. "6ter kongres fun arbeter-sport-farband in poyln," *Arbeter-tsaytung* 12, no. 11 (March 12, 1937): 6, 8.

35. A representative of the Morgnshtern, Lucian Blit, greeted the ZRSS at the third congress of the ZRSS in 1929, pointed to the continuing divisions within Poland among workers sports movements, and proclaimed that he hoped that these movements would work together for common goals in the near future. "Driter kongres fun poylishn arbeter-sport-farband," *Naye folkstsaytung* 4, no. 42 (February 17, 1929): 4. Blit's greeting was described by a Labor Zionist reporter as having made a "pitiful impression." N. "Driter kongres fun arbeter-sport-far-

band in poyln," *Arbeter-tsaytung* 4, no. 7 (February 15, 1929): 6. A small number of Bundist delegates attended the sixth congress of the ZRSS. "6ter kongres fun arbeter-sport-farband in poyln," 6. None bothered to attend the seventh congress (at which 24 of the 140 delegates represented Shtern, and 2 delegates represented Hapoel). "Der 7ter kongres fun arbeter-sport-farband in poyln," *Arbeter-tsaytung* 14, no. 4 (February 19, 1939).

36. Abraham Brumberg, "The Bund and the Polish Socialist Party in the Late 1930s," in *The Jews of Poland Between Two World Wars*, ed. Yisrael Gutman, Ezra Mendelsohn, Jehuda Reinharz, and Chone Shmeruk (Hanover and London: University Press of New England, 1989), 75–82; Piotr Wróbel, "From Conflict to Cooperation: The Bund and the Polish Socialist Party, 1897–1939," in Jacobs, *Jewish Politics in Eastern Europe*, 161–65.

37. A. V., "Di proletarishe sport-bavegung," 17.

38. Roni Gechtman, "Socialist Mass Politics though Sport: The Bund's Morgn-shtern in Poland, 1926–1939," *Journal of Sport History* 26, no. 2 (Summer, 1999): 336–37.

39. *Arbeter-gezelshaft far fizisher dertsiung "morgnshtern" in poyln. yidishe sektsie fun arbeter sport internatsional. varshever optaylung. barikht fun der tsayt 1.II.1936—1.II.1937*, (Bund Archives, MG 9–158).

40. B. Goldshtayn, *Tsvantsik yor in varshever "bund" 1919–1939* (New York: Farlag "unzer tsayt," 1960), 222. Cf. J. S. Hertz [I. Sh. Herts], "Der bund in umo-phengikn poyln, 1926–1932," in *Di geshikhte fun bund*, vol. 5 (New York: Farlag unzer tsayt, 1981), 90–91. The First International Workers Olympics had been held in Frankfurt am Main in 1925, before the creation of Morgnshtern and when Shtern was still in its infancy.

41. "Der 5ter internatsionaler sotsialistisher sport-kongres in prag," *Arbeter-tsaytung* 4, no. 44 (October 25, 1929): 2.

42. "Fun arbeter sport bavegung," *Arbeter-tsaytung* 6, no. 24 (June 12, 1931): 8. A report in the newspaper of the Poalei-Zion Left on the Vienna Workers Olym-pics accused the Olympics' organizers of having transformed the mass of worker athletes into a "golem of clay, without a trace of proletarian soul," pointed out that contingents in the various parades organized in conjunction with the Olym-pics lacked appropriate political slogans, and claimed that the delegation from Morgnshtern was scarcely in evidence. N. N. "Arbeter-olimpiada in 'roytn' vin," *Arbeter-tsaytung* 6, no. 32 (August 21, 1931).

43. Almost 200 members of Shtern were in its delegation to the third Workers Olympics. I. Gotlib, "Der yungster tsvayg fun unzer bavegung," *Arbeter-tsaytung* 14, no. 7 (March 3, 1939): 21. The Polish Workers Sports Association chose not to participate in the third Workers Olympics because it objected to the presence at that event of representatives of the Soviet Union. "Z.r.r.s. tsit zikh tsurik fun der arbeter-olimpiade," *Arbeter-tsaytung* 12, no. 26 (June 25, 1937): 5.

44. Hertz, *Di geshikhte fun a yugnt*, 208.

45. "Der ershter 'shtern' tsuzamenfli," *Arbeter-tsaytung* 8, no. 22 (June 2, 1933): 1.

46. "Farkhasmet dem lokal fun 'shtern,'" *Arbeter-tsaytung* 12, no. 16: (April 16, 1937): 7. A newspaper article dating from 1935, on the other hand, suggests that although local units of the Poalei Zion-Left had been subjected to legal pres-sure, Shtern may not have been under quite as much pressure: "In many places

the workers' societies for physical culture are the only legal workers' organizations." I. K., "In shelikhes fun klas!" *Arbeter-vort* 8–9 (April 19, 1935): 7.

47. "A reaktsionere hetse kegn dem a. s. k. 'shtern,'" *Arbeter-tsaytung* 5, no. 15 (April 11, 1930): 10.

48. "The management of the Workers Sports Association endeavors to instill comradely relations, but does not always succeed and workers sports competitions are sometimes disrupted by the appearance of anti-Semitism." Melekh, "Antisemitizm in sport," *Arbeter-tsaytung* 10, no. 39 (October 4, 1935): 6.

49. *Naye optaylung. Arbeter gezelshaft far fizisher dertsiung "morgnshtern" in poyln, optaylung in lodz,* March 1939, 3 (Bund Archives, MG 9–159).

50. "Alg. farz. fun varshever 'shtern,'" *Arbeter-vort* 2 (January 24, 1936): 6.

51. "Algemeyne farzamlung fun i.a.s.k. 'shtern' in varshe. Der bilans fun a derfolgraykher arbet," *Arbeter-tsaytung* 12, no. 7 (February 12, 1937): 7. The Shtern group in Warsaw had 300 members at the beginning of 1928 (P. Frim, "Fun varshever arbeter sport-klub 'shtern,'" *Fraye yugnt* 5, no. 2 [February, 1928]: 18), and approximately 460 members at the end of that year. Melekh, "Unzer sport-klub 'Gwiazda' ariber in clas A," *Arbeter-tsaytung* 3, no. 49 (December 7, 1928): 6. It claimed 500 activists in 1929. "Fun arbeter-sport," *Arbeter-tsaytung* 4, no. 29 (July 19, 1929).

52. *Arbeter-gezelshaft far fizisher dertsiung "morgnshtern" in poyln. yidishe sektsie fun arbeter sport internatsional. varshever optaylung. barikht fun der tsayt 1.II.1936 – 1.II.1937,* (Bund Archives, MG 9–158).

53. *Arbeter-gez. far fizisher dertsiung "morgnshtern" in poyln. varshever optaylung. a yor arbet. tetikayts-barikht far der tsayt fun II.1 1937 bizn II.1 1938.*

54. At the time of the last known annual meeting of the Warsaw Shtern, it was reported that the club had "over 400" activists, but that the total membership was much larger. "Yerlekhe alg. farzamlung fun varshever 'shtern,'" *Arbeter-tsaytung* 14, no. 2 (January 27, 1939): 2.

55. Bernard K. Johnpoll, *The Politics of Futility: The General Jewish Workers Bund of Poland, 1917–1943* (Ithaca: Cornell University Press, 1967), 220–24; Antony Polonsky, "The Bund in Polish Political Life, 1935–1939," in *Jewish History: Essays in Honour of Chimen Abramsky,* ed. Ada Rapoport-Albert and Steven J. Zipperstein (London: Peter Halban, 1988), 547–77; Daniel Blatman, "The Bund in Poland, 1935–1939," *Polin* 9 (1996): 35–82.

56. It has been asserted by Yankef Kener (who was editor of the Left Poalei Zion's periodicals in Poland for children and youth, *Kinder-velt* and *Di fraye yugnt*) that Shtern had a larger membership in Poland as a whole than did Morgnshtern. Warsaw was not favorable territory for the Left Poalei Zion—and seems not to have been particularly favorable territory for its sports affiliate. Lodz was also not among the strongholds of the Poalei Zion-Left. However, Kener, presumably describing the period immediately preceding the beginning of the Second World War, indicates that Morgnshtern had 6,000 members in Poland and that Shtern had over 16,000 members. Yankef Kener, *Kvershnit (1897–1947). Fragmentn fun zikhroynes, epizodn, geshikhtlekhe momentn, gedenkverter vegn umgekumene kedushim, martirer un kemfer* (New York: Tsentral komitet fun linke poyletsien in di fareynikte shtatn un kanade, 1947), 164, 171. If Kener is correct, than Gechtman's claim that Morgnshtern was the largest Jewish sports organization in Poland (Gechtman, "Socialist Mass Politics though Sport," 329) is unjustified.

It ought to be noted, however, that Kener's figures are not corroborated by contemporary sources and cannot be confirmed. Shtern, which had 146 local divisions, repeatedly claimed to be the largest Jewish workers sports organization in Poland. Gotlib, "Der yungster tsvayg fun unzer bavegung," 21. Hapoel is alleged to have had more than 5,000 members in Poland. Kantorowicz, "Die tsienistishe arbeter-bavegung in poyln," 32. Maccabi, a Jewish sports movement that did not have a socialist orientation and that included middle-class and Polish-speaking Jews in its constituency, was larger in some locations—e.g., in Vilna—than any of the Jewish workers sports movements. Rogoff, "Sport in vilne," 20.

PART III

Odd Contestants

HARVEY E. GOLDBERG

7   *Sabbath Sport on the Shores*
    of Tripoli: Muscles and Memory
    among the Jews of Libya

Introduction

The image of a successful sports competitor, who is also the
member of an ethnic minority, is familiar in modern societies. Their
accomplishments are seen to redound to the group as a whole, at the same
time that they serve the goal of individual social mobility. The admira-
tion of the physical skills of minorities existed in premodern times as
well, even as these groups occupied a fixed niche in a social structure
that was not defined by national identities and alternative minority status. In this paper I examine an account of "wrestling" matches among
teams of Jews, which took place on Sabbath afternoon, in Tripoli (Libya)
in the early nineteenth century. The account points to symbolic links
between these events and processes within the wider society. The Jewish "sporting event" became an arena in which issues crucial to the city
as a whole were aired. Competitive games between Jews are reported, in
less detail, from both Morocco and Algeria, and they also seem to take
on significance in terms of their wider social setting.

In addition to analyzing the meanings of traditional forms of competition, this historical case, when compared with more recent data on the
life of the Jews of Libya, suggests that there are certain characteristics of
sports events that, while clearly shaped by their specific cultural milieu,

transcend different periods and social settings. One such feature is the role of dramatic sports performance in collective memory. Although not predictable in advance, some of the outcomes of the sports activities emerge as affective group foci, and are symbolically preserved by groups for years later, even spanning the generations. In the case of the Jews of Libya, some of these sport-related memories resonate even after most of the community left their country of birth and moved to Israel.

Libyan Jews, Physical Prowess, and Sports

More than 30,000 Jews moved from Libya to Israel from 1949 to 1951, and only about 4,000 remained in that North African country after that time. I begin my discussion of sports among them with a recollection from the first months I was exposed to their way of life in 1963.[1] The setting was an immigrant moshav in Israel's Sharon plain, and much of my time at this initial stage of fieldwork was spent in the moshav office. On a window ledge in the office laid a pile of pamphlets telling the story of two sainted rabbis who had lived in Tripoli. The pamphlets were published by the Committee of Libyan Jewish Communities in Israel, under the auspices of the religious Hapoel Mizrahi party. They were sent out to locales where Jews from Libya congregated and were distributed free for the asking. I noticed that the pile in the office remained more or less static for several weeks, with only an occasional visitor thumbing through a booklet or taking one. I entertained a hypothesis that because the rabbis were from the city of Tripoli, and the members of the moshav were from a village in the interior of the country, they had no previous knowledge of these figures and therefore no interest in them. My hypothesis was disabused when several weeks later another pamphlet arrived, bearing a picture of a handsome man in traditional—but nonrabbinic—dress, sporting a broad moustache. He was also from the city of Tripoli and known as Moni Gabai. News that the pamphlet had arrived spread rapidly in the moshav and within a few hours it was gone from the windowsill. Clearly, Moni Gabai grabbed the imagination of the villagers in a manner that the rabbis did not.

Moni Gabai's formal name was Shim'on Bracha. A description of him appears in another book by the Committee of Libyan Jewish Communities in Israel (which was the basis of the pamphlet), and calls him the "National Hero" (gibor leumi) of Libyan Jews. His heroics were expressed first and foremost in his defense of Jews against Muslim toughs who would on occasion harass them.

According to the book, Moni Gabai did not seek self-aggrandizement, but

> had a special sense to "smell out" the weak points at which his Jewish brethren were in danger from groups of Arab toughs who would lie in wait for Jews during dark nights, or would come to disturb a wedding celebration, or generally harass them in different circumstances. He would hurry to such trouble spots, either by himself or with a group of young brave friends, and Woe to the toughs if they did not succeed in fleeing before feeling the weight of his heavy hand! Like a lion in a flock of sheep he would pounce, knocking down everything left and right, and would run after those who fled, not giving up until he succeeded in giving them the portion that they deserved.

The panegyric then continues: "The small and the mighty, the Rabbi and the craftsman, man and woman—all the segments of the people adored him."[2] The dramatic recollections of life in Tripoli upon which this description draws were evidently shared by the villagers in this moshav.

Rabbi Frija Zuaretz, the author of the book—who was also a member of Knesset for several terms (1955–1969), indicates that Moni Gabai spent long periods of time in jail (under the Italian colonial regime) as the price of his acts of ethnic self-defense. He presents this information without apologies, although the fact that the story of Moni Gabai appears at the very end of the volume suggests some ambivalence. The kind of heroism represented by Gabai does not easily fit into "classic" rabbinic or even respectable Zionist paradigms, but it also assumes that Zuaretz did not feel he was being true to the heritage of Jews from Tripoli without mentioning this popular hero. The response of the moshav villagers, depicted above, certainly confirms Zuaretz's decision to include a section on Gabai. His account also goes on to indicate that this paragon of physical prowess was attracted to the realm of sports: "He loved to watch young Jewish men in sports practice, and in exercise to put themselves in shape. In 1936 [two years before his death at the age of 44], he organized a soccer team giving it the name 'Tel Aviv.' He bought the equipment and uniforms with his own funds, and would also pay the young people a daily sum compensating for the wages they lost by committing themselves to practice. . . ." The account continues: "More than once, this team, or other Jewish teams, competed with non-Jewish teams in the stadium [including both Italian and Muslim teams], and often these competitions would end with blows and fisticuffs. He would step in, of course: Striking, wounding, and not stopping—ending up, as usual, in prison."[3]

We hear elsewhere of Jewish sports organizations in Tripoli beginning in the 1920s, in particular with regard to the Maccabee organization
which was also linked to Zionism.[4] The centrality of sports in the life
of Jews also receives expression in a film on the Jews of Libya, produced
in Israel in 1981, that recalls the competition between Jewish and Arab
soccer teams during the Italian period.[5] One popular rabbi, Bichor Sabban,
stressed in an interview with me how he was known both for teaching
the modern Hebrew spoken in Palestine and for being an enthusiastic
supporter of Jewish soccer teams. Rather than explore the connection
between sports and ethnic or national identity in the mid-twentieth century Tripoli, I consider a much earlier setting in which Jews engaged in
games of physical competition in that town.

Jewish Sabbath Games in the Nineteenth Century

This setting is described in the writings of Mordechai Ha-Cohen, who
was born in 1856 and died in the late 1920s, and who in the first decade
of the twentieth century wrote a book in Hebrew that deals with the
history, institutions, and customs of the Jews of Libya.[6] Ha-Cohen, who
at first was a merchant who traveled to the interior of Tripolitania, was
familiar with a wide spectrum of the culture of the Jews in the region,
including the life of the Jews in the villages. In discussing the early years
of the nineteenth century, Ha-Cohen notes that in the days of Yusef
Pasha, the last autonomous regent of Tripoli, many Jews came to settle
in the city after being ransomed from corsairs. He then indicates that at
that period, all the Jews resided in two adjacent quarters of Tripoli, the
hara kebira (large [Jewish] quarter) and the *hara zeghira* (small quarter),
and goes on to describe a Sabbath afternoon pastime giving saliency to
that residential division. Here is his narrative:

> In former days, each Sabbath after the morning meal, the Jewish toughs
> [he uses the Hebrew term *"biryonim"*] would gather on the western
> wall of the town, adjacent to the Jewish quarter. The members of the
> *hara kebira* (Large Quarter) with their special red flag would stand to the
> North, while the members of the *hara zeghira* (Small Quarter) would
> stand to the South with their white flag. They would exercise and then
> organize themselves as two armies, fighting without any weapons. Some
> would wrestle with their opponents, attempting to throw them to the
> ground, and others would box, skillfully hitting both head and foot.
> However, he who overcame his rival would be careful not to hurt him
> excessively. They would *take captives from one another and redeem
> captives* [italics added] with bravery and cunning.

The women and children would stand crowded, watching the two teams play on the wall, praising that which emerged as the winner. For the most part the members of the *hara zeghira* were victorious as they were both courageous and clever. But the *hara kebira* team had two heroes, light of foot, who easily jumped great distances. When the fighting became difficult they swiftly ran to release the captured members of their side.

Even though they liked and married one another, it was not possible for a member of one quarter to visit his friend in the other quarter during the fighting. But when the period set aside for fighting was over, a white flag was raised signifying peace, and one was able to visit the other.[7]

Ha-Cohen goes on to explain that these roughnecks constituted a "gang" that served, in an informal but definite manner, to defend the honor of the Jews.[8] According to his narrative, "the fear of the *biryonim* was upon all the high handed ones," and it was a terrible shame to the family of a Muslim if he were to be bested by one of the Jewish toughs. The account emphasizes that the members of the Jewish gang would not bow their heads to accept any authority.

The portrayal of the *biryonim* and the Sabbath games is followed, in the book, by several stories, written in an almost folklorelike manner, depicting confrontation between members of the gang and Muslim officials who unjustly opposed them. One story relates that an official, jealous of their skill and feats, tried to arrest members of the gang but that they escaped by a seemingly impossible jump from the wall of the Jewish quarter. When this official complained to the pasha, the latter supported the Jews saying: "if only all my soldiers were as brave as the Jews."

A second story, following the same general theme, is more elaborate. It tells of an official who forced a Jewish woman into having sexual relations with him and continued to visit her regularly. Her husband feared voicing a complaint. The head of the *biryonim* heard of the episode and slipped into the house of the woman to lay in wait for the official. His initiative came to the attention of the rabbinic court, which then summoned him before it for entering the house of a married woman while she was alone. Despite his protest that his action was for the purpose of defending the woman and the honor of the Jews, the court punished him with stripes, indicating that such an initiative was not acceptable. The council of judges then turned to the head of the community, who revised the tough's plan by giving it communal backing. In this framework, the *biryonim* succeeded in intimidating the Muslim and he desisted from molesting the woman.

The success of these Jewish toughs (as portrayed in the stories) is not due to their prowess alone, but their actions are embedded in specific cultural frameworks relating both internally to Jewish life and to the nature of relationships between Jews and Muslims. The *biryonim* are portrayed as accepting rabbinic leadership and bending their activities to its directives. In the realm of relationships with Muslims, the toughs are feared not only because of their strength, but because of the great shame a Muslim would bring upon himself (particularly a high-status official) if publicly exposed as having been bested by them. The Jews' low status itself could thus become a resource, using it as a threat vis-à-vis Muslim officials, and thus furthering Jewish interests. With this in mind, we return to the Sabbath games and examine how they may be placed in broad cultural and historical context.

The Sabbath Games and the Place of Jews in Tripolitan Society

Ha-Cohen's narrative, which is folkloristic in many of its features, clearly fills the compensatory function of raising an ethnic group, in verbal performance, above those who seek to oppress it. It would be a mistake, however, to relegate the stories to the realm of collective fantasy. Ha-Cohen states that he learned of the activities of the *biryonim* through the oral accounts of one Shabbetai Nahum, who was the second most influential "tough," and who passed away in 1872 at a ripe old age (Ha-Cohen was then sixteen years old).[9] In addition, the description of toughs who defended a quarter within a town dovetails with Ira Lapidus's discussion of such groups (called *zu'ar*) in the quarters of late medieval Mamluke cities.[10] Thinking in simple functionalist terms, the games would provide opportunities for the Jewish roughnecks to practice and test their skills. That this "practice" took place publicly meant that their abilities, and their potential power, became widely known and acted as a deterrent to behaviors that otherwise would disturb Jewish life. One might also speculate that demonstrating the prowess of the toughs was more important to the Jews than to other groups because, in the traditional setting, they constituted a "natural" target due to their societal weakness.

We thus move from viewing our account in terms of generalities about the "psychology of minorities" to placing it within the specifics of Tripolitan society at that period. The description of the games may also be linked, textually, to the section that precedes it: the author's statement that some Jews reached Tripoli after having been captured by pirates. This connection is reinforced by Ha-Cohen's use of the terminology of *taking and redeeming captives* in the course of the games. These textual links suggest that the game may be symbolic of central aspects of life in the society in general, both Jewish and Muslim, and may reflect the delicate balance of contradictions of which Jewish life in Muslim Tripoli was composed.

Although Ha-Cohen does not state so directly, the continuation of his story, in which the pasha compliments the Jews for their feats, implies that in addition to Jewish onlookers, at least some Muslims were among the spectators of the Jewish competition. This conjecture may be given further basis by recalling that in some traditional North African towns, much of the commercial activity of the city was at a standstill on the Sabbath because the Jews were pivotal in that sector of the economy.[11] Such a situation is depicted for Tripoli in the early twentieth century and documented in detail by Daniel Schroeter for the major port of Essaouira in Morocco in the middle of the nineteenth century.[12] Not only did many Muslims have time, on Saturdays, to "hang out" near the Jewish quarter, according to my guess, but what was happening on top of the wall of the *hara* attracted attention in other parts of the city as well. Shamelessly resorting to a forced analogy closer to home, I remember from the time when my sons were young that on Sabbath afternoons in Jerusalem, everyone throughout the city knew what was going on at the YMCA soccer stadium, including "religious young people" who ideally were not supposed to be attending to such matters. Further, parenthetically, if this reconstruction of the situation is on the mark, Ha-Cohen's description of the onlookers as "women and children" may represent an inversion of a typical (or stereotypical) Muslim perception of the Jews: either that they "do not count" or that they are assimilated to unimportant categories of people. Whatever the plausibility of these musings, I claim that the Jewish Sabbath games in Tripoli were of interest to residents of the city in general.

If "games," as Clifford Geertz has asserted with regard to Balinese cockfights, may be a story that people "tell themselves about themselves," it is helpful to add Victor Turner's perspective that "to look at itself a society must cut out a piece of itself for inspection."[13] Don Handelman gives an example of this process of "cut[ting] out a piece of itself" in his study of the Palio race in Siena, Italy, where each year different communes (*contrade*) take part in the competition that grips the attention of, and represents, the city as a whole.[14] We assert that the mock fights in the Jewish quarter constituted such an event of interest to all in Tripolitan society.

In contrast to the situation in Siena, however, where each *contrada* may be considered a conceptually equal segment to all others, and each year different contrade are selected to represent the whole commune, the Jewish quarter in Tripoli was an already-packaged sector, with properties making it conducive to this special symbolic role. As nonbelievers, the Jews were a category apart, encompassed by Muslim Tripolitan society. With their conceptual "cutting out," they were symbolically "rotated" and reworked so that their partition into two barrios came to stand for both Tripolitan society *and* for the nonbelieving Europeans who, at that period, threatened to encapsulate it. The Jews were an old local population that had been in Tripoli for centuries, but their section of the city was also the spot in or near which foreign consuls resided. The location of the mock battles, on the western wall of the town that faces the sea, a border zone par excellence, also encouraged this perception. Ha-Cohen's account hints, in a manner that does not make sense if focusing on Jewish life alone, that the competition entailed a temporary suspension of intermarriage between the two quarters. There is no Jewish religious or halakhic reason for members of the two quarters not to marry one another, suggesting that this statement has be read symbolically as representing behavior that befits the division between the faithful and infidels. At the same time, both sides remain in contact, each with its own heroes who make forays into enemy "territory." There are no permanent victories in this continued contestation, but rather individual successes and losses along with periods of truce, with the struggle destined to renew itself on a periodic basis.

The Jews thus came to momentarily stand for the whole society from which they were "officially" barred within the framework of the Islamic notion of "protected peoples." In addition, the salience of the games at the time has to be placed in a very specific historical context. The mock war on the wall of the Jewish quarter, in which the taking of captives was central, condensed the drama that pervaded the political-economic base of Tripoli at that era in which the activities of state-sponsored corsairs were crucial. Precisely at that time, this base was being threatened. The ability to maintain the corsair enterprise was nearly balanced against the foreign European forces seeking to suppress it. This period also touches upon American history and the sinking of the frigate *Philadelphia*, an event enshrined in the lyrics to the hymn of the U.S. Marines: "From the halls of Montezuma, to the shores of Tripoli." In this setting, the Jewish games, which were both remote and very close to home, became particularly compelling to Tripolitan Muslims. The metaphorical connection is expressed in the words placed by the narrative in the mouth of Yusef Pasha: "If only all my soldiers were as brave as the Jews, I would be pleased."[15] Just as the Jews were set apart socially as a collective, yet linked to Muslims through myriad individual ties, so they were circumscribed conceptually during the games, while the conceptual border was situationally transcended in the cultural interests of the wider society. Jewish sports condensed and represented a compelling tension-ridden theme running throughout the whole body politic.

Although this analysis is based on a single account relating to early nineteenth-century Tripoli, there is evidence that similar situations, in which Jewish games and competitions attracted the attention of the neighboring Muslim majority, were found elsewhere in North Africa, both from other areas of Tripolitania and elsewhere. Ha-Cohen describes how in the Jebel Nefusa south of Tripoli, Berber villagers gathered around to watch the water fights among Jews that took place on the festival of Shavu'ot.[16] A common interpretation among the onlookers was that this activity of the Jews would be a source of blessing to the land and region. In the Moroccan town of Iligh, according to Paul Pascon and Daniel Schroeter, the Jews were explicitly invited by the local Qaid to carry out these fights on the day after Shavu'ot.[17] In the Western Atlas, according to data I collected in Israel, Jews from the small settlements around Agouim would spend the festivals together in the central *mellah*. During the "intermediate days" of the festival, they would play a kind of "soccer." Berber villagers would gather around and watch, each cheering for "their own" Jews; that is, those under their tribal patronage. In the Mzab region of Algeria, as described by Lloyd Briggs and Norma Guède, the Jews of Ghardaia also split into two divisions that had water fights between them on Shavu'ot.[18] The authors suggest that the divisions were called *sof*-s, and, although they attribute no clear function or meaning to these units, the fact that the Jewish "sides" were given names normally designating Muslim factions suggests that they were significant to local society as a whole.[19]

These examples, although they have not been studied in great detail, point to a situation quite different from that of citizenship, as that term applies to contemporary nation-states. Jews take part in sport and games not as individuals demonstrating that they can fit into an arena in which all participants are formally equal and free to achieve what they can based on their individual skills, but as fixed tokens of a clearly delineated sector of society defined as subordinate to the reigning religious group. The athletic prowess of the Jews does not signify the possibility that they can reach social heights outside the realm of sports as well, but, anchored in the unchallenged assumption of the fixity of the place of the Jews, they are available for symbolic manipulation according to the current and variable cultural "needs" of the wider society.

It might also be added that in this situation, the term "sports" is probably inappropriate when referring to a conceptually distinct and organizationally differentiated realm of activity. The Shabbat "exercises" of the Jews of Tripoli flowed indistinguishably into their roles as defenders vis-à-vis aggressive Muslims. Another aspect of their social position and activities was to serve as enforcers of norms within the Jewish community when these were flouted or threatened by individuals and other mechanisms of social control did not seem to do the job. At the same time, these important historical differences notwithstanding, I suggest that there is something in the collective experience of these sportlike games that partially bridges the specificities of social context and temporal period. To explore this, I return once more to Ha-Cohen's text and its setting.

As mentioned, Ha-Cohen learned of the activities of the biryonim through an oral account given him by an old man who had been an influential "tough" in his youth. Ha-Cohen thus decided to include in his work events that took place about fifty years before he was born, and about one hundred years earlier than his writing of the book. These games, it appears, and the feats of the biryonim, continued to echo in the collective memory of the Jews of Tripoli just as the heroics of Moni Gabai continued to grab the imagination of moshav villagers in Israel twenty-five years after his death in North Africa. There even may have been some resonance of the nineteenth-century games in Moni Gabai's days. In the 1930s, in an area not far from where the wrestling on the wall took place, it was common for Jewish and Muslim youngsters to congregate on the Sabbath and throw stones at one another, an activity that was criticized by the adults but also described as a kind of sport.[20] I cannot claim that this involved any conscious continuity of an old tradition, but the hints of some sort of "collective memory" in this activity are intriguing. Contests of strength and dexterity are not organized for the *purpose* of becoming mental monuments, but it is not uncommon for them to end up serving this role in group life and identity. I therefore conclude with several thoughts on this theme.

Sports and Collective Memory

Everyone, I think, can supply his or her examples of the link between sports and memory. From my own childhood in the United States, Bobby Thompson's home run against Ralph Branca to win the National League baseball pennant in 1952 constitutes an image that resonates widely in the memories of my age cohort. It does not, from afar, seem to be a particularly Jewish event, but my own introspective truth tells me that the "Wait till next year!" Brooklyn Dodgers were indeed surrogate Jews. Another example from Israeli history, easily recognized by many Israelis, concerns basketball player Tal Brodie. His statement on camera (in Americanized Hebrew), after Israel won a game in 1977 against a team from Moscow that the next day's headlines called "the Red Army"—"Now we are on the map and will remain on the map, not only in sports, but in everything"—is familiar even to those who were born after that period.[21] Electronically preserved, it requires only a few reproduced bytes to evoke it more than a generation later. I might add that with regard to both these events, I did not have to take the trouble of looking up the year involved because I have clear recollections of where I was and what I was doing at the time they happened. In short, sports activities have the potentiality of becoming an organizing kernel in collective memory with mental resonance far beyond the sporting activities themselves.

Paul Connerton, while paying attention to bodily experiences, does not include a discussion of sports in his work on social memory, but noticing the linkage between the two realms is not entirely novel.[22] In the introduction to his translation of the work of Maurice Halbwachs, Lewis Coser remarks that upon immigrating to the United States, he found that he was able to make friends and feel at home in many settings, but could not participate in the identity-forming collective memories of his associates that drew upon American sports.[23] The insight, however, deserves to be placed within a comparative view of memory events and their impact. In the introduction to their book *Jewish Memories*, Lucette Valensi and Nathan Wachtel note a typical pattern of the vehicles of memory that emerged in their interviews: words, images, and then photographs. Then, they go on to state, "the ultimate reminders came in the form of sweet-smelling pastries. Almost without fail, important rituals and noteworthy events were associated in the memory with a particular food. . . . Soon enough, those memories would materialize before our eyes, like Proust's madeleines, in the form of cookies and cakes."[24]

For anyone who has carried out historical interviewing in homes, this description rings true, but I suggest that sports constitutes another important memory setting, perhaps less regular in its occurrence, but at the same time more public while still anchored in sensory experience that can produce lasting traces. Claude Lévi-Strauss, seeking a way to focus simultaneously on both structures and events, has explored the nexus between games and rituals, which are major loci of collective remembering.[25] It might be argued that games can be of cultural importance only by virtue of memory; memory is the only way of retaining traces of the triumph of victory or the significance of defeat.[26] In contemporary societies, dramatic victories and losses in the realm of sports become a locus of memory that integrates the engagement of the individual, the attention of the audience, and the tension of the situation. Moreover, these are events that are not engineered from above, but represent both the agency of individuals and the unpredictable flow of life, with its ups and downs, that pour into a collective image capable of summing up and preserving a whole historical setting.

To conclude with a final illustration, I cite a letter sent to the *Jerusalem Post* by Beatrice Magnes on July 4, 1967, a month after the eastern part of Jerusalem came under Israeli control:

> Forty years ago today on July 4, 1927, the first public game of American baseball was seen in Jerusalem. How were two entire teams of nine collected? There were several lively young American Jews here; there were eager young American teachers from the Quaker schools at Ramallah; there were students of the American School of Oriental Research; and one woman, the American wife of a British official.
>
> The captains of the opposing nines were Dr. Bluestone, then Director of Hadassah, and Mr. Magnes, formerly captain of the Oakland, California, high school baseball team and later President of Jerusalem's Hebrew University. The game was played at the Maccabi playing field behind the old Shimon Hatzadik Quarter. The first ball was pitched by the American Consul-General. The archaeologist-priest, Dr. Romain Butin, the director of the American School of Oriental Research, was the umpire.
>
> On a slight rise in the ground one saw puzzled camels and Arabs who were watching and perhaps picking up American phrases such as "Run you old stick in the mud" or "Kill the umpire."
>
> There are still a few octogenarians here today who recall with pleasure that jolly July the 4th, forty years ago.
>
> B. Magnes[27]

This letter (with its shades of "orientalism," and perhaps a bit of feminism), written by the wife of the former president of the Hebrew University of Jerusalem, finds significance in the memory of a sports event even without an element of outstanding accomplishment or of victory. Stimulated by the sharp shift in political and social reality in the wake of the 1967 war, it summons up an image of the social fabric of a remembered era. Not unlike the women onlookers to the Sabbath games on the wall of Tripoli, Magnes's mental involvement in the July 4th game testifies to how the event may be read as an encapsulation of processes reverberating throughout Jerusalem at that time. Whether such sports memories are called up solely in the interest of nostalgia or whether they implicitly place into view materials from a previous era that might be called upon in new emerging social constellations is now only a matter of speculation.

Notes

This paper has benefited from the comments of Vered Vinitzky, Don Handelman, and Barry Schwartz. The research was partially supported by grants from the Memorial Foundation for Jewish Culture and Machon Eshkol of the Faculty of Social Sciences of the Hebrew University of Jerusalem.

1. Harvey E. Goldberg, *Cave Dwellers and Citrus Growers: A Jewish Community in Libya and Israel* (Cambridge: Cambridge University Press, 1972).

2. F. Zuaretz, A. Guweta, Ts. Shaked, G. Arbib, and F. Tayer, eds., *Libyan Jewry* (Tel Aviv: Committee of Libyan Jewish Communities in Israel, 1960), 419–20 (in Hebrew).

3. Ibid.

4. Renzo De Felice, *Jews in an Arab Land: Libya, 1835–1970*, trans. J. Roumani (Austin: University of Texas Press, 1985), 96–97; Zuaretz et al., *Libyan Jewry*, 156–60.

5. *Yehoodei Loov*, VHS, produced by Gady Castel, directed by Steve Edwards (Israel: Hamerkaz Hatarbuti Le-Yahadut Yotzei Loov, 1981).

6. See Mordecaï Ha-Cohen, *Higgid Mordecaï: Histoire de la Libye et de ses Juifs, lieux d'habitation et coutumes, edité et annoté par H. Goldberg* (Jerusalem: Institut Ben-Zvi, 1978) (en Hebreu), and the partial translation into English, Harvey E. Goldberg, trans. and ed., *The Book of Mordechai: A Study of the Jews of Libya* (London: Darf, 1993). On the background of the publication of the book in Israel about seventy years after it was written, see Harvey E. Goldberg, "History and Experience: An Anthropologist among the Jews of Libya," in *Going Home*, ed. Jack Kugelmass, *YIVO Annual* 21:241–72, 1992.

7. Ha-Cohen, *Higgid*, 118–19.

8. Ha-Cohen, *Higgid*, 119–23.

9. Ha-Cohen, *Higgid*, 120, note 35.

10. Ira Lapidus, *Muslim Cities in the Late Middle Ages* (Cambridge, MA: Harvard University Press, 1967), 143–84.

11. A local proverb stated: "a market without Jews is like a document without witnesses." See Mario Martino Moreno, *Gli Ebrei in Libia: usi e costumi* (by Mordecai Ha-Cohen). Collezione di opere e monografie a cura del Ministero delle colonie (Roma: Sindicato italiano arti grafiche, n. d.), 51. This work by Moreno, an orientalist working in the service of the Italian Ministry of Colonies, was produced through collaboration with Ha-Cohen and portions of his text, *Higgid Mordecaï*. It was published around 1928 and was based on an earlier volume published in Benghazi in 1921.

12. Daniel J. Schroeter, *Merchants of Essaouira: Urban Society and Imperialism in Southwestern Morocco, 1844–1886* (Cambridge: Cambridge University Press, 1988), 81–90.

13. Clifford Geertz, *Interpreting Cultures* (New York: Basic Books, 1973), 448;

Victor Turner, *Process, Performance, and Pilgrimage: A Study in Comparative Symbology*, Ranchi Anthropology Series, vol. 1 (New Delhi: Concept, 1979), 96.

14. Don Handelman, "The Madonna and the Mare: Symbolic Organization in the Palio of Siena," in Don Handelman, *Models and Mirrors: Towards an Anthropology of Public Events* (Cambridge: Cambridge University Press, 1989), 116–35.

15. Ha-Cohen, *Higgid*, 119, 123.

16. Goldberg, *Book of Mordechai*, 111.

17. Paul Pascon and Daniel J. Schroeter, "Le cimetière juif d'Iligh (1751–1955): étude des épitaphes comme documents d'histoire sociale (Tazerwalt, Sud-Ouest Marocain)," *Revue de l'Occident Musulman et de la Méditerranée* 34 (1982): 34–67.

18. Lloyd C. Briggs and Norma Guède, *No More Forever: A Saharan Jewish Town*. Papers of the Peabody Museum of Archaeology and Ethnology 55, no. 1 (Cambridge, MA: Harvard University Press, 1964), 44.

19. Briggs and Guède, *No More Forever*, 20, 59–60.

20. Hayyim Khalfon, *Lanu u-Levanenu* [For Our Children After Us]: *The Life of the Libyan Jewish Community* (Netanya: published by the author, 1986), 71 (in Hebrew).

21. *Anahnu ba-mapah, va-anahnu nishaer ba-mapah, lo raq be-sport, ela be-kol.*

22. Paul Connerton, *How Societies Remember* (Cambridge: Cambridge University Press, 1989).

23. Lewis Coser, "Introduction: Maurice Halbwachs 1877–1945," in Maurice Halbwachs, *On Collective Memory*, trans. and ed. Lewis Coser (Chicago: University of Chicago Press, 1992), 21.

24. Lucette Valensi and Nathan Wachtel, *Jewish Memories*, trans. B. Harshav (Berkeley: University of California Press, 1991), 7.

25. Claude Lévi-Strauss, *The Savage Mind* (Chicago: University of Chicago Press, 1962), 30–32.

26. It is curious to note that in Hebrew, the same tri-literal stem, N Ṣ Ḥ, connotes both "victory" and "eternity."

27. Beatrice Magnes, Letter, *Jerusalem Post*, July 4, 1967.

ANDRÉ LEVY

8 On Matching Unmatchables: Soccer Games between Jews and Muslims in Casablanca

Colonized Sports

Morocco was decolonized in 1956, after a forty-four-year, and by some accounts painless, period of French rule. To be sure, decolonization did not mean an abrupt and simple termination of external domination, but a continuing "dialogue with the colonial past."[1] And that dialogue added special fuel to the fire by virtue of the fact that various groups were differently exposed to the colonial force, and either suffered from it, or enjoyed its fruits, according to their socioeconomic, cultural, and political situation. As I discuss below, Jews, as a subordinate religious minority, had much to gain from French rule. Moreover, the colonial past today provides the platform upon which dialogue between Jewish and Muslim groups takes place.[2] Because, as in many postcolonial societies, the decolonial factor is an integral part of the organization and spirit of Moroccan sport, the Jewish-Muslim dialogue has particular poignancy on the playing field.

Very few scholars describe sport games between Jews and Muslims in North Africa, and those who do merely mention them in passing. These depict the games as corresponding ethnic and religious cleavages, as strengthening them or at least reflecting them, and thus helping to keep the groups apart while also maintaining some degree of social contact.

This understanding mirrors, more or less, the way in which researchers articulate the functional relationships between Jews and Muslims in general. Indeed, as Bilu and Levy argue:

> Games in which children or young adults of the two groups took part provide an impressive example of the ambivalent undercurrents in Jewish-Muslim relations. These ethnically mixed games were presented as an emblem of intimacy and closeness. . . . It appears . . . [however] that [these games] constituted socially acceptable means for expressing aggression against the other group.[3]

The studies mentioning interethnic sport games in the North African context usually rely on post factum or secondhand materials. Some lean on retrospective interviews.[4] Others draw on autobiographic memories,[5] while a few extract their insights from written testimonies of eyewitnesses or reports of outside institutions like the AJDC (American Joint Distribution Committee).[6] As a result, researchers tend to employ static concepts in their articulation of the relationships between Jews and Muslims during the games. This is not to say that their conclusions are necessarily simplistic or wrong, but the methodological limitations obfuscate the social dynamics of the games. They accept willy-nilly the definition of the game as static social encounters, limited by rules, and ignore its dynamic and cybernetic features.[7] They also overlook the ways in which the game and its outcome is shaped by changing sociopolitical contexts.

The ethnographic account is a product of fieldwork that I conducted primarily in Casablanca between July 1990 and September 1991. Since then, I visited Morocco on several occasions. My goal was to comprehend how Jews cope with their (seemingly or not) imminent extinction as a minority community and to understand what kind of social mechanisms and discursive articulations are developed in order to face this prospect. The basic claim I made was that Jews aspire to limit and control their contacts with Muslims, and try to handle them within well-defined and protected frames of interaction.[8]

Contemporary Casablanca

Muslims and Jews have lived together in Morocco for many centuries,[9] long before European political forces dramatically changed the sociocultural landscape. The main change that redefined Jewish-Muslim relations in the past century was the rapid and massive Jewish emigration from Morocco, especially during the 1950s and 1960s. At their peak, Jews numbered about a quarter of a million souls; nowadays they are no more than four thousand. Although demographically insignificant, as a cultural category, Jews are still a key feature in Morocco's cultural landscape.[10]

One can trace the split between Jews and Muslims long before the modern era, but the sharpening and widening of the schism between them grew as a result of European imperialism and its lingering influence. True, the divide between Jews and Muslims dates back before the beginning of direct colonial rule in 1912, the impact of the establishment of the state of Israel (1948), or the re-creation of the Maghrebi Monarchic State following the end of the Protectorate regime in 1956. The Jewish concentration within the limited spaces of the *mellah* (Jewish quarter) is only one of many examples to this long *durée* separation. However, colonial processes contributed considerably to the exacerbation of a socially structured and religiously based split because Jews were perceived as collaborators or, at the very least, as sympathizers with the French. Jews were also considered Zionists—an ideology anathema to all Arab and Muslim states.[11]

Following these and other developments, Jews became a tiny minority whose existence hinged on domestic and international political oscillations.[12] Contemporary Casablancan Jews minimize their contacts with Muslims and contain them within well-defined and controllable frames of interaction. These frames enable them to conceive of, and articulate, the minimized relationships along an ethnoreligious divide. Not only do they grant a sense of stability but these frames also enable the shaping and manipulation of relationships, therefore controlling Jewish fears and apprehension when encountering Muslims.[13]

One of these complex frames of interaction is the relatively rare soccer matches between Jews and Muslims. It is complex because, at least at face value, their results are unpredictable. Of course, there is more to social discourse than what meets the eye.

Sports in Morocco

Occasional visitors to Casablanca might notice that sport activities are popular among Moroccan males.[14] Indeed, varied sorts of athletic activities are represented in the spatial organization of the city: golf fields, soccer stadia, tennis courts, and even hippodromes for dog and horse races. Some of the late King Hassan's II formal portraits depict him as genuinely devoted to sport. The most frequent of these depict him as a golf player and a horse rider. Yet, athletic activities are not limited to the elites. Frequently, one notices runners jogging along the side streets and garden paths of the metropolis. This popular engagement with running was boosted, of course, after Said Aouita's impressive gold and bronze medal winnings in the 1984 Olympics.[15] His outstanding accomplishments made him a national hero, so much so that the fast train from Casablanca to Rabat is nicknamed "the Aouita"![16]

Morocco's fame in athletics comes from its world-renowned runners. Yet, as in many countries around the world, soccer is the most popular sport. Like running long and medium distances, playing soccer is not limited to those with financial means. It is no surprise then that this game has a popular aura and engages many Moroccan men, mainly youths. Soccer is played during school breaks and is a major afternoon recreational activity among youngsters. Despite the shortage of good stadia, soccer matches are played throughout Casablanca—and in fact throughout the entire country—in nearly every village, frequently on dusty roads.

Like their Muslim peers, young Jews prefer to play soccer during school breaks. They do so, with lots of passion. Along with these schools, Jewish clubs offer a relatively protected environment for engaging in sport; that is, an environment that is practically devoid of Muslims. Out of the four Jewish clubs in Casablanca, two offer athletic activities. The more luxurious one is the SOC (Stade Olimpique Casablanca). Beyond engaging in card games typical of all adult Jewish clubs,[17] the SOC has two reasonably good clay tennis courts. Its members are both wealthier and older than are those of the other club—the DEJJ (Département Educatif de la Jeunesse Juive). The latter appeals to youngsters who play soccer, basketball, table tennis, and even pinball. The DEJJ building also hosts regular Scouts activities.

Jews who are not necessarily members of either of these clubs can find "safe haven" at the shore. Mostly, they go to a beach named Tahiti.[18] In accordance with their quest for protection and disassociation from Muslims, they concentrate in a restricted zone, where they keep themselves busy, mainly with card games, although they also swim in the small pool and enjoy the waterslide. This, however, is only a partial picture because, to a large extent, Casablancan Jews are engaged with the all-Moroccan sportive activity as well. Certainly, they are enthusiastic spectators and gamble on soccer tournaments while following the national sport news on TV, including dog and horse races. Indeed, as much as Jews strive to dissociate themselves from their local surroundings, they too join the excitement when the Fédération Royale Marocaine de Football manages to send a promising team to the international arena. They follow the games closely, and national soccer teams are pointed to with a strong sense of local and national pride. They are elated when the team wins and depressed when it loses.

Still, Jewish identification with French sport is greater than their identification with Moroccan teams, especially when it comes to soccer. Most Jews believe that French cultural capital is of high value. Some "objective" parameters are evident: Many know all the French soccer groups of the first and second league, know the biographies of key players, and follow French matches that are broadcast on TV 5, the French channel to the Mediterranean.

Playing for Survival

The DEJJ organizes soccer tournaments about every six months. Jews are totally captivated by these games. Practically everyone has his or her favorite team, and all clubs are composed of different ages, ranging from about fifteen to twenty-five. The composition of the groups is rather steady, and players prefer to remain faithful to their original team. Each organization has its unique uniform, worn in the final round of the tournaments. Every team has a coach who is also the team captain and is considered the best player.

The three "internal" tournaments I have witnessed revealed the existence of some fairly good players. The games take place in the narrow courtyard of the DEJJ so that one can easily follow the mistakes and heroic exploits of every player. The narrow courtyard enforces a very fast and energetic game, and the lack of physical separation between player and spectators makes the tournaments particularly frenzied.

As a rule, Muslims are excluded from the DEJJ, as they are from all other Jewish clubs. This is a policy that causes many problems for the organizers and managers of these institutions, and they are quite imaginative in finding ways to exclude Muslims without insulting them publicly. Amran, a forty-year-old man who was responsible for these tournaments as well as for the Jewish Scouts, told me about his efforts to bar Muslims from the DEJJ:

> When I first came to the DEJJ there were lots of Arabs hanging around. And I didn't like it. At the moment I took charge of the place I decided to get rid of them. I wanted to expel them as soon as possible, but I didn't know how to do it. At first I just demanded that they leave pronto, but one of the [Muslim] parents asked the police to intervene. He claimed that I cannot be impartial and that this is racism. So, in order to solve this problem I went directly to the commander of the policemen and asked him: "Are you ready for your son or your daughter to hang around

with Jews? Will you allow that they'll get emotionally involved with a Jew?" The commander was embarrassed, and that's the way I managed to get the cooperation of the police. They never intervened again. But even today there are some Arabs who wish that their sons could join our activities. We have truly nice activities [He lists them]. In such cases I tell them calmly that in order to allow their sons to join they must wear a *kippah* on their heads and drink wine for *kiddush*. I tell them that we drink lots of wine. This discourages them totally because even if they are not practicing the religion they are too embarrassed to admit it publicly; especially if they have to breach their religious *dinim* [laws] because a Jew demands it.

Yet, such elaborate cultural mechanisms of exclusion indicate the existence of a general inclination that has many exceptions. In practice, personal considerations and structural limitations compel Jews to have a more flexible attitude. Thus, Amran's Muslim neighbor was able to convince him to include his son in one of the soccer teams. Amran explained it simply: "He is a wonderful player."[19] For exactly the same reason, the son of the Muslim gatekeeper of the DEJJ was also recruited. Jews are no longer spatially segregated in the mellah and therefore they do not live their lives in total separation. They must compromise with their neighbors, especially those whom they meet on an everyday basis.

Only Muslims can offer protection to Jews because Jews are the minority group. Gatekeepers of the clubs, like those of many other institutions such as schools, cemeteries, community institutions, and so on, must be Muslims. So, those who are in charge of the practicalities of exclusion cannot be other than Muslims. The partial incorporation of these liminal Muslims is a basic tactic in dealing with the exposure to them. Amran explained the recruitment of the Muslim players in terms of merit. His subtext, however, was that he could not rely on Jewish human resources exclusively because it was too small a community. He needed players from the larger human pool.

Besides the two players, referees in tournaments among Jews were also Muslim. The most popular was Bocha, who was frequently invited to serve as a referee, especially in semifinals and finals—the most fiercely competitive tournaments. Bocha, like the other Muslim referees, worked as a referee in one of the lowest professional leagues. He received a special salary from the DEJJ for his efforts.

Like the gatekeepers, the referee is appropriately locked within the social structure. Like any other referee, he should act impartially and be considered fair, indifferent to the interests of the competing groups. A Jewish referee within the tiny Jewish community might favor his own kin and, even if impartial, he runs the risk of being accused of nepotism. Moreover, the personal and social price of such an accusation would be considerable for a member of the Jewish community. Hence, the structurally exterior Muslim referee. This is a crucial consideration because Jews relate to these tournaments quite seriously. Parents do their best to attend all the rounds in which their sons are involved. They encourage them with loud shouts and cheers. Often violent quarrels erupt among the parents or other kin about the course of the game.

Of course, as Muslims, these referees enjoy a sense of political power, which allows them to rule without hesitation. With no risk of being accused of nepotism, they are free to make unpopular rulings. Still, they are not exempt from suspicion. In fact, it is exactly because of their structural positioning that Muslim referees are accused of being partial. They make excellent scapegoats because allegations of partiality do not risk causing a cleavage among Jews. Indeed, in *all* the games I witnessed, the referee was always accused of being partial: Bias was because of a bribe offered before the tournament began. Interestingly, the bribe always took the same paradoxical form—a bottle of whiskey.

Alcohol is an often-used idiom by Jews in the manipulation and definition of their relationships with Muslims. Without elaborating, I wish only to note that by using a marker of distinction that risks humiliating Muslims publicly for violating a religious prohibition, Jews regain control over situations where Muslims enter supposedly purely Jewish frames.

Although most soccer matches among Casablancan Jews occur solely within the Jewish community, in certain limited instances, Jews do play against Muslims. This is an intriguing and risky practice for several reasons. To begin with, interethnic games go against Jewish inclinations not to voluntarily get involved in an activity that includes Muslims. Also, soccer is an inherently competitive game. Thus, it may bring into sharp focus the ethnic cleavage that in everyday life has a less focused quality to it. Moreover, Jews might win the game, and thus symbolically reverse the roles of dominant and subordinate that constitute Moroccan social structure. Then what?

The Gulf War

I witnessed two occasions in which Jews played soccer against Muslims. The first one took place a few days before the eruption of the Gulf War in January 1991. The DEJJ Jewish junior soccer team headed to one of Casablanca's soccer stadia. The team was about to play against their Muslim peers. Those days were quite tense for Jews, especially because it was apparent that Israel would be imbricated in a war against an Arab state. Jews tried to minimize their visibility in Casablanca. Jewish schools changed the hours of recess so that the students would not encounter their Muslim peers in the streets. Headmasters did not allow the youngsters to go home during the lunch break, and later they closed the schools entirely. Jewish clubs also minimized their activities so that they would not be conspicuous. Yet, activities continued behind closed doors. Community officials repeatedly stated this double message: "We must carry on with our lives. We cannot show them that our routine is damaged in any way." However, they encouraged community institutions to minimize their activities and deter from any public and open-door events. Therefore, the Jewish junior soccer team participated in this sport event as a face-saving effort on behalf of the Jewish community.

Moshe Amran, who organized the match, was tense. He paced nervously back and forth in the bus that took us all to the stadium. He could not sit still. After a while, he took the bus's microphone and reminded everyone, players and fans alike gathered anxiously around him, that these are extremely tense and sensitive days and that every gesture can be interpreted the wrong way. Then he added: "I warn all of you to act appropriately. Do not get involved in any sort of provocation, and do not respond to any provocation!" Joe Malcka, his aide, took the microphone and added nervously to the already anxious youngsters in the bus: "We didn't come to win this game—only to play!"

Everyone sat quietly and looked anxious, pensive and reflective. No one talked, exchanged jokes, or laughed. Needless to say, they did not make racist jokes about Muslim drivers on the road, which at all other times was par for the course. They looked as if they were going to their own funeral.

When they arrived at the stadium, the scene there did little to alleviate their mood. The brand new uniforms that Moshe Amran bought especially for this match looked ostentatious against the simple and even modest clothing of their Muslim opponents. They appeared as if they were overinvested in the match. The Jewish girls who came to cheer the team were the only females in the stadium, a fact that added to the feeling of discomfort. The aroma of their expensive French perfumes wafted over the balcony. Their colorful and risqué short skirts stood out, and the Muslim players and spectators—all men—stood and stared. To their dismay, the match did not start immediately because another game was still going on. Like frightened sheep, the team gathered around Moshe Amran and Joe Malcka. They sat in the balcony watching the game and waiting.

When their game finally began, it was quick and ruthless. Within the first forty-five minutes of the first half, the Jewish team was down by five goals. They played as if weights of lead were tied to their feet. Unlike their games in the DEJJ, they were slow, uncoordinated, and did not show any spark. Things looked hopeless. The cheerleaders, girlfriends, and friends were stunned. At halftime, Amran was uncharacteristically quiet. Then the coach appeared, who turned out to be Bocha, the popular Muslim referee. His appearance was a surprise because he did not say a word before or during the first half of the game. To a bystander, he looked like a disinterested spectator. I thought he was there to serve as a referee in one of the upcoming matches.

Bocha took charge with typical élan. Unlike Amran, he did not spare the players' feelings but used instead "shock therapy." After gathering the team around him—and at considerable distance from their opponents—he started to scream: "How dare you play like this? You are a disgrace to your people! How come you let these miserable Arabs defeat you? Don't you have self-dignity? Don't you have any pride?" Bocha's words worked like magic, as if he had woken the players from a stupor. In the second half, the team was much more energetic and the players effectively defended the net. Yet even with some wonderful opportunities to score, they missed. The final score was 5–0.

Bocha was no longer a go-between. And he had spoken in a way that no Jew would dare to at that time. His provocative conduct reversed deeply rooted categories and shook the players up. The need to maintain a kind of duality of conduct troubles Jews and keeps them constantly on edge. Bocha's tactic threatened the separation Jews work so hard to maintain. Perhaps that is why his tactic met with only partial success. He could not get them to reverse the power hierarchy of Moroccan social reality. What the Jewish players were up to was to defuse the explosive component of the game—competition between unequals. The Jews had indeed "come to play" but not to win.

The second soccer match between Jews and Muslims took place several months after the Gulf War ended, and the lingering effects of the international conflict seemed to have dissipated. The match occurred during a summer camp in Immouzer, a small picturesque village in the mountains of the Middle Atlas, some forty kilometers south of Fez. Tourists from abroad know Immouzer for its surroundings; it has plenty of gorges and valleys, colorful mountains, and wonderful waterfalls. For the Moroccan middle class, however, the village itself serves as a pleasant yearlong resort. It is cool during summer, and a good spot to ski in the winter.

Like their Muslim middle-class compatriots, Jewish schoolchildren attend summer and winter camp in Immouzer. The JCC (Jewish Community Council) supports those who cannot afford the modest fees. While the winter camp was canceled because of the tension resulting from the Gulf War, camp resumed over the summer, signaling that things were back to normal. Three groups of children were sent sequentially, each for ten to fourteen days. During the stay of the last group, the camp's organizers got an invitation from a neighboring Muslim school headmaster for a soccer match. The children accepted enthusiastically. The organizers of the camp were encouraged by the invitation and announced to the children that "we are happy to meet our friendly Muslim neighbors." I was told confidentially by the head of the summer camp that "it is a good lesson for our children. They must realize that we have to keep good rapport with the Arabs [meaning Muslims]. Also, we couldn't refuse this invitation! It is not done."

The ambivalence on the part of the head of the summer camp was telling. On the one hand, he was glad to take part in the normalization of the relationships with the Muslim majority. Yet, the encounter would only accentuate competition and rivalry.

Unlike the previous soccer match, the atmosphere this time was quite relaxed. The Jewish youngsters who attended the summer camp walked in a row toward the neighboring Muslim camp. When we arrived, officials of the camp greeted us in Arabic, and they were replied to in Arabic but with a heavy French accent. Everyone exchanged smiles. The two teams took only a few minutes to get started. The crowd was concentrated at one end of the field. Muslim and Jewish spectators started singing without paying attention to the game. They mainly sang Scouts songs, known to both groups, and all in French. This was highly unusual because soccer matches are always laden with tension, as evidenced by screaming spectators.

I myself was so taken by the spectators' behavior that I did not notice much of the game. I clearly saw that no serious tackles were taking place, and no screams were heard among the players. It seemed as if the serene atmosphere of Immouzer influenced everyone. When the game was over, the spectators clapped their hands to show respect for the two teams. Yet no one had made even the slightest effort to follow the game, or the score!

The singing continued even after the game was over. Later, the children changed the songs' style, still singing in French but imitating with humor the *Achouach* way of singing.[20] After a while, the Jewish group got ready to leave. The Muslim youngsters stood, waved good-bye, and sang farewell songs in French. The Jewish group marched in a straight line back toward camp, sang to the Muslim group, and also waved goodbye.

Conclusions

As mentioned at the outset of this essay, scholars depict games between Jews and Muslims in North Africa as predetermined by ethnic and religious cleavages. Moreover, they tend to employ static concepts in their articulation of the relationships between Jews and Muslims during these contests. To some degree, this perspective is a result of the underlying assumptions about the nature of these events. Many theorists argue that games, like rituals, ceremonies, and so on, work as sociocultural frames that are constructed by rule-bound activities. These frames, in turn, rigidify these activities as they demand compliance with moral and behavioral codes relevant to the game.[21] However, according to Arjun Appadurai, these frames are not universally rigid. Some of them do allow themselves to be altered to accord with specific cultural settings. To account for this, Appadurai distinguishes between "soft" cultural forms that "permit relatively easy separation of embodied performance from meaning and value, and relatively successful transformation at each level" and "hard" cultural forms that "come with a set of links between value, meaning, and embodied practice that are difficult to break and hard to transform."[22] Cricket exemplifies the former, soccer the latter.

The distinction between the two types may be useful in understanding games in interethnic contexts, in part because it encourages us to refine the older understanding of games as static social encounters, limited by rules. At the same time, Appadurai's model leaves something to be desired because his distinction between the two types is based on the logic of the game itself while overlooking other important parameters such as the sociopolitical contexts that shape the game. For example, what we have seen in the two soccer matches does not fully accord with either of the approaches mentioned above. Although in the first match between Jews and Muslims great importance was attributed by the players and spectators to the outcome of the encounter, in the second it was totally ignored. In both cases, the players were less interested in the mechanics of the game and were mostly preoccupied with reestablishing good relationships between the two groups. In other words, both games were context-sensitive. Their dynamics were shaped by regional political circumstances.

The cases I have presented demonstrate the "mutual entailing of sport and politics,"[23] and thus contest the literature that accentuates the "hard" or "soft" character, or the bounded nature, of the game and the rigidity of its rules. Games cannot be totally resistant to sociocultural or political contexts because, unlike the ideology of equal opportunity and fair play in sports (supposedly granted within the bounds of the turf), interethnic tensions and particularly the ever-present possibility of violence seeps into the game and become part and parcel of the over-all atmosphere for player and spectator. Interethnic tensions disturb the game's ability to constitute itself as a *framed* activity. The boundedness of the game on the one hand, and its stylistic behavior or poetics on the other, grant the tiny Jewish minority a calming sense of predictability, which explains why Jews dare to enter it in the first place. Partly they participate because they have no choice, as stated by the head of the summer camp in the second match: "We couldn't refuse this invitation! It is not done." Behavior is "done" or not, among other things, in accordance with power relationships. Jews could not refuse the second match, just as they could not cancel the first one "due to the [political] situation."

The fact is, the importance of these games for Jews is that they are structured and framed by rules and are outside everyday social interaction. And yet the games are dangerous because if Jews were to dominate, they would upset the social balance and reevoke old, continuing, or new animosities that pit Arab against Jew. So it is precisely because the results can be manipulated that encourages Jews during difficult times to utilize such events to "normalize" their relationships with the Muslim majority. Thus, despite being a rule-bound activity, the outcome of the game is influenced by political and historical contexts and is clearly manipulated by one group according to its own best interests.

Notes

1. Arjun Appadurai, *Modernity at Large: Cultural Dimensions of Globalization* (Minneapolis: University of Minnesota Press, 1996), 89.

2. André Levy, "Playing for Control of Distance: Card Games between Jews and Muslims on a Casablancan Beach," *American Ethnologist* 26, no. 3 (2000): 632–53.

3. Yoram Bilu and André Levy, "Nostalgia and Ambivalence: The Reconstruction of Jewish-Muslim Relations in Oulad-Mansour," in *Modern Sephardi and Middle Eastern Jewries: History and Culture,* ed. H. E. Goldberg (Bloomington: Indiana University Press, 1996), 296–97.

4. Joëlle Bahloul, *The Architecture of Memory: A Jewish-Muslim Household in Colonial Algeria 1937–1962,* trans. C. Du Peloux Ménagé (Cambridge: Cambridge University Press, 1996), 47–48; Bilu and Levy, "Nostalgia and Ambivalence," 296–97.

5. Armand Etedguy, *The Three Mirrors Garden* (Ashkelon, Israel: 1990) (in Hebrew).

6. Michael M. Laskier, "Developments in the Jewish Communities of Morocco: 1956–76," *Middle Eastern Studies* 26, no. 4 (1990), 465–505.

7. C.f., Don Handelman, *Models and Mirrors: Towards an Anthropology of Public Events* (Cambridge: Cambridge University Press, 1990), 22–41.

8. André Levy, "Controlling Space, Essentializing Identities: Jews in Contemporary Casablanca," *City and Society* (1998): 175–99; Levy, "Playing for Control of Distance," 632–53; André Levy, "Notes on Jewish-Muslim Relationships: Revisiting the Vanishing Moroccan Jewish Community," *Cultural Anthropology* 17, no. 4 (2003): 365–97.

9. André N. Chouraqui, *Between East and West: A History of the Jews of North Africa*, trans. Michael M. Bernet (Philadelphia: Jewish Publication Society of America, 1968); Haïm Z. Hirschberg, *A History of the Jews in North Africa: From Antiquity to Our Time* (Jerusalem: Bialik Institute, 1965) (in Hebrew); Mohammed Kenbib, *Juifs et musulmans au Maroc, 1859–1948. Contribution a l'histoire des relation inter-communautaires en terre d'Islam* (Rabat: Faculté des lettres at des sciences humaines, 1994).

10. Levy, "Controlling Space, Essentializing Identities," 175–99; Levy, "Notes on Jewish-Muslim Relationships," 365–97.

11. See, for example, Doris Bensimon-Donath, *Evolution du judaïsme marocain sous le Protectorat français, 1912–1956* (Paris and the Hague: Muton, 1956); Albert Memmi, *Portrait du Colonisé* (Paris: Payot, 1973).

12. See, for example, Michael M Laskier, "Developments in the Jewish Communities of Morocco: 1956–76," *Middle Eastern Studies* 26, no. 4 (1990): 465–505; Lawrence Rosen, "A Moroccan Jewish Community During a Middle Eastern Crisis," *The American Scholar* 37, no. 3 (1968): 435–51; Mark A. Tessler, "Moroccan-Israeli Relations and the Reasons for Moroccan Receptivity to Contact with Israel," *The Jerusalem Journal of International Relations* 10, no. 2 (1988): 76–108; Mark A. Tessler, Linda L. Hawkins, and J. Parsons, "Minorities in Retreat: The Jews of the Maghreb," in *The Political Role of Minority Groups in the Middle East*, ed. R. D. McLaurin (New York: Praeger, 1979), 188–220; Yaron Tsur, *A Torn Community: The Jews of Morocco and Nationalism, 1943–1954* (Tel Aviv: Am Oved, 2001) (in Hebrew); Yaron Tsur and Hagar Hillel, *Les Juifs de Casablanca: Études sur la modernisation de l'élite politique juive en diaspora coloniale* (Tel Aviv: L'Université Ouverte, 1995) (in Hebrew).

13. Levy, "Playing for Control of Distance," 632–53.

14. The following ethnographic sections are published, in a slightly different version, in Levy, "Notes on Jewish-Muslim Relationships," 365–97.

15. The Moroccan runner won a gold medal (5,000 m) and a bronze medal (800 m) at that Olympics. Aouita also won the 5,000 m at 1987 World Championships. Also, he formerly held two world records recognized by IAAF: 2,000 m and 5,000 m.

16. This echoes with Emile Zatopec's nickname "the Czech Locomotive."

17. Levy, "Playing for Control of Distance," 632–53.

18. Levy, "Controlling Space, Essentializing Identities," 175–99.

19. Interestingly, Amran told me that he himself used to play "in a Muslim soccer team" when he was younger. He was the sole Jew there and, according to him, he suffered "more then anyone in the field" from blows when tackling Mus-

lim players. He insisted that a Jew can play and "prove himself without fear" in such games. Yet, he failed to see the connection between the inclusion that he experienced and the exclusionary mechanisms he employed to prevent Muslims from participating.

20. The Achouach, probably corresponding to the Ahidous of the High and Middle Atlas, is part of a rite that is performed under the open sky inside the *kasbahs*. It is danced only by women, and sung in a dialogic style with men. In this case, however, dialogue was between Jews and Muslims.

21. See, for example, Don Handelman, "Framing, Braiding, and Killing Play," *European Journal of Anthropology* 37:145–56; Don Handelman, "Postlude: Towards a Braiding of Frame," in *Behind the Mask: Dance, Healing, and Possession in South India*, ed. D. Shulman and D. Thiagarajan (Unpublished manuscript, n. d.).

22. Appadurai, *Modernity at Large*, 90.

23. John J. MacAloon, "*La Pitada Olimpica:* Puerto Rico, International Sport, and the Constitution of Politics," in *Text, Play, and Story: The Constitution and Reconstruction of Self and Society*, ed. Edward M. Bruner (Prospect Heights, Ill.: Waveland Press, 1984), 315–55.

TAMIR SOREK

9 *Arab Soccer in a Jewish State*

As a part of the fiftieth-anniversary celebrations of the state
of Israel in 1998, the Israeli Broadcast Authority produced a television
series called *Tkuma* (*Revival*). The section about the Arab Palestinian
citizens of the state[1] opened with a black-and-white clip of a soccer
match, showing Rif'at Turk, a famous star and a former member of the
Israeli National Team, scoring a goal for Hapoel Tel Aviv. The choice
of soccer as a starting point for the discussion about Arabs in Israel is
no coincidence, but rather stems from the unique status of the game in
Arab-Jewish relations.

On the one hand, this choice reflects the relative convenience for
Israeli Jews in dealing with Arab citizens as athletes, rather than in any
other social role. In sharp contrast to the discriminative character of most
Israeli institutions,[2] the integration of Arab soccer teams and players
into the Israeli leagues, and their relative success in them, enables the
portrayal of Israel as a liberal society impartial to the players' ethnic or
national identities. On the other hand, the choice reflects the relative
convenience of soccer for Arab citizens in channeling their social aspirations. The Palestinian citizens of Israel have learned to create imaginary social wedges between different spheres of life; these boundaries
and distinctions aim to relieve the tension created by the contradictory
expectations stemming from their identities as Palestinians by nationality and Israelis by citizenship. In this context, sports in general—and
soccer in particular—is constructed as an integrative arena, where a sense
of "normal citizenship" is created, albeit bounded by space and time.

Arab Soccer

The most popular sport in Israel, by number of spectators, television ratings, and money involved, is soccer. The last two decades of the twentieth century saw a marked rise in the number of Arab teams playing in the Israeli soccer leagues. In the 1976–77 season,[3] only eight Arab teams played in the top four leagues. In 1992, twenty-one Arab teams were playing in those leagues, and by 2001, that number had almost doubled to forty teams. The percentages of Arab teams in these leagues grew from 7 percent in 1977 to 35 percent in 2001.

The Arab teams' achievements are even more striking when taking into account the strong correlation between the size of a team's hometown and its representation in the higher divisions. Because the Arabs in Israel are spread out in settlements smaller than those of the Jews, the starting point from which they must climb to the senior divisions is lower. To bring this point home, the median number of residents of settlements represented in the National League in 1997–98 was about 154,000; in the second division, the median was about 50,000[4]; and in the third division, about 29,000. In contrast, the Arab teams represented much smaller settlements: In the 1997–98 season, three Arab teams played in the second division, representing settlements whose residents numbered between 15,000 to 25,000; in the third division, ten settlements were represented, whose median number of residents was about 13,000.

Also, Arab fans' interest in their teams rose during the 1990s in comparison with Jewish fans, demonstrated by the large number of tickets sold by Arab teams relative to Jewish ones. Table 1 presents the number

Table 9.1. Ticket Sales for the Second Division in the 1997/98 Season[a]

Team*	Population in 1996 (in thousands)	Ticket sales in 1997/98[b]	Number of tickets per 1000 pop.
Kufr Kana (A)	13.0	5651	434
Taibeh (A)	25.3	7245	287
Sakhnin[c] (A)	19.4	2925	151
Nes Tziona (J)	22.3	2759	124
Kiryat Gat (J)	46.1	4493	97
Yavne (J)	28.9	2298	90

* A=Arab town, J=Jewish town
a. Not including season-ticket holders.
b. Data from the Israeli Football Association.
c. Given a punishment of eight away games, five of which were closed to supporters.

of tickets sold by different clubs in the second division for the 1997–98 season, relative to the settlement's population. The Arab teams are compared with Jewish teams that represent similarly sized towns.

The success of Arab teams was accompanied by the success of the individual players—more and more Arabs earned positions on Israel's senior teams and even on the national squad. As I explain below, because of the symbolic power of soccer, this multidimensional success confronts the Arab fans with critical questions about identity.

An Arab Presence

Arabs in Israel are socially inferior. This applies to politics, economy, education, and in practically every realm where they compete with Jewish citizens. Soccer, therefore, constitutes a unique subsphere of Israeli public life where Arab citizens have made remarkable achievements.

In any situation of group conflict, it can be said that the empowerment of minorities in the general public sphere is a double-edged sword. On the one hand, such empowerment always has its "subversive" aspect, which is identified with separatist tendencies or an aspiration to construct isolated social enclaves. On the other hand, when this empowerment is achieved within the framework of a state-oriented institution, it reaffirms the legitimacy of the majority's domination and represents the society's integrative tendencies.

The success of minorities in certain sports often turns the sports arena into a key location for the expression of nationalist feelings. For example, during athletic performances, well-known soccer teams bear the flag of their supporters' separate national identities. The Celtic soccer team in Glasgow represents the Irish-Catholic minority in the city,[5] and the Athletic Bilbao team represents the Basque minority in Spain.[6] The Barcelona soccer team represents Spain's Catalonian region, and al-Wahdat—the Palestinian team in Jordan—gives its fans an opportunity to vocalize their identity as a national minority.

At the same time, supporting a soccer team with a clear ethnic identity may constitute an opportunity for collective integration into the majority society, especially when the minority faces serious difficulties accepting the common symbols of the majority. For some of the Catholic working-class supporters of the Celtic team in Glasgow, fandom is not only an expression of their ethnic identity but also a collective integrationist channel into Scottish society. With the exception of soccer, these fans consider all other symbols and institutions of the majority Presbyterian.[7]

This duality is fully evident in the public discourse on the involve-

ment of Arab teams and players in the Israeli leagues. The potential symbolic power of the soccer game has made it a battleground of meanings:
Different social agents try to articulate differing meanings based on ideology or interests. These meanings reflect alternative definitions of collective identities for the Arabs in Israel. Hence, the soccer game in Israel
is played on two different levels: The first is on the field, where professional excellence is needed for winning; the second is the broader public
sphere, in which power relations between various agents of identity are
expressed in the battle over consciousness. The main axis of this battle
is the above-mentioned dialectic—an opportunity for integration into
Israeli society and acceptance by the Jewish majority versus a stage for
promoting national pride. Because there is an inherent tension between
these two goals,[8] emphasizing one usually means confronting and challenging the other.

The power relations between the meaning shapers are not equal. The
hegemonic meaning produced by the Hebrew media describes soccer as a
meritocratic and integrative sphere in which the national identity of the
players and supporters is irrelevant. As such, soccer may contribute to
the integration of Arabs as individuals into Israeli society. But it simultaneously blurs their national identity. By way of contrast, most of the
Arab sports journalists attempt to emphasize the national identity of the
players and clubs, aiming to build around them a sense of national Arab
or Palestinian pride. At the same time, if one might make such a broad
generalization, the Arab players on the field, the Arab soccer bureaucrats,
and the Arab audience in the bleachers tend to adopt the hegemonic
interpretation, emphasizing professionalism and the shared experience
with the Jewish fans.

The Bleachers

For Arab soccer fans in Israel, the soccer sphere serves as an "integrative
enclave"[9] where they attempt to blur national and ethnic tensions, emphasize the common denominator with the majority, and suspend protest.
Excluded from most of the collective myths and symbols and discriminated against in the distribution of public resources, Arab fans have still
something to lose in terms of political rights, economic conditions, and
day-to-day relations with the majority. The construction of the enclave is
the combined results of the majority's effort to maintain the status quo and
the minority's interest in smoothing its relationship with the majority.

The sports field is a suitable site for the production of an integrative
sphere because the ethic of modern sports is based on the principle of

equal opportunity[10] and the celebration of achieved status.[11] These attributes have made the sports sphere very attractive to national minorities all over the world.

In the following section, I refer to three concrete practices that mark the soccer bleachers as an integrative territory: the extensive use of Hebrew, the ungrudging attitude toward the Jewish players, and the exclusion of Palestinian symbols.

The Use of Hebrew

Most of the Arabs in Israel are bilingual, speaking both Arabic and Hebrew. Arabic is their first language, spoken at home, and it serves as the language of instruction in Arab schools. Hebrew is used for daily interactions with Jews and with most of the state's institutions. In addition, Arab citizens are consumers of the Hebrew media as a main source of information and entertainment. Many Hebrew words also have been integrated into the day-to-day language of the Arabs in Israel. Furthermore, the level of use of Arabic may be taken as an indicator of the speaker's frequency of interactions with Jews.[12]

Although the adoption of Hebrew by Palestinian citizens undoubtedly stems from the power relations between Jews and Arabs in Israel, Arab citizens should not be conceived of merely as passive actors in their linguistic behavior. Their bilingualism enables them to maneuver between different social spheres—and to construct the character of these spheres. More specifically, the use of Arabic versus Hebrew in a certain social interaction tells us about the integrational quality of the interaction.

For the Arabs in Israel—a national minority among a majority of non-Arabic speakers—the Arabic language has become central to Palestinian national identity.[13] Meanwhile, Hebrew, which was first acquired in order to survive, became a signifier; whenever the Arabs in Israel want to color an interaction as integrative, they use it. For example, Arab Knesset members use Arabic in their addresses to the Knesset assembly only when they want to demonstrate a very strong protest. By doing so, they remind the Israeli establishment of their separatist aspirations, culturally and sometimes politically. On the other hand, the choice of an author such as Anton Shammas to write in Hebrew is compatible with his claims, at least in the past, to be recognized as an Israeli. The extensive use of Hebrew in the soccer field should be interpreted in the same way.

The songs, cheers, and curses heard in soccer stadia are largely taken from the verbal repertoire of Israeli soccer supporters as a whole. For example, the fans of Ittihad Abnaa' Sakhnin, the most successful Arab club and the winner of the Israel State Cup in 2004, cry: *"Yalla, yalla Sakhnin, ha-rishon ba-derekh"* ("Let's go, let's go. The first goal is on the way"). The fans of Maccabi Kafr-Kana shout "Maccabi, Maccabi!" imitating the intonation of the Maccabi team's Jewish fans. Fans of both teams encourage the players with expressions such as *"Ten lo"* ("Give it to him; hit him") and singing *"Hu gadol!"* ("He is great!"). The curses are also in Hebrew: *"Zevel!"* ("Garbage!"), *"Titpater!"* ("Resign!"). An extreme example, even though not very frequent, is the adoption of anti-Arab racist cries. These curses, such as *"Aravi melukhlakh!"* ("Dirty Arab!") are shouted, a little tongue in cheek, by Arab fans against Arab players who play on Jewish teams.

One could dismiss the extensive use of Hebrew by describing it only as a tool that enables the minority to communicate with the majority. It is true that soccer competitions expose the Arab citizens of Israel to extended interaction with the Jewish majority. Every Saturday, thousands of Arab fans face a Jewish soccer audience, in addition to the Jewish players on the Arab teams. Majority-minority relations dictate that the main influence of this interaction will be the adoption of Jewish behavior and patterns of expression by the Arab audience.

And yet, inter-Arab public interactions in soccer also are governed by Hebrew. The Hebrew language is dominant even when all involved are Arabs. For example, an Arab referee is compelled to hear Hebrew curses, and even in inter-Arab games, the fans of opposing teams taunt each other in Hebrew. A striking example of the status of Hebrew as the "soccer language" appeared during a game between the two most successful Arab teams from Sakhnin and Nazareth in the 1998–99 season. During the week before the game, the managers of Nazareth attacked Sakhnin's coach, Azmi Nassar, in the Arab media as a part of their long and complex relationship with him.[14] Sakhnin's reaction was more than symbolic. Two large signs were set on the field, facing most of the audience and the television cameras, stating in Hebrew: *"Azmi, ohavim otkha lanetzah!"* ("Azmi, we love you forever!"), *"Azmi, hame'amen ha-bakhir bamigzar ha-'Arvi!"* ("Azmi, the best coach in the Arab sector!") In this case, the writers are Arab, the readers are Arab, and the context is an internal Arab quarrel of which the Jewish fans are totally unaware.

As I have already pointed out, Hebrew for the Arabs in Israel is the "public language" that enables them to communicate with the state's institutions and the Jewish majority. However, choosing Hebrew as a language for announcing messages regarding an internal conflict between Arab soccer fans indicates that there is something beyond Hebrew's status as a public language; Hebrew is undoubtedly the soccer language in Israel. In order to maintain the role of soccer as an integrative sphere, Hebrew has gained importance and prominence both on the field and in the bleachers.

Jewish Players, Arab Teams

One can find at least one Jewish athlete on almost every Arab team that plays above the lowest division. This presence is partly a result of the "commodification of Israeli football,"[15] but it is also a concrete practice used by Arab sports functionaries in order to influence Arab-Jewish interactions. The participation of Jewish players on Arab teams reduces the potential of the event to become an Arab-Jewish conflict, and I tend to think that the Arab managers who hire them are aware of that.

Indeed, most of the Jewish players gain sympathy and respect from the Arab audience. Whoever witnessed the very emotional farewell of thousands of Arab fans of Sakhnin to the Jewish goalkeeper Me'ir Cohen[16] crying "Stay, stay!" could recognize that Arab-Jewish relations on the soccer field is governed by a unique dynamic. Sakhnin's manager at the time, Mazen Ghnaim, emphasized to the media his love and appreciation for Cohen, saying that he will miss Cohen not only as a player but also as a person. In the context of Arab-Jewish relations, the subtext of this statement and similar others are clear: Although we are an Arab team and he is a Jewish player, our national identity is irrelevant when it comes to soccer. Likewise, the violent turmoil in Arab-Jewish relations that erupted in October 2000 has not translated into hostility toward the Jewish players by Arab audiences (in sharp contrast to the accelerated hostility toward Arab players on Jewish teams by Jewish audiences).

Azmi Nassar is a former player in the Israeli first division and the most successful Arab coach in Israel. In an interview with the Hebrew newspaper *Haaretz*, he referred to the differences between the social condition of Arabs in Jewish teams and Jews in Arab teams:

> We, in Bnei Sakhnin and Akhi Natzeret[17] have progressed several years ahead of the State of Israel. We don't see any difference between Arabs and Jews. And we also want to integrate into Jewish society. We are tired of looking at people as Arabs or Jews. We feel good with the Jews; we want to live with them. We are happy that they are in our society and accept them. But for Jewish society—this is difficult. In soccer, as everywhere, they look at us as second class.[18]

As a fascinating illustration to Nassar's argument, some of the Jewish players even earned Arab nicknames. A Jewish player in Sakhnin, for example, whose name in Hebrew is *Tsabar*, was named by Sakhnin's audience *Sabri* (a common Arab name). These nicknames are not only an unambiguous expression of acceptance and sympathy but also another attempt to blur the ethnic-national boundaries between Arab and Jew.

Palestinian Symbols

Dan Rabinowitz[19] describes the discursive ways in which the state of Israel denied the Palestinian national identity of its Arab citizens, and how it tried to create a new, local Arab identity, loyal to the state of Israel. And indeed, in the first decades of Israel's existence, its Arab citizens downplayed the Palestinian elements of their identity. The absence of the Palestinian exiled leadership, as well as many years of worry about the reach of the arm of Israeli law and the reaction of the Jewish majority, forced demonstrations of Palestinian national identity into the private sphere. Today, as in the past, the interiors of many Palestinian houses in Israel are decorated with national symbols, such as maps of Palestine or Palestinian flags. On the other hand, the few public attempts to express a national identity, such as the political organization of the al-'Ard group in the early 1960s, were so efficiently suppressed as to increase their rarity in the years to come.[20]

Nonetheless, since Land Day in 1976 (in memory of the six Arabs who were killed by Israeli police in March 1976 during protests against governmental land expropriation), and even more so since the first Intifada in 1987, public manifestations of Arab and Palestinian nationalism are no longer rare. The collective calendar contains certain "dates of national identity," such as the Nakba (the destruction of Palestine in 1948), Land Day, and the annual commemoration of thirteen demonstrators who were killed by Israeli police in October 2000. These dates are marked by widespread public rallies and demonstrations, which include Palestinian flags and nationalist songs.

Memorials to the dead—important pillars in the construction of European nationalism (and, following that, in Zionism)—have been established in various Arab towns. Some Arab schools even take their students on "heritage trips" to destroyed Palestinian villages, outings that emphasize the fate of the Palestinian collective more than that of the actual villages that were razed. Furthermore, since the signing of the Oslo Accords, Palestinian national symbols are no longer illegal, and the Palestinian flag is commonly seen at political demonstrations.

Given all this, one might expect that soccer would provide an arena for a dramatic expression of the conflict between Jews and Arabs—and particularly so among the fans. This is not the case. Despite the significant place that Arab men in Israel give to sports in general, and to soccer in particular, soccer bleachers are far from being a site of national identification. One sees no Palestinian flags and the nationalistic character of the fans' songs and slogans is marginal. Even though the conflict between Jews and Arabs constitutes the deepest chasm in Israeli society, the processes of Palestinization, undergone by Arab society in Israel since 1967 and accelerated by the two Intifadas, have not broached the soccer bleachers. The main reason is that soccer in Israel is identified by the Arabs with "Israeliness," with taking part in a shared public sphere. Soccer is seen as an opportunity for integration, while expressions of Palestinian nationalism within the sports arena are taken as a threat to that opportunity.

The Limits of Isolation

To what extent are the processes taking place in the soccer bleachers really detached from other spheres of life? Actually, the findings that I present below imply a certain spillover from the soccer stadium to wider social contexts.

The data are based on a countrywide survey held with 448 Arab citizens of Israel, men aged eighteen to fifty, who constitute a representative sample of this subpopulation. They were interviewed during January 2000 in their homes by Arab interviewers using a closed questionnaire. The interviews included questions about habits of soccer consumption and questions about their political behavior and sense of belonging to different social groups and categories. Interviewees were then asked to choose three out of nine identities that they were most proud to belong to: the Palestinian people, the Arab nation, their religious group (Muslims or Christians), Israeli citizens, their *hamula* [extended family], their town or village, their region (Galilee, Triangle, or the Negev), and as men.[21]

The research design enables us to explore whether soccer consumption correlates with senses of identity or with political behavior. The results support the argument about the integrative function of the soccer stadium. The first dimension probed is political behavior. Since the end of military rule in 1966, Arab voting patterns are considered by scholars as a barometer for their identity orientation, especially regarding the state of Israel and the Palestinian people. In a very crude categorization, Arab voters in 1999 had two options: Arab parties or Zionist parties (mainly "left-wing" parties like the Labor Party or Meretz, but also some religious or right-wing parties). Despite many disqualifications, voting for a Zionist party may indicate an aspiration to integrate into Israeli society (without referring to the motives for integration or to how realistic these aspirations are). A simple distribution analysis reveals a strong positive correlation between attendance in the local stadium and the tendency to vote for a Zionist party. Among people who attend local games (at least once during the period of the research), 29 percent voted for a Zionist party in the 1999 Knesset elections. Among those who did not attend, only 18 percent voted for a Zionist party.

In the identity questions, a strong negative correlation was found between attendance in the stadium and the tendency to choose Palestinian identity as a source of pride. Between those who did not attend games, 49 percent chose Palestinian identity as a source of pride. Among "occasional spectators" (attending between one and sixteen games in the season), the ratio was 38 percent. Only 15 percent (two out of thirteen) of the "heavy spectators" (seventeen games or more) chose Palestinian identity. On the other hand, no correlation was found between pride of being Israeli citizens and involvement in soccer.

What is fascinating about these correlations is that they exist independently of other variables that potentially predict political behavior or sense of identity. For example, even within each level of education or age, these correlations are valid. Table 2 presents the coefficients calculated from logistic regression in order to isolate the peculiar contribution of the soccer bleachers from the tendency to vote for a Zionist party or to choose Palestinian or Israeli identity as a source of pride. The other

Table 9.2. The Contribution of Each Different Variable for Predicting Voting Behavior or Choosing Certain Identity as a Source of Pride
(the numbers are standardized logistic coefficients—ß)

	Voting for Zionist Parities	Pride in Palestinian identity	Pride in Israeli identity
Attendance in local games	0.22*	−0.31**	0.10
Active use in Hebrew	0.59**	−0.01	0.55**
Reading newspapers	−0.20	0.15	0.04
Age	0.12	0.21*	−0.01
Education	−0.16	0.25*	−0.59**
Constant	−1.18**	−0.24*	−2.04**
N=	368	431	427

*p < 0.05   **p < 0.01

independent variables in the equations, in addition to attending local games, are age, education (number of years), active use of Hebrew (self-rated on a scale of 1 to 5, as an indirect indication of interactions with Jewish citizens), and the number of days in the week that the interviewee reads the newspaper.

The table proves that the correlations between attendance in the soccer bleachers and political behavior are independent of age, education, written media consumption, or other interactions with Jewish citizens. These findings imply that the integrative atmosphere of the soccer stadium leaves traces on some individuals' sense of belonging and even influences their voting choices in elections. These findings also support my previous argument that many Arab fans identify soccer with "Israeliness." This identification is not enough to develop a shared national pride with the Jewish majority, but it is significant enough to distance them from Palestinian nationalism conceived as contradicting integrative aspirations.

This is an apparent paradox. On the one hand, I argue for a dynamic of enclave—the integrative atmosphere of the soccer stadium is opposed to Arab-Jewish relations in most of other public spheres. On the other hand, the survey supplied evidence for a certain degree of spillover from the stadium outward. The key to solving this paradox is to differentiate between the collective and the individual level. Although the Palestinian citizens of Israel as a collective assign soccer an integrative role and therefore suspend any demonstration of separate identity or protest (but keep them for other opportunities), on the individual level, many fans who are actively present in the stadium carry the integrative experience with them to other spheres of life.

Representing Israel, Pride to the Arab Nation

In the evening of May 18, 2004, while Israeli troops stormed Palestinian refugee camps in the Gaza Strip in another attempt to crush the Palestinian uprising against the occupation, both Israeli Prime Minister Ariel Sharon and Palestinian President Yasir Arafat found time for phone calls concerning seemingly trivial issues. Both leaders called Mazen Ghenayem, the director of Ittihad Abna' Sakhnin soccer club, who that evening became the first Arab team to win the Israeli National Cup. Sharon emphasized his confidence that the team would represent Israel in an honorable manner in Europe, while Arafat claimed that the team brought pride to the Arab nation.

This dual congratulation, while seemingly paradoxical, was possible because of the peculiar and multifaceted image of Arab soccer in Israel and the attempts by different agents to use it for their political purposes. Furthermore, these attempts are evidence that soccer is not only an "interesting angle" to probe questions of identity; the dominance of soccer in the leisure culture of Arab men in Israel also makes it a central social sphere by itself and should be treated as such.

Arab soccer fans and players prefer to stress the common denominator with their Jewish counterparts. It is clear that the "soccer language" in Israel is Hebrew, and the ideological language is the meritocracy that produces the image of soccer as an autonomous impartial sphere, where the formal and informal state-regulated discriminative mechanisms do not exist. Consequently, soccer is seen by many Arab fans as an opportunity to receive legitimacy as citizens from the Jewish majority. The integration into a public sphere, which is identified with the state, and even represents the state, may enable them to feel a partnership with Jewish citizens.

The integrative orientation of soccer should not be misidentified with the "normal development" approach,[22] a term used to describe an academic tendency to see the Palestinian minority in Israel as moving toward the normalization of its political orientation, seeking integration in the state's fabric and equality in the allocation of common resources, such as ethnic minorities in other states. The Arabs in Israel are not "normal citizens" in any sense except for their formal citizenship. Israel is by definition a Jewish state, and the political practices that derive from this definition set Arabs in Israel in a permanently marginal position within Israeli society. This marginality is reflected in a multifaceted predicament that cannot be solved very easily.

As my research shows, involvement in sports is a strategy for coping with this predicament. The intensive involvement offers Arab soccer fans a diversified arsenal of meanings concerning their status in the state and their relations with the Jewish majority. Their choice in adopting the integrationist interpretation and reproducing it does not change their formal status. The Arab minority uses the sports arena only to maintain an enclave of normal relations with the majority, and reserves protest for other occasions.

Interestingly, despite the evidence of some spillover in political orientation of Arab fans from the stadium to other spheres, there is no evidence of a similar spillover among the Jewish fans. At the same time, by their massive support for an Arab team who won the Israel National Cup and by their desire to represent Israel on the international level, Arab soccer fans presented the Israeli public with a dramatic proposal. Their consistent endeavors to articulate their success in Israeli, even patriotic terms, undermine the basic assumption of the hegemonic definition of Israeli identity. They offer, therefore, an Israeliness that is not necessarily Jewish and has nothing to do with the IDF and the ethos of "security." This Israeliness is bilingual, speaking both Arabic and Hebrew and vibrantly switching between or integrating the two. It is secular in its institutional form but tolerant of any religion, and can even tolerate Muslim prayer in the national sphere, like the collective prayer of Sakhnin's Muslim players right after their victory. It is based on active participation in the Israeli arena and on a dialogue between the various ethnic and religious groups within it. It is competitive and achievement oriented but not predatory and manipulative. As soccer in Israel is a masculine institution that marginalizes women, this "identity proposal" is far from offering a utopian model for equality. But given the road that needs to be traveled in regard to solving this ethnonational and religious conflict, the model presented is a very good start, indeed.

Notes

This article is based on a study supported by research grants from the Israel Foundation Trustees and the Shaine Center for Research in Social Sciences.

1. The Palestinian citizens of Israel number one million, representing 19 percent of Israeli citizens. They consist of Arab Palestinians who did not escape or were not expelled during the 1948 Arab-Israeli war, and received Israeli citizenship with the establishment of the state.

2. Shalom Dichter, *Sikkuy's Report on Equality and Integration of the Arab Citizens in Israel 2000–2001* (Jerusalem: Sikkuy, 2001).

3. This was the first season of the league's format that prevailed until 1998–99 (two top nationwide divisions, with various levels of local divisions below them).

4. The calculation only includes a settlement when the team representing it is the settlement's top team. For instance, teams based in Tel Aviv are not counted for the second division, because the city is represented in the first division.

5. Peter Bradley, "The Irish in Scotland: Football, Politics and Identity," *Innovation* 7 (1994): 423–39.

6. Jeremy MacClancy, "Nationalism at Play: The Basques of Vizcaya and Athletic Club de Bilbao," in *Sport, Identity and Ethnicity,* ed. Jeremy MacClancy (Oxford: Berg, 1996), 181–99.

7. Gerry Finn, "Racism, Religion and Social Prejudice: Irish Catholic Clubs, Soccer and Scottish Identity. I. The Historical Roots of Prejudice," *International Journal of the History of Sport* 8 (1991): 72–95.

8. Azmi Bishara, "The Arabs in Israel: Reading a Fragmented Political Discourse," in *Between the "Me" and the "Us,"* ed. Azmi Bishara (Jerusalem: Van Leer Institute and Hakibbutz Hameuchad, 1999) (in Hebrew).

9. Tamir Sorek, "Arab Football in Israel as an 'Integrative Enclave,'" *Ethnic and Racial Studies* 26, no. 3 (2003): 422–50.

10. Allan Guttmann, *From Ritual to Record: The Nature of Modern Sports* (New York: Columbia University Press, 1978).

11. Christian Bromberger, "Football as World-View and as Ritual," *French Cultural Studies* 6 (1995): 293–311.

12. Muhmmad Amara and Sufian Kabaha, *A Split Identity: Political Division and Social Reflections in a Divided Village* (Giv'at Haviva: The Institute for Peace Research, 1996).

13. Ramzi Suleiman and Benjamin Beit-Hallahmi, "National and Civic Identities of Palestinians in Israel," *The Journal of Social Psychology* 137 (1997): 219–28.

14. During his career, Nassar served as coach of the teams from both Sakhnin and Nazareth several times. Nassar was also the coach of the Palestinian National Team in the West Bank and Gaza Strip.

15. Amir Ben-Porat, "The Commodification of Football in Israel," *International Review for the Sociology of Sport* 33 (1998): 269–76.

16. Cohen left Sakhnin in the middle of the 1999–2000 season after receiving an offer from a team in the highest division. In his half-season in Sakhnin, he exhibited his excellent athletic skills and quickly became the crowd's favorite.

17. He used the Hebrew pronunciation of the two leading Arab teams' names, both having been coached by Nassar.

18. *Haaretz,* November 2, 2000.

19. Dan Rabinowitz, "Oriental Nostalgia: How the Palestinians Became the Arabs of Israel," *Teoria Uvicoret* 4 (1993): 141–51 (in Hebrew).

20. Sabri Jiryis, *The Arabs in Israel* (Beirut: Institute for Palestine Studies, 1969).

21. The survey was part of wider research and therefore included many questions not discussed in this article.

22. Nadim Rouhana and As'ad Ghanem, "The Crisis of Minorities in Ethnic States: The Case of Palestinian Citizens of Israel," *International Journal of Middle East Studies* 30 (1998): 321–46.

PART IV

Civilizing the Body

EDWARD SHAPIRO

10 *The Shame of the City: CCNY Basketball, 1950–51*

A half century ago there occurred two of the great events in the history of Jews and American sports: the victory of City College of New York in 1950 in the National Invitation Tournament and the National Collegiate Athletic Association tournament, the two major postseason basketball tournaments, and the 1951 basketball scandal, the most famous gambling scandal in college sports history. This scandal implicated the entire starting lineup of the previous year's championship CCNY team as well as players at several other New York colleges. The scandal soon spread to colleges throughout the country. Thirty-two players from seven different schools were accused of accepting bribes to throw a total of eighty-six games in twenty-three cities between 1947 and 1950, and twenty were convicted. At least twenty games at Madison Square Garden had been fixed. Of the fifteen New York City college ball players ensnared in the scandal, eight were Jews. Gamblers with such Jewish-sounding names as Jackie Goldsmith, William Rivlin, Jack Rubinstein, Benjamin and Irving Schwartzberg, Joseph Aronowitz, Saul Feinberg, Eli Kaye, and Nathan "Lovey" Brown participated in the scandal. The detective who arrested the CCNY players was Abraham Belsky. Jews were also prominent among the lawyers and judges involved in what *Newsweek* called "the most sickening scandal in the history of American sports." Although several histories, one novel, and an HBO special, "City Dump: The Story of the 1951 CCNY Basketball Scandal," have discussed the scandal, none has analyzed its ethnic dimension.[1]

For half a century, City College had played an increasingly important role in the social and economic ascent of the city's Jews. They, in turn, had a close and deep emotional attachment to CCNY, and took pride in its academic and athletic accomplishments. "We knew it as a gospel that this plain College was for each of us a passport to a higher and ennobled life" said one Jewish graduate of the class of 1906. In *The Rise of David Levinsky*, Abraham Cahan described the almost religious awe of his eponymous character on viewing the CCNY building, then on Twenty-third Street.

> I would pause and gaze at its red, ivy-clad walls, mysterious high windows, humble spires; I would stand around watching the students on the campus and around the great doors, and go my way, with a heart full of reverence, envy, and hope, with a heart full of quiet ecstasy. It was not merely a place in which I was to fit myself for the battle of life, nor merely one in which I was going to acquire knowledge. It was a symbol of spiritual promotion as well. University-bred people were the real nobility of the world. A college diploma was a certificate of moral as well as intellectual aristocracy. My old religion had gradually fallen to pieces, and if its place was taken by something else, if there was something that appealed to the better in me, to what was purest in my thoughts and most sacred in my emotions, that something was the red, church-like structure on the southeast corner of Lexington Avenue and Twenty-Third Street. It was the synagogue of my new life. Nor is this merely a figure of speech: the building really appealed to me as a temple, as a House of sanctity, as we call the ancient Temple of Jerusalem.[2]

Jews such as Cahan saw CCNY as an institution that offered the brightest of the city's working-class Jewish youth the best of Western civilization and the vocational tools to succeed in this new and fabulous country.

The Jewish Harvard

The role of CCNY in the Americanization and embourgeoisement of New York's Jews was at its height during the 1940s and 1950s. By mid-century, the great majority of its students (and athletes) were Jews and the college was at its peak, both academically and athletically. Prior to World War II, relatively few Jews attended college, and business rather than the university was the major avenue for economic and social advancement. This changed after the war when a college degree became the ticket of admission into the middle class, and universities dropped their anti-Jewish quotas and increased their enrollments. In the 1940s and 1950s, however, most New York Jews could not afford expensive residential colleges, and they saw no need to leave the city when the city's free public colleges had an excellent academic reputation. CCNY was the jewel of the city's higher education system. It had the most rigorous admission policy and its graduates had little trouble finding employment or being admitted to prestigious graduate and professional schools. Indeed, CCNY became known as the "Jewish Harvard."[3]

Although Jewish immigrant parents saw sports as frivolous and goyish, their children believed involvement in sports, even if only as spectators, would hasten their Americanization and counter the anti-Semitism of people such as Henry Ford. Jews, the Flivver King said in 1921, "are not sportsmen. . . . Whether this is due to their physical lethargy, their dislike of unnecessary physical action or their serious cast of mind, others may decide. . . . It may be a defect in their character, or it may not; it is nevertheless a fact which discriminating Jews unhesitatingly acknowledge." Sociologist Edward A. Ross agreed. "On the physical side," he wrote, "the Hebrews are the polar opposites of our pioneer breed. Not only are they undersized and weak-muscled, but they shun bodily activity and are exceedingly sensitive to pain." For Jews, prominence in athletics would refute this stereotype of the Jew as bookish, emaciated, and disdainful of physical activity. "We have been branded as weak and physical cowards," a Yiddish daily declared in 1923. "While we are proud to emphasize our interests in matters intellectual, we must not brand ourselves as physical weaklings, but by displaying an all-around development, we will best gain the respect of the world."[4]

Participation in sports enabled American Jews to affirm simultaneously their Americanness and Jewishness. As historian Peter Levine has noted, sports nurtured among Jews' "communal beliefs tied closely to Jewish tradition and culture while at the same time reinforcing mainstream American values." They encouraged their "claims to legitimacy and full participation while . . . providing a sense of ethnic solidarity and identity." Eager to become fully American, Jews avidly read the sports pages of their daily newspapers and delighted in the exploits of Jewish athletes such as Barney Ross, Marshall Goldberg, and especially Hank Greenberg, the latter arguably the most admired Jew of the 1930s and 1940s.[5]

Jews and the City Game

The Jewish presence in sports during the 1930s and 1940s was particularly notable in basketball, then the nation's most popular spectator sport. Sociologists and sportswriters often resorted to genetics to explain this phenomenon. Jews, they claimed, were quicker, better balanced, and had better eyesight. According to sportswriter Paul Gallico, the reason that basketball appealed "to the Hebrew with his Oriental background is that the game places a premium on an alert, scheming mind and flashy trickiness, artful dodging, and general smartaleckness." Although Gallico's explanation is half-baked, basketball was in fact the favorite sport of New York's Jews at this time. Even Jews argued that there was an almost natural affinity between Jews and basketball. No other sport, a former Jewish athlete at CCNY said in 1936, demanded "the characteristics inherent in the Jew . . . mental agility, perception . . . imagination and subtlety. . . . If the Jew had set out deliberately to invent a game which incorporated those traits indigenous in him . . . he could not have had a happier inspiration than basketball."[6]

What the sportswriter Peter Axthelm has called "the city game" was very popular among New York City Jews at a time when most still resided in poor and lower-middle-class, densely populated Jewish neighborhoods of Brooklyn, Manhattan, and the Bronx. The favorite game at the city's many Jewish community centers was basketball. The 1930s and 1940s were also the golden age of New York City collegiate basketball. CCNY, New York University, Manhattan College, Long Island University, and St. John's annually fielded strong teams, and college doubleheaders featuring New York City colleges at Madison Square Garden were major events. Beginning in 1938, the annual National Invitation Tournament, the unofficial national college championship, was held at the Garden.

Also at this time, gambling on college basketball became more popular in New York City and elsewhere, due in part to the press's publicizing of the point spread. The point spread was the margin of points by which one team could normally be expected to defeat another team. The point spread encouraged gambling on games in which the two teams were not evenly matched. If the stronger team's supporters were to be rewarded, it not only had to win, but it also had to win by more points than the point spread. Conversely, those betting on the weaker team would win if their team lost by a smaller margin than the point spread. The point spread encouraged gamblers to approach players to "fix" games. The gamblers could argue that they were not asking players to "throw" any games, but merely to win by a smaller margin than the point spread.

New York City Jews starred on the great St. John's, New York University, Long Island University, and CCNY teams of the 1930s and 1940s. Local Jewish ballplayers such as Max Zaslofsky, Red Holtzman, Sonny Hertzberg, Dolph Schayes, and Sid Tannenbaum were neighborhood heroes. The Jewish press followed the exploits of Jewish basketball players, particularly those at CCNY. The basketball team at City College had been viewed by Jews as virtually their own and for good reason. During the thirty-eight-year tenure of its legendary coach Nat Holman—"Mr. Basketball"—438 of its 518 players (83 percent) were Jews. When in 1917 CCNY defeated Yale's quintet, one Jewish paper saw it as "a striking example of real democracy" that the children of immigrants defeated the bluest of American blue bloods. The future of the country, the paper concluded, rested with the boys from the tenements, "the red-blooded aristocrats of America's future." It was an accurate prophecy. Eight decades later, the president of Yale would be named Levin.[7]

This passionate attachment of the city's Jews to basketball reached its apex in 1950, precisely at the time when the Jewish presence at City College was at its highest. The college's victories in the National College Athletic Association and National Invitation tournaments was a unique feat, and will never again be duplicated. One excited City College professor called it the greatest event in the college's 102-year history, ranking even ahead of its move from lower Manhattan to Harlem and its postwar expansion in enrollment. The road to the victories of March 1950 had not been easy for a team that Ned Irish of Madison Square Garden called "the best collection of players ever gathered at a New York school" and potentially "one of the great college teams of all time."[8]

The CCNY quintet finished the 1949–50 season with a record of 17–5, acceptable but hardly up to the standard to which its fans had become accustomed. It had lost to UCLA, Oklahoma, Niagara, Canisius, and Syracuse, and had never ranked higher than seventh in the Associated Press poll, finishing the regular season at twenty-seventh. It was one of the last of the sixteen teams selected for the NIT. Because it had defeated St. John's and Manhattan College during the regular season, CCNY was considered to be the best team among the New York City area colleges. The NIT wanted a local school to be represented in the tournament, and CCNY was the logical choice. Entering the tournament, the City College squad's problems were obvious. Its tallest starting player was only 6'5" and the team lacked experience. The only senior in the starting lineup was Irwin Dambrot. Few observers gave CCNY much of a chance, particularly since Bradley University, the nation's number one team, as well as two other powerhouses, the University of San Francisco and the University of Kentucky, had also been invited.

In 1950, the NIT was more prestigious than its NCAA counterpart. In the first round of the NIT, the unseeded CCNY Beavers easily defeated the Dons of San Francisco, 65–46. Their second round game was against Adolph Rupp's storied Kentucky Wildcats, the NCAA champion in 1949.

CCNY slaughtered Kentucky, 89–50, the worst defeat in Kentucky basketball history. One member of the Kentucky state legislature was so
distraught that he introduced a bill calling for a day of mourning and
flying the flag at the state capitol at half-mast. In the semifinal round,
CCNY defeated Duquesne, 62–52. CCNY then met Bradley. "Win or
lose," the New York Times editorialized, "the City College quintet's
accomplishments have stirred the imagination of the sporting world
and well rewarded the ardent undergraduates and loyal alumni who for
so long have been hoping that something in the nature of this miracle
would take place." Further miracles were about to take place. Although
an underdog, CCNY defeated Bradley 69–61, and Ed Warner, its outstanding forward, was selected as the tournament's most valuable player, the
first time this award had gone to a black.[9]

The Pride of New York

All New Yorkers, and not merely CCNY students and alumni, were
excited by CCNY's victory. Mayor William O'Dwyer held a reception for
the team on the steps of City Hall where he congratulated it "for making the City of New York so proud." A noon rally took place on the City
College campus. School president Harry N. Wright praised the team for
displaying "the true spirit" of CCNY. One aspect of this "true spirit"
continually emphasized by New Yorkers was that CCNY's unsubsidized
players had defeated hired athletes who had been highly recruited while
in high school and then pampered while in college. The CCNY players,
by contrast, had not been heavily recruited, came from the lower economic rungs of society, were attending a tuition-free institution, and were
students first and athletes second. Their victory of 1950 was viewed as
a triumph of the underprivileged—ethnically, economically, and athletically—and this endeared them to all New Yorkers. In Charley Rosen's
Barney Polan's Game: A Novel of the 1951 Basketball Scandals, the
leading character is a Jewish graduate of CCNY and a sportswriter for a
Brooklyn newspaper. "If God would grant me the power to decide," he
says, "I would never trade City's miraculous NIT title straight-up for
even a Dodgers World Series championship come September. Definitely
not. Not even if it meant sweeping the Yankees."[10]

Many considered CCNY's victory in the NIT a fluke, and few thought
it could do the unprecedented and win the NCAA tournament also. Only
eight teams were selected for the NCAA, four from the east and four from
the west. CCNY was invited to participate while it was competing in
the NIT, and it soon proved that the selection committee had not made

a mistake. CCNY defeated Ohio State, 56–55, in the eastern semifinals, and then North Carolina State, 78–73, in the eastern finals. Despite its loss in the NIT, Bradley, the winner of the western finals, was favored over CCNY in the championship game held at Madison Square Garden. CCNY again shocked Bradley in a thriller, 71–68, and Irwin Dambrot was chosen the tournament's most valuable player. "Under the greatest of pressure," wrote one historian of college basketball, CCNY had "won through two tournaments in which all ten of the country's top-rated teams were playing. They beat the previous year's defending champions from both tournaments and twice beat the number one team." This was truly one of the greatest accomplishments in the history of American intercollegiate athletics.[11]

New Yorkers, especially Jews, seemingly could not get enough of this "team of destiny," as it came to be known. The *New York Herald-Tribune* contrasted them with the hired gladiators at other colleges. "The cult of athletics has never taken hold in the municipal colleges," it stated approvingly. "Students go there to get an education. They are New York's own, born to the taxpayer's privilege, admitted to free advantage strictly on the basis of high school scholarship." At CCNY, it continued, "sports are incidental; nobody goes to tuition-free City College for a four-year outing. The educational process is just as serious and functional as the subway." This emphasis on the CCNY athlete as a student first and an athlete second was quite widespread, and was encouraged by a college administration eager to bolster the institution's academic reputation.[12]

Manhattan Borough President Robert F. Wagner, Jr., whose father had played basketball and football at City College a half century earlier, presented engraved scrolls to the CCNY players at a ceremony on the college campus, and swore in Coach Holman as an "Honorary Deputy Commissioner of the Borough of Manhattan." (Holman had to pay a fee of six cents for the appointment to be legal.) In order to enable students to attend a massive March 30th rally in honor of the team, the CCNY administration took the unprecedented step of canceling classes for one hour and announced that no action would be taken against students not attending classes for the rest of the day. At the rally, President Wright declared that this was one of the proudest days of his life. "This team came here to study, not to play basketball. . . . I want to point out that they are given no scholarships to play ball . . . and they have not been imported to play basketball. I am particularly proud of their high scholastic rating."[13]

Arthur Daley, the sportswriter for the *New York Times*, noted that the CCNY players were "from the sidewalks of New York," and the *New York*

Herald Tribune called them "our boys." Even Frank McGuire, a native New Yorker and coach of archrival St. John's, admitted that he had been rooting for CCNY. The victories were particularly gratifying considering the less-than-friendly view of the rest of the country toward the city as an outpost of immigrants, Wall Street, and un-American ways. That CCNY defeated schools located in Peoria, Illinois; Lexington, Kentucky; Raleigh, North Carolina; and Columbus, Ohio, in a sport invented and perfected in America made its victories especially sweet, and sweetest of all was the defeat of Kentucky. Adolph Rupp had not heavily recruited Jewish athletes, and he had vowed that blacks would never play for Kentucky as long as he was coach. Marvin Kalb, a member of the CCNY class of 1951, remembered the NIT game between CCNY and Kentucky as "a cultural war."[14]

Yet despite the pride of New Yorkers in CCNY, the team and coaching staff were hardly representative of the city's ethnic makeup. The team consisted of four blacks and twelve Jews (the student manager was an Italian American). Three of its starters (Irwin Dambrot, Ed Roman, and Al Roth), its two most important substitutes (Norm Mager and Herb Cohen), and its coach and assistant coach (Nat Holman and coach Bobby Sand) were Jews. Holman, an unusually well-read and erudite person by the standards of his profession and the author of several books on basketball, was aware of the sociological significance of CCNY basketball in general and of the victories of 1950 in particular. Four years earlier, he had almost come to blows with the coach of the University of Wyoming team when the latter shouted anti-Semitic taunts at his CCNY players. In a 1960 speech given at a dinner in his honor, Holman recalled that "the small and often undernourished boys, coming for the most part from the crowded tenements of the Lower East Side, Bronx, and Brooklyn, who made up our squads year after year, typified so many Davids doing battle with the Goliaths of collegiate sports." "I think," he continued, that "millions of non-college people, residing in New York City and in other parts of this country, regarded our City teams as theirs. The City College team was a symbol, a symbol of the underprivileged who through hard work, through training, and the use of natural intelligence, was able to conquer, despite overwhelming odds." And of these underprivileged, none had more reason to be gratified than New York's Jews. In March 1950, Holman became a celebrated figure to the city's Jews, and he received invitations to speak at Congregation Rodeph Shalom and the Ramaz School, an Orthodox day school on Manhattan's Upper East Side. Holman himself had been raised in the Jewish ghetto of the Lower East Side and had a strong Jewish identity. He was a generous contributor to the United Jewish Appeal, was active in promoting sports in Israel, and spent the last years of his life in a Jewish old-age home in the Bronx. He needed no reminding, nor did he have to remind his Jewish listeners, of the ethnicity of the residents of these "crowded tenements."[15]

American Verities

But for most Americans, the significance of the CCNY triumphs lay elsewhere. *Sport* magazine selected Holman as its man of the year for 1950. In its February 1951 issue, appearing one week before the sporting world had an additional reason for focusing on the CCNY basketball team, it noted that Holman's success "served to re-state in a troubled time the vast opportunity that beckons in this free country to the young man who has the guts to go after what he wants." For *Sport*, the most important athletic magazine in America, the "what" the young man should go after was so obvious that it was left unstated. The magazine would be as surprised as everyone else to discover that Holman's young men defined it solely in financial terms. This award to Holman came at a difficult period in the nation's history. The Korean War had broken out in June 1950; financial scandals had been uncovered within the Truman administration; charges of communist infiltration of the media, the churches, academia, and government were being aired daily by demagogues; and the atomic espionage trial of Ethel and Julius Rosenberg was proceeding. In contrast, the CCNY achievements seemed to affirm deeply held American verities and were a refutation to the siren calls of socialism and communism. This theme of Americanism was helped when former and graduating CCNY players withdrew from participation in a 1950 May Day exhibition game at St. Nicholas Arena in New York City sponsored by the Communist *Daily Worker.* The paper claimed the withdrawal was because of the influence of the red-baiting Hearst press on a spineless CCNY administration. Without the former college players, the May Day game organizers substituted players belonging to left-wing publications and unions in New York and Baltimore.[16]

Newsweek magazine predicted in December 1950 that, notwithstanding the "Cinderella team" of 1949–50, the 1950–51 team could be Holman's best team. He agreed. Of the key players from 1949–50, only Dambrot had graduated. Returning were four outstanding juniors, Ed Roman, Al "Fats" Roth, Ed Warner, and Floyd Layne, two Jews and two blacks. The inexperience that had hindered the championship team early in the season would no longer be a factor. "Because they were a young team," a March 1950 *New York Times* editorial said, "they lost games they could have won. Often, before the big crowds at Madison Square Garden, the Beavers passed wildly and missed shots that should not have been missed." As the newspaper would soon find out, there were other reasons besides inexperience for these errant passes and muffed shots.[17]

Rumors regarding point-shaving and the throwing of college basketball games had been circulating within the world of New York basketball for several years before 1951. It was common for spectators to berate players for not doing their best and to wait until the end of lopsided games to find out the final point spread. In January 1951, the newspapers reported that two players for Manhattan College had been fixing games. Junius Kellogg, the star of the Manhattan College team, became a national celebrity for telling his coach that he had been offered one thousand dollars to fix a game with De Paul University and for helping law enforcement authorities catch the culprits. It was initially assumed that Manhattan College was an isolated case. This would soon change.

On Saturday, February 18th, a spokesman for Manhattan District Attorney Frank S. Hogan revealed that his office was questioning witnesses who were likely to implicate players from two other area colleges. A further statement was promised on Sunday morning. Almost simultaneous with this announcement, a train from Philadelphia carrying the CCNY team, fresh from thrashing Temple University 95–71, pulled into Grand Central Station. The police arrested Roman, Roth, and Warner and charged them with receiving bribes. The arrests were the result of a monthlong investigation by twenty New York detectives. Roman, Roth, and Warner were booked, along with Harvey (Connie) Schaff, a former player at New York University, Salvataro T. Sollazzo, a jewelry manufacturer and the gambler behind the scheme, Sollazzo's sidekick Robert Sabbatini, and Eddie Gard, a former player at Long Island University and Sollazzo's go-between with the players.

The City College players were charged with fixing games against the University of Missouri, the University of Arizona, and Boston College at Madison Square Garden during the 1950–51 season. CCNY was a heavy favorite in each game and yet lost all three, 54–37 to Missouri, 41–38 to Arizona, and 63–59 to Boston College. (It was later revealed that the games against UCLA and Niagara that CCNY had lost during its miracle season of 1949–50 had also been fixed.) It was now clear why a team from which so much had been expected had won only eleven out of eighteen games. At the arraignment, Chief Magistrate John M. Murtagh of Felony Court, an alumnus of City College, claimed Sollazzo had "corrupted these young men and brought disgrace on a great institution."

In fact, the CCNY players, as well as three from Long Island University who were arrested on February 22nd, had needed little enticement, as they later admitted. The players were adults, knew precisely what they were doing, and had pocketed thousands of dollars each. But it was more convenient to blame Sollazzo than those who had brought so much credit to CCNY and the city.[18]

The involvement of City College, coming after the glorious season of 1949–50, was front-page news throughout the country and came at a time when the Senate Crime Investigating Committee, chaired by Senator Estes Kefauver of Tennessee, was investigating organized crime. The CCNY situation became even bleaker when four additional members of the 1949–50 CCNY team were arrested—Dambrot, Layne, Mager, and Cohen. City College responded by canceling the remainder of its basketball season. Journalists and the nation's moralists wondered how those who had been so highly praised for their fortitude and character less than a year earlier could have been so easily corrupted. "It just makes you wonder," District Attorney Hogan said, "what has happened to our moral values. The entire business is loathsome and pathetic."[19]

Contemporary explanations of the scandal emphasized broad cultural trends such as a national decline in morality, an overemphasis on collegiate athletics, and an obsession with the almighty dollar. "Only last year there was a team of young athletes who achieved for their college and their classmates an almost impossible dream," the *New York Times* said on February 20th. "They represented in a small but significant way, something we call democracy—freedom of opportunity and choice, including the right to an education regardless of race or creed, financial or social standing. By winning . . . they brought glory to their college and their city and were a vindication of the democratic process." The *Times* at first argued that the onus rested on the gamblers and not the players. "Shall we permit a situation to exist which corrupts young men and turns college athletics into a hunting preserve for gamblers?" the paper asked. "It is time to rid ourselves of this cancerous growth— these youth-ruining gamblers and their little runners and payoff men and suborners of corruption who cover everything they touch with slime." Two days later, the *Times* added to its list of villains. "Somehow the home, the neighborhood, the campus, the college fostered a crooked, distorted sense of values and produced moral shipwreck," it said. "College sport grew into a misshapen monster, until the hippodromed team wagged the college. Perspective and proportion were lost in a chase for fame and the dollar. The very things that education is supposed to stand for and inculcate took a back seat." Holman, by contrast, argued that "a general relaxation of morals in the country" was more responsible for the scandal than any overemphasis on college athletics.[20]

The *Daily Worker* and *Chicago Tribune* provided alternative political explanations of the scandal. The *Daily Worker* argued in a front-page editorial that "profiteering chairmen of Wall Street corporations," bankers, "big-shot politicians grabbing the war contracts," and the "profit system" were responsible for what it called "one of the tragedies of our time." The scandal was also due to the demoralization among the young caused by the military draft, the Korean War, and a "war-ridden morality in which they are being drenched by their college presidents and trustees." The elimination of future scandals thus depended on the destruction of capitalism and militarism. Until that golden age, the paper declared, "let us determine to save our children from the crooks, gamblers and profit hogs—the big ones at the top as well as the small fry around Madison Square Garden." The *Chicago Tribune* disagreed. It argued rather that the scandal stemmed from the greed, demise of the sense of honor, and moral "degradation" associated with the New Deal. The buying of votes by the New Dealers and Franklin Roosevelt's betrayal of his office led directly to the buying of college athletes and to their betrayal of their teammates, coaches, and colleges.[21]

The Revenge of the Hinterland

Other explanations focused on social factors. One major scapegoat was the moral values of New York City, a longtime target of the hinterland. The problem supposedly was not gambling per se, but urban gamblers. *Newsweek* claimed that as a result of the scandal, New York City stood before the nation "like a latter-day Sodom." Phog Allen, the coach of the University of Kansas, contrasted the virtues of the metropolis with those of the Great Plains. "Out here in the Midwest," he said, "this condition, of course, doesn't prevail. But in the East, the boys . . . are thrown into an environment which cannot help but breed the evil which more and more is coming to light." Sportswriter Stanley Woodward asserted that betting on college basketball games was an eastern urban phenomenon. The residents of Lexington, Kentucky, home to the University of Kentucky, "are probably as basketball-conscious as any men and women in the country," he said, "but they don't bet much, and there is absolutely no organized bookmaking such as you find in the larger metropolitan areas." In fact, nearby Louisville, Kentucky, was one of the most important bookmaking centers in the country, and gambling on college basketball games was popular in the Bluegrass state.[22]

Coach Rupp of Kentucky agreed with Woodward. He said he was not surprised by the scandal in New York City. "The newspapers there quote odds and play directly into the hands of the gamblers." Gamblers, however, "couldn't reach my boys with a ten-foot pole." Furthermore, Rupp continued, "our boys are under constant and absolutely complete supervision while they're on the road, especially in New York." Woodward, Allen, and Rupp would have to eat their words. The scandal soon spread to players at Bradley University, located in Peoria, Illinois, nearly a thousand miles from New York City, and to some of Rupp's own fabled Kentucky Wildcats. Gamblers did not need a ten-foot pole to reach players at Kentucky. Cold cash had been sufficient for Alex Groza, Ralph Beard, and Dale Barnstable, stars on the great Kentucky teams of the late 1940s, to dump a game against Loyola of Chicago in the 1949 NIT. The fixing of Kentucky games continued into the 1949–50 and 1950–51 seasons, long after Groza, Beard, Barnstable had left. In court, the Kentucky players testified that Rupp was friendly with a leading Lexington bookmaker and familiar with the point spreads on Kentucky games.[23]

For many, Madison Square Garden was a convenient symbol of the moral decadence of New York City. Almost immediately, college presidents and basketball coaches throughout the country declared that their teams would no longer play in this den of iniquity. The Bradley University team unanimously rejected participating in the 1951 NIT in order to avoid the "unsavory atmosphere" of the Garden. The National Collegiate Athletic Association recommended to its members that they should play their games in campus facilities rather than at off-campus sites such as the Garden. It also announced that, for the first time since 1942, none of the NCAA tournament games would be at the Garden. Even New Yorkers could not resist blaming Madison Square Garden. Although CCNY wanted to continue playing there, the New York City Board of Higher Education banned all the municipal colleges from playing at the Garden. The Board also decided to deemphasize athletics at the city's colleges. In an effort to "restore sanity to intercollegiate basketball," it banned the recruitment and preferential treatment of athletes and declared that emphasis would now be placed on intramural, rather than intercollegiate, sports. The problem faced by City College and other institutions, declared CCNY President Wright, was the "incompatibility between our educational objectives and the requirements and practices of big-time basketball. The situation is made more acute by a low public sensitivity to moral standards and to the responsibility of the individual." This incompatibility had existed in 1950 as well, but then, of course, the CCNY basketball team projected a different image.[24]

Another suggestion concerned that other den of corruption, the Catskill summer resorts. Grossinger's, the Concord, Kutsher's, and other hotels in the Jewish Alps catered to a largely Jewish clientele from New York City and its suburbs, and were celebrated for their abundant Jewish cuisine and entertainment. They also were famous for basketball. Hundreds of college basketball players worked as bellhops, counselors, lifeguards, waiters, porters, and busboys during the daytime at some forty resorts, and in the evenings they provided entertainment for the guests by playing other resort teams. The games attracted gamblers who had little difficulty in bribing players eager to supplement their meager summer earnings. Many of the players implicated in the 1951 scandal had first been approached by gamblers in the borscht belt.[25]

One reform to clean up college basketball suggested by Phog Allen and others was to forbid players from participating in the summer resort games. The New York City Board of Higher Education did prohibit their players from playing for the summer hotels. The resort owners predictably denied they were responsible for the scandal. "Temptation and the opportunity to mislead these boys is not confined to any particular area, and the avenues of approach to them will be developed by unscrupulous persons, wherever they may be found," said Milton M. Kutsher, the president of the Sullivan County Resort Council. The resorts survived the demise of basketball. After the scandal, one hotel person said, "the gyms were quiet. The big sport was Simon Says. For entertainment, we went back to singers and dancers and stand-up comics. The only kind of scandal they would ever cause was sexual. That was one problem we could always handle."[26]

Roth and Warner were the only CCNY players involved in the scandal who received jail sentences. At their sentencing, General Sessions Judge Saul S. Streit excoriated the commercialization and corruption of collegiate sports in general and CCNY athletics in particular. He stated, and the CCNY administration confirmed, that Roth and Cohen had been accepted to City College on the basis of records rife with "deliberate fraud and probable forgery," including doctored high school transcripts. Floyd Layne and Ed Warner also should not have been admitted to CCNY (Warner had even been considered retarded while in junior high school). Nevertheless, as Streit noted, both Layne and Warner had made "unaccountable improvement" as students, despite having to devote many hours to basketball. Streit justifiably suspected that academic standards had been bent on their behalf. CCNY, the judge concluded, was part of an educational system in which fame "depends less and less on education as a center of learning and more and more on the prominence of . . .

football or basketball teams." Things went from bad to worse for CCNY's academic reputation when it was announced just prior to the opening of the 1951–52 season that the college had barred three players, including two starters, from the team because their college admission records had been "altered." The college also revealed then that Irwin Dambrot had also been admitted on the basis of forged admission records. This was particularly embarrassing for the CCNY administration because it had prided itself on not offering inducements to athletes and had emphasized their academic accomplishments. Roman, for example, was a candidate for Phi Beta Kappa. For CCNY alumni and students, these revelations of academic chicanery depreciated the worth of a CCNY degree and the image of their alma mater. CCNY would never have the same place in the hearts of New York Jews that it had prior to February 1951. Its glory years on the hardwood are now a distant memory, and the role of Jews in the 1951 scandal has disappeared down the memory hole. Neither the triumph of 1950 or the scandal of 1951 are discussed in the standard histories of American Jews or of American anti-Semitism. Harold U. Ribalow even deleted the chapter on Nat Holman from the postscandal editions of his book *The Jew in American Sports,* which first appeared in 1948, and replaced it with a chapter on the professional basketball player Dolph Schayes. Later editions even failed to mention the Cinderella season of 1949–50.[27]

The Dog That Did Not Bark

The scandal of 1951 should have been a gold mine for anti-Semites, and yet there is no evidence that Jews were held uniquely responsible for the scandal. Jews naturally feared an anti-Semitic backlash. It had been only a decade since the activities of Murder Incorporated, a gang spawned in the Jewish ghetto of Brownsville, Brooklyn, had been front-page news. Jewish criminals such as Bugsy Siegel, Mickey Cohen, Snags Lewis, and the Purple Gang of Detroit were active in the 1940s, and they reinforced the anti-Semitic canard associating Jews with crime. Even more troubling for Jews was the arrest of Julius and Ethel Rosenberg, Harry Gold, and David Greenglass during the summer of 1950 for spying on behalf of the Soviet Union. And now there was the CCNY basketball scandal with its predominately Jewish cast. Yet the anti-Semitic dog did not bark either during the Rosenberg trial or during the basketball scandal. The press did not delve into the Jewish aspect of the scandal, just as it had not dwelled on the Jewish dimension of CCNY's miraculous season of 1949–50.

The basketball scandal occurred at the height of the Cold War and while fierce anti-Semitic campaigns were under way in the Soviet Union and Czechoslovakia. American anti-Semites thus found themselves in the unanticipated position of supporting America's mortal enemies. There was also little room for anti-Semitism in an era when Marjorie Morningstar had become an icon for American bobby-soxers and when the most famous literary defense of American institutions had been voiced by another of Herman Wouk's characters, the lawyer Barney Greenwald in *The Caine Mutiny*.

Anti-Semites were also unable to capitalize on the basketball scandal because it involved gentiles as well as Jews. While Jews comprised over half of the basketball players from New York City implicated in the scandal, there were still over twenty gentile players from City College, Long Island University, Manhattan College, Bradley University, Toledo University, and the University of Kentucky who were convicted of taking bribes. Nor was Salvatore Sollazzo, the chief fixer, a Jew. It became even more difficult to claim that corruption in collegiate athletics was an exclusively Jewish phenomenon when an even more important collegiate scandal surfaced in August 1951 at West Point. Ninety-six cadets, half of whom were football players, were expelled from the academy for cheating on examinations. One was the team's quarterback and the son of Earl "Red" Blaik, the Army coach. The findings of the Kefauver Committee emphasized that gambling was a national problem involving small and large cities alike and all ethnic groups. The disgraceful place of athletics on the college campus and the seeming moral decline of the nation's youth evidenced by the basketball scandal were national problems and not restricted to Jews and to New York City.

Coming four and a half years after Bess Myerson was selected as the first (and still only) Jewish Miss America, midway in the period that the historian Arthur Goren has called the "golden decade" of American Jewish history, and four years before the yearlong celebration of the American Jewish tercentenary, CCNY's victory in 1950 was further evidence that America's Jews, even those from the tenements of New York City, had become part of the American mainstream. Stanley Cohen, a quarter of a century later, remembered the significance of the 1950 NIT and NCAA tournaments when "five street kids from the City of New York—three Jews and two blacks . . . whale[d] the shit out of Middle America." For Jews, the 1950 CCNY basketball team, comprised of the sons of immigrants and the grandsons of slaves, was a symbol of the triumph over bigotry and a confirmation of America as truly a golden land. Five years after CCNY's victory run, Will Herberg published a book with the revealing title *Protestant-Catholic-Jew*. Truly, Jews were part of the national mainstream if they could win the NIT and NCAA and be elevated to parity with Protestants.[28]

Notes

1. Stanley Cohen, *The Game They Played* (New York: Farrar, Straus, Giroux, 1977); Charles Rosen, *Scandals of '51: How the Gamblers Almost Killed College Basketball* (New York: Holt, Rinehart, and Winston, 1978); Charley Rosen, *Barney Polan's Game: A Novel of the 1951 Basketball Scandals* (San Diego: Harcourt, Brace, 1998) (Charles Rosen and Charley Rosen are the same); Albert J. Figone, "Gambling and College Basketball: The Scandal of 1951," *Journal of Sport History* 16 (Spring, 1989): 44–61; "Basketball: Who's Clean?" *Newsweek*, March 5, 1951, 81.

2. Irving Howe, *World of Our Fathers: The Journey of the East European Jews to America and the Life They Found and Made* (New York: Harcourt, Brace, Jovanovich, 1976), 282; James Traub, *City on a Hill: Testing the American Dream at City College* (Reading, MA: Addison-Wesley, 1994), 28–32; Abraham Cahan, *The Rise of David Levinsky* [1917] (New York: Harper and Row, 1960), 168–69.

3. This was, of course, before the experiment with open enrollment and affirmative action devastated City College's academic standing. See Traub, *City on a Hill*, passim.

4. Peter Levine, *From Ellis Island to Ebbets Field: Sports and the American Jewish Experience* (New York: Oxford University Press, 1992), 4, 11, 16.

5. Levine, *Ellis Island to Ebbets Field*, 7.

6. Jon Entine, *Taboo: Why Black Athletes Dominate Sports and Why We're Afraid to Talk About It* (New York: Public Affairs, 2000), 202–3; Paul Gallico, *Farewell to Sports* (New York: Alfred A. Knopf, 1938), 325; Levine, *Ellis Island to Ebbets Field*, 27.

7. Levine, *Ellis Island to Ebbets Field*, 75–76.

8. *New York Times*, March 30, 1950, 43; Stanley Frank, "Easy Doesn't Do It," *Collier's*, February 18, 1950, 66.

9. *New York Times*, March 18, 1950, 12.

10. *New York Times*, March 21, 1950, 37; Rosen, *Barney Polan's Game*, 13.

11. Neil D. Isaacs, *All the Moves: A History of College Basketball* (New York: Harper and Row, 1984), 100.

12. *New York Herald-Tribune*, March 30, 1950, 26.

13. *New York Times*, March 30, 1950, 43; *New York Herald-Tribune*, April 7, 1950, 31. One CCNY alumnus wrote Holman that the victories of March 1950 had increased the respect for CCNY graduates and the status of CCNY diplomas, and that there was no longer any reason for CCNY students and alumni to feel inferior. Noel Simmons to Nat Holman, April 12, 1950, Box 1, "Congratulatory Letters on Grand Slam," Folder 1, Holman Papers, CCNY Archives.

14. *New York Times*, March 28, 1950, 36; *New York Times*, March 31, 1950, 39; "City Slickers," *Newsweek*, March 27, 1950, 78; *N.Y. Vue—Daily News*, March 22–28, 1978, 69. Rupp backtracked on recruiting black players after his all-white 1966 Kentucky team was thrashed by Texas Western in the NCAA championship game. All of Texas Western's starting five were blacks. Historians consider this

to have been arguably the most important game from a sociological and political perspective in the history of intercollegiate basketball.

15. "Farewell Speech," Nat Holman Papers, Basketball Hall of Fame, Springfield, MA.

16. "By the Editors," *Sport* 10 (February, 1951): 16, 80–81; *New York Times*, April 11, 1950, 4; *Daily Worker*, May 1, 1950, 16.

17. *New York Times*, March 18, 1950, 12; "Drive, Drive Drive!" *Newsweek*, December 4, 1950, 76.

18. *New York Times*, February 18, 1951, 60; *New York Times*, February 19, 1951, 1, 40; Cohen, *Game They Played*, 146–47; for Sollazzo, see Robert Rice, "Annals of Crime: The Bewildered Fixer," *New Yorker*, March 5, 1955, 38–66.

19. *New York Times*, February 19, 1951, 40; *New York Times*, June 20, 1951, 33.

20. *New York Times*, February 20, 1951, 24; *New York Times*, February 22, 1951, 30; "Catching the Fix," *Time*, March 5, 1951, 50; Nat Holman, "How Can We Save Basketball," *Sport* 11 (November, 1951): 13.

21. *Daily Worker*, February 21, 1951, 1, 7; *Chicago Tribune*, February 22, 1951, 16.

22. Cohen, *Game They Played*, 105; "Basketball: Who's Clean," 81; Figone, "Gambling and College Basketball," 55–60.

23. "The Police Blotter," *Newsweek*, October 29, 1951, 80. John Rocker, a pitcher for the Atlanta Braves, would get in hot water in 2000 for saying some politically incorrect things about New York and New Yorkers. "The biggest thing I don't like about New York are the foreigners. I'm not a very big fan of foreigners. You can walk an entire block in Times Square and not hear anybody speaking English. Asians and Koreans and Vietnamese and Indians and Russians and Spanish people and everything up there. How the hell did they get in this country?" When asked what he would do if traded to the New York Mets, he responded, "I would retire first. . . . Imagine having to take the [Number] 7 train to the ballpark, looking like you're [riding through] Beirut next to some kid with purple hair next to some queer with AIDS right next to some dude who just got out of jail for the fourth time next to some 20–year-old mom with four kids. It's depressing." Jeff Pearlman, "At Full Blast," *Sports Illustrated*, December 17, 1999, 60ff.

24. *New York Times*, February 20, 1951, 19; *New York Times*, March 3, 1951, 9; *New York Times*, March 27, 1951, 1, 24; *New York Times*, April 4, 1951, 24; *New York Times*, May 1, 1951, 1, 19; *New York Times*, December 26, 1951, 33; *New York Times*, December 9, 1951, 52; Cohen, *Game They Played*, 176.

25. "Borscht Basketball: Best U.S. Collegians Play for Catskill Resorts," *Life*, August 28, 1950, 63–64.

26. *New York Times*, February 21, 1951, 19; *New York Times*, February 25, 1951, sec. 2, 17; Stefan Kanfer, *A Summer World: The Attempt to Build a Jewish Eden in the Catskills, From the Days of the Ghetto to the Rise and Decline of the Borscht Belt* (New York: Farrar, Straus, Giroux, 1989), 219.

27. *New York Times*, November 20, 1951, 26; *New York Times*, December 1, 1951, 1, 28.

28. Cohen, *Game They Played*, 45–46; Arthur Goren, *The Politics and Public Culture of American Jews* (Bloomington: Indiana University Press, 1999), 186.

JEFFREY S. GUROCK

11   The American Orthodox Athlete: From Contradiction in Terms to Institutional Standard-Bearer

A traditional community that celebrates the cerebral and the intellectual while historically according minimal recognition and respect for physicality and aggressiveness should find sports generally foreign, if not threatening, to its social and cultural consciousness. Such clearly was the attitude of the traditional Jewish community of the premodern period toward most forms of athletics. Although the Talmud does require a father to teach his son to swim as a lifesaving precaution and sources can be found that encourage Jews to be physically fit to more properly observe the commandments, Jewish men, respectful of the evolving traditions, did not strive—nor were they honored for—athletic excellence. After all, the paradigmatic Jewish male was always Jacob, the scholarly man of the tents (figuratively, the sedentary, reflective spectator) and not Esau, the man of the field. Although this peripatetic of Jewish forefathers had a real, or dream-sequence, main event with an angel, he was projected within rabbinic tradition in his passive mode. As far as Jewish women were concerned, they were neither lionized for their learning nor marginalized for personal activism. And although, as we will see, informal "ball playing" was not unknown to Jewish girls and women, because formal contests in pre–modern times Olympics, tournaments, and the like were for men only, Jewish women, like their non-Jewish counterparts, had to have been, at most, sideline spectators.[1]

Moreover, as long as these formal sports were associated with ancient religious rites and symbols, such endeavors were for a minority of Jews who wanted to staunchly or to partially separate themselves from the Jewish way of life. How profound, and how widespread, was the players' disaffection from their ancestral past differed from place to place and from source to source. Predictably, the pro-Hasmonean chroniclers of the second-century BCE Maccabean revolt castigated as apostates those Jews who frequented gymnasia, reversed their circumcisions, and otherwise "joined to the Gentiles." For these polemicists, such activities led, in part, to divine punishment through Antiochus's decrees. Along similar lines, the rabbis of the Mishnaic period condemned those who sat in "the seat of scorners" (i.e., stadium seats, if you will), homes to idolatry and heresy.[2]

However, other Greco-Roman period sources—from Josephus, to Philo, to papyri, to the Talmud itself—speak of another minority of Jews who surely sought to emulate the gentile sporting life, but who were neither desirous, nor who were perceived as anxious, to leave the Jewish faith or community. They, for the most part, stopped short of participating in formal gentile-run contests, or at least in showing obeisance to the gods. But, on their own, boys and girls alike played the same games as did their non-Jewish neighbors. Apparently, ball playing was so widespread among those with at least some concern with Jewish practice as it evolved that the rabbis of the Talmud both set parameters for what sort of athletic activity might be performed on the Sabbath as well as expressed concerns about how a Jewish male's or female's interest in sports might lead to even more problematic forms of assimilation. In so doing, these rabbis of the first centuries of the common era adumbrated concerns that their successors would address almost two millennia later in other highly assimilatory cultures.[3]

As the Middle Ages unfolded in Christian Europe, the Jews' sorely disadvantaged social and political position within their unfriendly host societies severely limited their possibilities for participation in organized sports. The medieval tournament was the foremost place to be for this epoch's formal athletic activities. These events, a "brutal medieval cross between sport and warfare," were for the "baronial and fighting class" alone. And Jews, who were generally barred from military service even if, here or there, they had the right "to bear arms" to defend their community or locality, most probably could never have been invited to duel, arch, or joust competitively.[4]

Within their own Jewish communities, youngsters—and some adults—did play ball, did recreate, albeit within their own spheres. There is evidence that children occasionally engaged in foot races and in what we would call today "Blind Man's Bluff," and men and women partici- pated in a primitive form of tennis. Women, reportedly, were particu- larly fond of that pastime and some rabbinic authorities even permitted them the right to do so in festivals.[5] However, it is hard to really gauge how deep or widespread was the passion for play within Jewish quar- ters. Historian Salo W. Baron has asserted that as boys were socialized and educated within their traditional society that valued learning and honored the scholar above all else, little time was allocated within the school experience for leisure-time activities.[6]

But, no one really knows whether the best, or even most, yeshiva students of that time always stood by their books as their rabbis would have wanted and did not sneak outside for "recess." Besides which, clearly the schools of the Tosaphists, for example, did not provide education for all. Thus, even in the best of situations in the twelfth- or thirteenth-cen- tury France or Germany, there had to have been masses of hardscrabble youngsters who occupied themselves with tossing a pelota (jai alai ball) around, while their most erudite contemporaries pined away in the halls of the yeshiva. Moreover, there is even a reference in rabbinical response literature that suggests that Jews tutored each other in the martial art of fencing, although, like swimming instruction, knowing how to duel might have been more than a game. With potential enemies all around them, even if physical attacks against Jews were not a constant occur- rence, such self-defense training might have been a very serious lifesav- ing measure.[7]

In the modern period, the decline in the power and values of the tra- ditional Jewish community in Western and Central Europe, as that group sought freedom and equality, was mirrored through the rise of widespread Jewish interest in sports. Jews then began not only to play like gentiles did, but, more importantly, seek to compete arm in arm with their coun- terparts. Jewish males, in particular, did so to disprove romantic and racist canards against them as physical degenerates incapable of taking their places as soldiers, athletes, and patriots within their host societies. In Germany, for example, Jewish university students tried to show that they possessed the "Teutonic ideals of virile virtues" by "testing their courage in dueling and through physical training in the *Turner* clubs." Essentially, in an emancipatory era and context, the right to play sports was a community-defining situation and Jews wanted in.[8]

Traditional Jews in Central Europe of the nineteenth century—we might now begin to call them Orthodox Jews—increasingly a minority within the Jewish group, did not aspire to compete with, among, and against gentiles. But, they too wanted to share in the bounties of eman-cipation. Accordingly, they began to socialize their youngsters as repre-sentative members of their larger society and culture, even as they still strove to maintain within them a great regard for their ancestral faith. In that Enlightenment milieu, physical training became part of the educa-tion of the modern Orthodox youngster, the *Mensch-Yisroel*, even if the "Mensch" was a young woman. Rabbi Samson Raphael Hirsch, the apos-tle of "Torah with Derekh Eretz," pointed to the cultivation of "physi-cal powers" as among the three key "resources which the child requires for living as an Israelite." For him, it was a parent's obligation to "see that his limbs are firm and supple and exercise them—our Sages, as we know, included swimming among the subjects of education." Accord-ingly, physical training was part of his Frankfurt school curriculum. However, a full embrace of sports within the Orthodox community did not begin until well into the twentieth century.[9]

These real concerns about educating generations of well-integrated, all-around persons were of little moment to the Jewish religious commu-nity of Eastern Europe of that same time period. There, traditional Jews resisted czarist efforts to have them act as their aggressive gentile neigh-bors did. In the nineteenth-century shtetl, reverence and concern for the head, for the intellect—far more than the cultivation of the body—was where these Jews' emphasis lay. Although few in the community were rich and knowledgeable enough to engage in full-time study, most people looked up to these *sheyne Yidn*, these Jewish "beautiful people." With that ideal squarely in mind, parents hoped to raise their sons to be schol-ars, to work with their minds and not with their muscles, even if most fathers were butchers, bakers, porters, coachmen, and so on. Whiling away time as an athlete was no way for a kid to move up in class. Rather, the superstars of the Jewish town were the sedentary types who stuck to their books. Of course, in keeping with Jewish tradition, even the most committed students participated in outdoor games on Lag B'Omer—the Jewish field day. But, there was no social sanction for daily and violent pastimes—"fighting [was] 'un-Jewish' in the extreme."[10]

Interestingly enough, toward the end of the nineteenth century, a leading Russian rabbi, Israel Mayer ha-Kohen Kagan, in ruminating about how he was raised and educated, publicly regretted that he had not devoted enough time in his youth to physical fitness. A sounder body, in his view, would have helped him become an even greater scholar. Speak-ing in 1893 to his disciples in the Yeshiva of Radun, Rabbi Kagan said:

> Do not study overmuch. Man must preserve the body so that it is not weakened, so that it does not fall ill, and for that it is crucial to rest

and relax, to breathe fresh air. A walk should be taken toward evening, or sit at home and rest. When possible, a swim in the river is good for strengthening the body.[11]

Apparently, too many hours at his books had weakened his eyesight. As an adult, he was obliged to abstain from reading for two years. However, not withstanding Rabbi Kagan's reputation and prestige, his remarks did not inspire a physical training movement within the world of the yeshiva. The more commonly held position was that such activities were frivolities—a *"bitul* Torah"—a waste of valuable time that should be spent in Torah study.[12] And, of course, it was the image and continued reality of "the underdeveloped and frail body of Jewish men . . . produced by the experience of studying in a yeshiva" that spurred Max Nordau in 1898 to call for the creation of a new, "muscular" Jew and Judaism. Needless to say, this secular Zionist's call for a proud, athletic Jew who would help his (and, I imagine, her) people take their respected places within the modern world did not resonate at all positively within most of the East European Orthodox Jewish community.[13]

It remained for twentieth-century America to witness a noticeable and highly noteworthy shift that took place in this traditional community's attitude toward physicality and, ultimately, sports. There and then, fascination with, and involvement in, athletics—including participation in competitive sports—emerged as a significant part of the lives of Orthodox Jews in America. Everywhere, even the children of rabbis from Eastern Europe not only followed closely what went on in the "majors," but took part in both violent and noncontact sports. Moreover, these second-generation youngsters received, at least, the passive (and sometimes the active) approbation of most of their religious leaders and authorities. Ultimately, for some members of that group, their personal affinity for and success in sports became a way of promoting Orthodoxy positively to Americans and American Jews as a modern, accommodating faith, worthy of the allegiance among the masses of their people. Still, as with all such encounters with modernity, Orthodox Jews in America established and frequently redefined limits to their group's participation in this nontraditional form of cultural expression. These decisions provide another useable way of differentiating among the varying strains that made up twentieth-century Orthodoxy.

I must emphasize that in speaking here about Orthodox Jews in twentieth-century America, my focus is on a very small segment of that ethnic and religious group's population. By definition, I am looking only at those people, be they immigrants or native-born Jews, who were staunchly committed to upholding in their lives what the ancient traditions taught. These were those Jews who were, and are, for example, recognizable through their punctilious observance of the Sabbath and the laws of kashruth as prescribed in the *Shulkhan Arukh*. All other American Jews—even those masses who attended Orthodox synagogues—were, to a great extent, emancipated from the telling questions of when, why, and to what extent sports' secular values might be permitted to permeate, or could even be openly encouraged, to enter religious lifestyles.[14]

For Orthodox Jewish immigrants who arrived in the early decades of the twentieth century, two momentous decisions determined that they, and especially their children, would be caught up in the culture and challenge of American sports. The first, the most monumental choice any East European Jewish family could make during this time period, was their very opting to come to America itself. There, the lures and pressures to Americanize—to be like gentiles, who might become their friends and teammates—would prove pervasive and profound. In other words, once these Orthodox Jews decided to depart for this country, they risked that their youngsters, once opened to the streets of New York, might come to harbor new and troubling religious and social values.[15]

The second critically important decision, which speaks to the immigrant Orthodox generation's conscious willingness to allow their children to rapidly acculturate, was their decision to send their sons in overwhelming numbers and all of their daughters to the public schools. In these temples of Americanization, Orthodox youngsters—like all other Jewish and non-Jewish students—were exposed daily to a new social system, new role models, and different definitions of appropriate behavior. For our purposes, it is imperative to note that physical education—sports training—was an important part of the ongoing curriculum of acculturation. And, of course, when school was out, a myriad of Christian and Jewish settlement houses beckoned, offering their sports and recreational programs, which built upon what was inculcated from 9 A.M. to 3 P.M. These were lures that Jewish kids of all religious stripes were wont to resist and their parents were hard-pressed to deny them.[16]

What this meant was that youngsters came home from school, or up from the streets, with new heroes—a coach and not a rebbe—and with new interests—like "how did the local fighter or team do last night"— and with new aspirations—"maybe I too can be a 'star of the ghetto.'" Moreover, if a youth from an Orthodox home tried to act on his fantasy, he—and we are talking here primarily about boys—immediately found that practice and game-match schedules did not take Judaism's clock and calendar into account.

Some Orthodox families eventually were able to make their peace with their sons' ambitions to be fighters and not scholars. One turn-of-the-century Yiddish author wrote of the ambivalence a fictional rabbi, "a rabbinical scholar of the old type" and his wife came to feel toward their son, "the professional pugilist." Initially, they were "shocked . . . who ever heard of decent people fighting like peasants." But, eventually they became "reconciled to his vocation," and even felt a degree of pride when he was victorious against a gentile fighter. But what of the now formerly Orthodox athletes' breaks with Jewish law to pursue their American sports dreams? Here, affinity for athletics, as much as any other aspect of Americanization, effected massive tensions within Orthodox families.[17]

Fortunately for the survival not only of Orthodoxy but also of American Judaism in general, this same era witnessed the slow evolution of the "shul with a pool" concept to address the needs of these second-generation youngsters. A small group of rabbis and teachers, men and women both, themselves scions of religious families from Eastern Europe and trained at the Jewish Theological Seminary of America (JTSA), began to develop, under synagogue auspices, sports, recreational, and other American social activities—a panoply of events scheduled with the demands of Jewish tradition squarely in mind. Certainly from the 1910s on, it was possible for observant Jewish youngsters, particularly in New York, to play ball during the week under the banner of the Young Israel, Institutional Synagogue, or Jewish Center against both Jews and Christian settlement house clubs.[18]

As important, these modern religious institutions used the availability of sports on their premises as a lure to attract a larger segment of second-generation Jews to synagogue life—those who hailed from families whose interest in religious practice was in decline. The idea was that for the shul and/or the Talmud Torah to possibly compete against settlement houses and the like for the allegiances of Jewish children, many of their fun activities, sports included, had to be brought into a Jewish religious milieu. The modern thinkers and activists who led these modern Orthodox movements fervently believed that the road to the sanctuary, to commitment and observance, could begin with a synagogue-sponsored gym, pool, or dance program. Not incidentally, what made these incipient synagogues Orthodox—clearly an Orthodoxy far different from the one transplanted from Eastern Europe—was that if, and when, a player, swimmer, or dancer prayed, he or she did so in a service that adhered to the strictures of the Code of Jewish Law.[19]

A young Orthodox rabbi, Mordecai M. Kaplan deserves the lion's share of credit for these moves toward bringing the culture of America—sports very much included—into the twentieth-century synagogue. Undoubtedly, this son of an East European rabbi acquired his first youthful interest in sports as a public school pupil. As a teenager, he did a bit of boxing—one of his rabbinical school classmates with whom he sparred once chipped the edges of Kaplan's front teeth. Kaplan also dreamed of playing football for Columbia University. But he was too busy with his studies to follow through on his ambition. In any event, by his own account, his troubling observation of children of devout Jews playing baseball in the streets on a Sabbath afternoon while their elders listened in shul to a rabbi drone on about a traditional text convinced Kaplan and his financial supporters to found in 1918 the Jewish Center synagogue. Ultimately, the Jewish Center synagogue idea would find its greatest acceptance within the Conservative movement. (Kaplan himself would soon depart theologically and institutionally from all ties with Orthodoxy.) Still, the idea that the American Orthodox synagogue—no less than its Conservative counterpart—might use sports within its precincts to both accommodate the observant and to attract the uncommitted long remained a cardinal rule of that expression of modern Judaism.[20]

In the meantime, while the vast majority of immigrant Orthodox Jews did little to shield their children from the pressures of Americanization and thus were readily caught up with the pressures sports wrought, there was, at the turn of the century, a small, transplanted yeshiva culture, based almost exclusively in New York, that did its utmost to control its youngsters and to raise them as they themselves had been reared in Eastern Europe. Indeed, when established in 1886, Etz Chaim, America's first yeshiva, provided its grammar school–aged students with only a meager general education. There is no record of Etz Chaim, at its inception, providing any time-out for physical training or sports. Over the next thirty years, as the so-called Jewish parochial school movement grew ever so slowly to encompass Etz Chaim and three other like-minded schools, educating at most 1,000 boys, these yeshivas grudgingly began to offer a very modest range of general studies and a few moments a day for "physical training, recess and organized games." To do less might have brought down upon them the censure of state education department officials. Besides which, for all their efforts to insulate themselves from Americanization, these early yeshiva families demanded some secular training for their sons to enable them to advance economically in America. However, the acquisition of sports skills was not seen as necessary for advancement in America.[21]

A sea change took place within the American yeshiva community in 1915 with the appointment of Dr. Bernard Revel as president of the Rabbinical College of America—an institutional forerunner of Yeshiva University. His master game plan was to build a modern Orthodox seminary, competitive with JTSA, capable of training Torah-learned and acculturated English-speaking rabbis to address the social and religious needs of fellow native-born Jews. A quality preparatory school that would willingly—not grudgingly—impart secular training to budding rabbis was an essential part of the program. Accordingly, the Talmudical Academy (TA) was established a year after Revel's arrival—a school that proudly conformed to the educational protocols of the state education department.[22]

Longtime school principal Dr. Shelley Safir was especially anxious to produce well-rounded American boys. For him and his staff of both Jewish and gentile teachers, that meant "scholastic achievements" had to be balanced by some proficiency in sports. Toward that end, by 1919, not only did he have a gym teacher on staff "licensed to teach physical training in N.Y.C. schools" but he also encouraged his students to do "their full share in activities pertaining to their . . . physical well being." "Athletic activities" were described as among the students' most "outstanding enterprises." In fact, the annual student-faculty baseball game, held appropriately on Lag B'Omer, was one of the noted highlights of the school year. Safir, himself a tennis buff, played center field in the 1923 tilt. Joseph Lookstein, a young rabbinical student, handled the pitching chores.[23]

TA students were very proud of their athletic involvements and asserted that it in no way detracted from "their achievement in the 'mark book.'" In that regard, they crowed, "there is 'something' different in the Yeshiva student. He knows just where to stop." Their only complaint, albeit an important one, was that the school did not have adequate sports facilities. Safir admitted as much when he reported to state authorities that, ensconced as they were then in a small building on the Lower East Side, they used "public parks" for outdoor activities and "class rooms for indoor work."[24]

Dr. Bernard Revel, who received his rabbinical training in Eastern Europe, had no personal affinity for sports activity. He never spoke out publicly about the value of athletics in molding an integrated American Orthodox personality. He certainly had no interest in participating in a school sports event. Nor, for that matter, did, his old-line Orthodox Talmud faculty. However, he clearly shared, or at least understood, Safir and the students' hope that someday his yeshiva might have an adequate physical education facility. After all, Revel was a realist and understood that American boys, even his disciples whom he called "the few, the saving remnant," loved sports. Besides which, we may reasonably project that, committed as he was to raising up generations of American Orthodox Jews "possessed of a full education in modern thought and culture," to his mind, athletics could be part of the message of "synthesis" that he always preached.[25]

Significantly, if he ever had to defend this part of his modern yeshiva program to those who would down it as a "bitul Torah" (i.e., a waste of valuable time that would be better spent studying Torah), Revel could claim his contemporary Rabbi Abraham Isaac Kook as a supporter—the famous chief rabbi of Palestine who was then speaking out explicitly on the value of physical fitness and even of sports among Orthodox Jews.[26] This religious Zionist ideologue, responding in part, and implicitly, to Nordau's critique, clearly stated as early as 1920 that the incipient national revival of the Jewish people—within which Orthodox Jews had to take a part—required that they develop sound bodies to complement their bright minds and holy souls.[27]

Rabbi Kook's activist views did not sit well with most of Palestine's old-line Orthodox rabbis, and he had his outspoken detractors back in Eastern Europe and even in America. But his message may have resonated positively in the 1920s with Revel and elements of his Rabbinical College community at the very time that the yeshiva's president was in the process of linking his school institutionally with the nascent American branch of Mizrachi (religious Zionists). Revel never acknowledged publicly any affinity for this part of Kook's Torah, even as the Palestinian rabbi's works were read with pride, interest, and devotion. But Revel's actions, as we will immediately see, suggested a kinship with Kook's physical-fitness message. Later on in Yeshiva's history, Rabbi Kook's teaching would be evoked to support the expansion of sports' presence at the New York Torah institution.[28]

In all events, the moment the New York yeshiva athletics enthusiasts hoped for seemed to have arrived in 1928 when Revel finalized plans not only to append a college to the Talmudical Academy, but also to move the entire operation to a commodious campus on Washington Heights in northern Manhattan. A "physical culture building" was among the eight structures contemplated for the new uptown campus. Had this vision become a reality, it then would have been possible for these Orthodox undergraduates—who were taking their secular studies to the next level even as they were on the road to the rabbinate or just preparing for careers as religiously informed laymen—to while away some time exercising on the parallel bars or still rings or shooting some baskets in the gymnasium.[29]

As fate would have it, Yeshiva College (YC) would open its doors uptown in 1929, but without a gym. Seven of the eight buildings for the envisioned campus would not be built because when the Great Depression hit America that year, Revel and his followers found that they barely had sufficient funds to complete even one structure. The "temporary gymnasium" situated in the basement of the lone school building, noteworthy for its low ceilings and poor ventilation, would long be the locus for the four one-credit courses in "physical education" required of college freshmen and sophomores. A generation would pass before the financially strapped institution would even begin to think of constructing a first-rate gym.[30]

Still, student interest in sports at the Talmudical Academy and Yeshiva College continued unabated. Indeed, the "program" took a major step forward in the 1930s when the two sister schools began fielding interscholastic and intercollegiate teams.[31] Even when they lost, Yeshiva students were proud of their teams because the very existence of their competitive squads evidenced to the world that they, second-generation American Orthodox students, were regular guys. In 1935, *Commentator* editors spoke for many on their campus when they declared that "more than any other college organization, the Yeshiva College basketball team has been instrumental in uprooting [the] misconception . . . that Yeshiva College . . . is an eastern anachronistic product transplanted artificially to a soil totally inimical to it."[32]

However, for Yeshiva to maintain its hard-earned reputation, its most "regular" of college guys, the Blue and Whites players, had to deport themselves as American "Mensch-Yisroel" when they took on gentile opponents in Orthodoxy's home. So, in 1939, student journalists were outraged that "visiting teams" were reportedly subjected to "poor refereeing, unsatisfactory timekeeping, excessive roughness and poor sportsmanship on the Yeshiva court."[33]

As the 1940s unfolded, a few Yeshiva graduates, some of them young American Orthodox rabbis anxious to make their mark within the larger Jewish community, dreamed publicly that sports at Yeshiva—especially, but not exclusively, basketball—could do more than just refute canards about the alleged orientalism of their school. Moving from a defensive to an offensive stance, now it was thought that through a high profile in athletics, Yeshiva could project Orthodoxy as a faith to which the masses of American Jews could relate. Implicit in this game plan was the belief that American Orthodoxy had to become more competitive against Conservatism and Reform Judaism in the battle that was just beginning in suburbia for the next generation of Jews. Had not Rabbi Solomon Schechter, Conservative Judaism's first twentieth-century leader, been on record years earlier as asserting that "unless you can play baseball . . . you will never get to be a rabbi in America?"[34] And clearly his and Kaplan's disciples, as we have noted, had taken that message seriously and were playing out the Judaism-through-sports theme in the synagogues under their domain. Accordingly, it was said presently, if Yeshiva was truly interested in producing rabbis "who will go out into the spiritual desert that is America today and revive and resuscitate Orthodoxy among the Jews of this land," they had to come from a school that was known for its "cognizance of the mores, customs and traditions of . . . young Jews as Americans." Yeshiva had to institute a more "invigorated, diversified sports program" for all students. And the elite "regular" guys—the Yeshiva varsity sportsmen—should be put on the road as institutional standard-bearers.[35]

However, any plan to place sports in higher relief upon Yeshiva's map required a level of funding and institutional commitment that previously had not been forthcoming. Until then, students themselves had run the intramural and intercollegiate sports program. They had raised the pittances that were paid to volunteer coaches. Remarkably, they had succeeded in attracting some top-flight men to the challenge of Yeshiva athletics. Their greatest coup was their securing Bernard "Red" Sarachek's services as college varsity basketball coach beginning in 1942. Abraham "Doc" Hurwitz was a one-man (full-time) physical education department. And, of course, there was the continuing problem of the absence of a real gym.[36]

Yeshiva's second president, Dr. Samuel Belkin, like his predecessor also a product of the East European yeshiva world before securing a secular education in American Ivy League schools, had no personal sports background. And although he desperately wanted his Bureau of Community Service to succeed in reaching the unaffiliated, he had to be sensitized to the usefulness of sports in that crusade. Fortunately for Yeshiva's sports devotees, Belkin's aide-de-camp, the school's public relations director Samuel Hartstein, himself a former YC basketball player, was constantly on the scene to advocate for the promotion of Yeshiva athletics. More than that, he used his own office to grind out press releases, sports brochures, and the like to the Jewish and general media. He also was instrumental in forming in 1948 the Yeshiva University Athletic Association [YUAA]—an Orthodox sports booster club, if you will—to raise money for coaches and to dream the dream of the up-to-date gym. Among its earliest achievements was its involvement in the long-term engagement of Olympians Henry Wittenberg and Arthur Tauber to coach the fledgling wrestling and fencing teams and the hiring of tennis teaching-pro Eli Epstein to lead the netmen. For a while, Edward Lowenstein of the Maccabee Sports Association coached an impermanent soccer team. Plans also were hatched to take Yeshiva varsity teams to visit outlying Jewish communities to prove, as Hartstein's media alerts put it, that "they can pray and play . . . that religious observance and sports can go hand-in-hand." Yeshiva sports came fully of age in 1953 when Sarachek was appointed by Belkin as the school's first athletic director. In celebrating his new position, Sarachek pledged that "we have no intention of going big-time, but of increasing student interest and participation in our programs. Moreover, we expect to launch a program to provide much needed physical and recreational facilities."[37]

Red's and YUAA's efforts received a warranted symbolic, religious boost some three years later when Rabbi Joseph Lookstein—that erstwhile 1920s Yeshiva pitcher, now one of American Orthodoxy's most influential rabbis—publicly linked what they were doing to "Rabbi Kook's view that one who is indulged in building up his body, is as much performing the will of God as the pious scholar, thus lending to an athletic program as much significance in an institution of higher learning as a *s'micha* [ordination] program."[38]

But how big could sports really become at Yeshiva? Fortuitously, just in time for the 1949–50 campaign, a young athlete arrived on campus whose background and orientation captured the imagination of the YUAA and, of course, Sarachek. Bronx-born Marvin Hershkowitz, an All-City selection from basketball powerhouse De Witt Clinton High School, hailed from a marginally observant family. By his own estimation, his "family had a tendency towards Orthodoxy and attended an Orthodox synagogue," but his father "worked on Shabbat" to help make ends meet. While at Clinton, Hershkowitz played games on Saturday, but "tried to do as least wrong as possible." For example, he would arrange to bring his "gym stuff" to the game site before the Sabbath to avoid carrying it outside in violation of rabbinic precepts. Significantly, Hershkowitz recalled that he never did play well in those Saturday games and as a kid attributed his failures to some guilt over his quasi-Sabbath violations. Nonetheless, this highly recruited star went off to the then-local big-time basketball school, CCNY, and played quite well on the freshman team. However, he was troubled about upholding his growing traditional religious values. How would he deal with "[unkosher] training tables and Saturday travel dates" that would be part of varsity life? His personal journey to be both an athlete and an Orthodox Jew led him to Yeshiva University, where he felt privileged to play for Sarachek, an outstanding tactician who became his personal friend, even if he had to travel downtown by subway to practice and play at the Central Needle Trades school on Lower Seventh Avenue. As important, he found a number of rabbis and professors who welcomed him and were ready to tailor a Jewish studies program to his needs. They loved his attitude and recognized that he only had a Talmud Torah background and, upon arrival, could not have handled either a Talmud-track or Hebrew-intensive program.[39]

Sarachek was excited to acquire a young man of Hershkowitz's caliber. The competitor in the coach saw the possibility on the horizon of more wins for his team and greater public recognition for the school. And the recruiter in him figured that if Hershkowitz worked out, other public school athletes might follow in his footsteps. And, in fact, Hershkowitz did speak to potential student-athletes about "the coach, the school and that you did not have to be a rabbi." But, maybe more important, as a committed, if non-Orthodox, Jew and Belkin loyalist, Sarachek wanted these fellows to enroll at the school for more than just basketball stardom. Rather, he believed that Yeshiva would grant them a quality secular and Jewish education. And he hoped that upon graduation they would contribute to the Jewish community.[40]

Sarachek's visions, including his creed that "not only is the athletic program of immeasurable profit to the student, but the athletic teams are the only ones in the nation fostered by a Jewish college . . . [which] creates intense interest both within the Jewish community and without," coincided completely with Harstein's oft-repeated formula of "Friends, Funds and Freshmen," for the expansion of Yeshiva. And by 1956, Hartstein and his comrades were able to convince their president that this incipient preparatory track—within which Hershkowitz blossomed Jewishly and that had subsequently brought in some additional highly skilled players—should be formalized as a new "Jewish Studies Program" (JSP). This division would attract more and more students, not only athletes, with public school backgrounds. Hopefully, as adults, they would give much back to their community. The sportsmen would become American Jewry's team and increase the number of friends who would donate funds to Belkin's institution; maybe someone who might even be moved to help them build a gym.[41]

Belkin agreed and in February 1956 announced that in the coming fall, "a limited program in Hebraic studies and the principles of Judaism will be offered to accommodate students who are not prepared to take even a partial program" in Yeshiva's existing religious studies programs, with the proviso that these new students subscribe to the school's Orthodoxy and comport themselves accordingly. This announcement, coming as it did in the midst of the Mighty Mites greatest basketball season to date, constituted a moment of triumph for Sarachek. This team, led by public school youngsters that Sarachek recruited—and with some helpful words from Hershkowitz—would compile a 16-2 record. And now, even more help was on the way. Indeed over the next four years, the team compiled a 46-20 record. Not incidentally, by the 1959–60 season, eight of the eleven varsity members were public high school kids. Yeshiva basketball seemingly was on the upswing to stay.[42]

However, this sports heyday did not last long, as Sarachek was unable to sustain the flow of stars into his system. A combination of religious forces within the institution and social circumstances without conspired to chill his dreams. To begin with, the decision to actively recruit public school guys never sat well with many within Yeshiva's community, especially the old-line Talmud faculty, who felt that "the influx of a non-Yeshiva type element into the Yeshiva environment might affect the climate and morale of the Yeshiva itself." And they exerted pressure to restrict admission to only the most committed. Their carping also played no small role in making the newcomers uncomfortable. Red's men were the most visible of the school's new recruits. And admittedly or allegedly, some of the ballplayers, certainly not Hershkowitz, did not always walk the school's straight and narrow. Very uncharitable elements on campus derogatorily referred to the JSP students as members of the "Jewish Sports Program" who "came to shoot baskets, take the college courses and go home." Some highly intolerant students even referred to JSP men as *shkotsim* or (pejoratively) gentiles.[43]

Concomitantly, a gradual change in Yeshiva's larger student recruitment strategies cut, or refined, the pool of public schools students, sportsmen included, whom the school actively pursued. Increasingly, as the 1960s unfolded, "freshman" would be drawn from the then-burgeoning nationwide Orthodox day school movement. And although Yeshiva was still committed to "outreach," school officials began, quite quickly, to look for and at a somewhat different type of public school prospect. Now, the typical second-generation of JSP student was a graduate of the Bronx High School of Science, if he were a Bronxite, who had attended an elementary-level day school before attending a superior secular high school. And he had never really "dropped out" of the Orthodox fold within which he was initially reared, because he often spent his spare time in the ever-expanding network of Orthodox youth groups. In a word, the "true freshman" with no real Jewish background but with a strong athletic profile was no longer appearing at Yeshiva. Besides which, as this era unfolded, there was the other, undeniable reality that generally there were fewer top-notch Jewish ball players on urban high school varsities to even pursue. The coach, consequently, would have to rely on day school products to lead the club. And the 1960s record reflected the fact that young men who as high schoolers had never played against high-level competition did not adjust well to the pressures of college ball, even as the competition grew stronger. In a typical year, 1962–63, the team, with only one good public school player in the starting lineup (two others were role players) went 6-14. One veteran of that squad has reported that there was "some tension between the yeshiva and non-yeshiva players." A frustrated Sarachek, his raised expectations shattered, suffered through nine consecutive losing seasons (1960–61 through 1968–69), winning only 61 of 178 ball games (.353 winning percentage).[44]

Meanwhile, as if losing on the hardwood was not annoying enough, Red also had to have been troubled in 1964 when questions were raised publicly, and debated angrily, about whether basketball players, whatever their pedigrees, were worthy institutional standard-bearers at Yeshiva and whether Saracheck was an appropriate role model for this Orthodox institution.

The flashpoint now in the debate over whether sports and athletes either personified or undermined a true yeshiva environment was a proposal for a "Homecoming Weekend"—including a ball game and a post-game social—to honor past and present players and "to arouse student and alumni interest in athletics." Its protagonist, *Commentator* sports editor Neil Koslowe, not incidentally the son of an early player-coach of the "Blue and White," held still to the YUAA vision of the late 1940s and 1950s. He argued that a vibrant sports program was essential for Yeshiva's growth, that the recruitment of outstanding athletes from all corners of the Jewish community was a desideratum, and that athletes who "give of themselves so that the Yeshiva name would be respected . . . surely [should] have the respect, praise and appreciation of . . . fellow Yeshiva students."[45]

However, Koslowe was to find that many within his generation of students did not view athletes as among "Yeshiva's best," as highly appropriate institutional standard-bearers. One such critic, who seemingly spoke for the student council majority that rejected his proposal, pointedly asserted that "if we wish to do honor; if we wish to create heroes; if we must have idols, let them be those *roshey yeshive* [Talmud faculty] who wage the war to conquer the contradictions of Torah and *khokhma* [secular learning] and who with G-d's help, will win the battle." As important, he protested that the image of a Yeshiva homecoming weekend—with basketball and a postgame social as its centerpiece—smacked of an attempt to secularize his school. Another fellow critic coined the phrase "the collegification" of Yeshiva to underscore his concerns.[46]

As this cultural battle continued, Koslowe was bombarded with canards that his event was a poorly masked effort to bring large numbers of "enticing" Stern College students (Yeshiva's sister school) to the weekend's activities. Everyone knew that young Orthodox women had always attended Yeshiva sports events. Saturday night at Central Needle Trades was traditionally "date night." But now it was alleged that this proposed official social event would lead to an unconscionable *kalus rosh*, a level of libertine behavior inappropriate for Yeshiva. And even as Koslowe's critics were pillorying his intentions, the attacks turned uglier still as students turned on his hero, Coach Sarachek.[47]

Koslowe had said that "Yeshiva College is Bernard Sarachek. He came and he taught and he fought and he yelled" as he preached that "we're Yeshiva we are just as good as anybody else—in fact, we are better in all respects." Red's enemies riposted and blistered the fiery, earthy, old-school coach who punctuated his pep talks with unprintable metaphors as "a vulgar, uncouth person [who] has no place in a university . . . [and] to say that one who has such 'qualities' exemplifies and represents Yeshiva, of all places, is a slander on its good name and reputation."[48]

In response, one of Red's legion of followers tried to put "ribald" Red's rhetoric in its appropriate sports context. In his view, the "spirited coaching of Red Sarachek never seems to have a deleterious effect on the athletes." Besides which, "it is difficult to imagine that the use of phrases like, 'Oh my gracious, fellows, stop throwing passes away . . .' would serve a better purpose." Still, it remained for Victor Geller, Yeshiva's rabbinic placement director and a YUAA loyalist, to silence angry student opponents by reminding everyone of the services Sarachek had rendered to Orthodoxy in his off-the-court communal activities. For Geller, Sarachek was not "a paragon" nor "an exemplar of Yeshiva. . . . But let the record be clear that there are large numbers of people within Yeshiva and outside who respect and admire" him.[49]

In 1969, Sarachek left Yeshiva's coaching lines to assist his disciple Lou Carnesecca in the latter's own quixotic pursuit of professional sports glory as coach of the New York Nets. Red had always given valuable advice to some of America's best-known coaches, from Dean Smith to Joe Lapchick, among others. And now he was tapped to officially bring his special expertise to the highest level. Subsequently, he served as a consultant to Carnesecca when Louie returned to St. John's University. And upon retirement to Florida in the 1980s, Red helped out Kevin Loughery, an erstwhile "Redman," in schooling the Miami Heat.[50]

Sarachek initially willed the Yeshiva job to Sam Stern, the last of his outstanding public school protégés. But Stern was no more successful than Sarachek in bringing in top-flight talent from a diminishing outside pool into an increasingly selective Yeshiva. After two frustrating seasons, Stern departed and Red turned to Jonathan Halpert to head up and give new direction to the program. Captain of the 1966 team, one of the best of his generation of TA athletes, and a second-generation member of the Yeshiva family, Halpert, in his early years, tried to use his connections to attract the best players from the ever-growing day school community to his squad. Occasionally, he would reach out with care and discretion to a public school youngster whom he was certain could toe Yeshiva's now well-defined mark. He also, wisely, downgraded the team's schedule somewhat to afford his club the possibility of being competitive.[51]

In his more than thirty years as Yeshiva's coach, Halpert continued to teach, albeit without the off-color histrionics, Red's style of basketball. Moreover, he preached, as his mentor had, that the club was American Jewry's team and his men were institutional standard-bearers. And he had been proud to take his guys on the road to visit outlying Jewish communities. But unlike Red and Marvin Hershkowitz, a different type of Orthodox community hosted Yeshiva. Whether the team went to Miami or Brookline or Hartford, it interacted primarily with day school products, like themselves. In a sense, the winnowing out of contemporary Orthodoxy of its nonobservant segment was reflected by the fact that neither the Floridians, Bostonians, nor Connecticutites who cheered the team on were at all surprised that the players could "play and pray." So did they.

Like Saracheck, Halpert is a highly competitive sort and knew that in order to win—like what Red always understood and Hershkowitz exemplified—he had to have a few non-Yeshiva-trained stars. Day school products would be the complementary role players. Interestingly enough, he found "public school" kids, almost without exception, from within Israeli "public schools." With Hershkowitz's help, he migrated to Israel in the 1980s where he recruited young men from traditionally leaning, *masorti* families who had expressed enough of a commitment to Orthodox values to pass muster with Yeshiva officials. With these older army veterans as the hub, Yeshiva teams from 1980 to 2000 amassed a respectable 246–207 (.553) record against a decent level of opposition.

Part of the team's success was attributable to the presence on campus since 1985 of the magnificent Max Stern Athletic Center, complete with a 1,100-seat gym with a pool, next door to a shul. School officials realized that to attract late twentieth-century American Orthodox students from day school environments to their university they would have to provide them with the type of recreational facilities to which they were accustomed at home or at their summer camps. Fortunately, the institution had, by then, developed enough friends and funds to help them impress potential freshmen. Of course, Yeshiva's sports teams were the immediate beneficiaries of these improvements.

Still, this contemporary era has not constituted a heyday in Yeshiva University sports. Certainly, sports are front and center every spring when the Max Stern Center hosts the Henry Wittenberg Wrestling Tournament and the Red Sarachek Basketball Tournament, major admissions department events that bring together day school grapplers and hoopsters from around the nation. Nonetheless, with all these available facilities and winning teams to cheer on, there has been a noticeable decline, which began in the mid-1990s, in student interest in campus sports and even in physical fitness. All too often, the pool and gym are empty or underutilized, frequented by an identifiable minority of students who love to work out, play on varsities, or simply like to cheer in the stands. The others, in keeping with the tenor of these times within the committed Orthodox community, prefer to spend their extracurricular hours in voluntary Torah study. They are, in their own way, of a mind-set far different from their grandfathers, who desperately wanted to be seen as "all-American boys," or even of their fathers, who wanted Yeshiva to be respected through a high sports profile.

Notes

1. For the famous requirement incumbent on a father to teach his son to swim, see *Kiddushin* 29A. For a listing and some analysis of Talmudic sources that relate to varying forms of athletic activity, see Jehosua Alouf, "Physical Culture in the Period of the Talmud" (in Hebrew), in *Physical Education and Sports in Jewish History and Culture: Proceedings of an International Seminar,* ed. Uri Simri (Netanyah, Israel: Wingate Institute for Physical Education and Sport, 1973), 5–11, 39. On Maimonides' attitude toward physical activity, see also Meir Baskhi, "Physical Culture in the Writings of Maimonides" (in Hebrew), in Simri, ed., 11–18, 50. For early rabbinic discourses on the different characters of Jacob and Esau, see *Genesis Rabbah* 63: 10; cf. *Gen* 25: 27. See also Louis Ginzberg, *Legends of the Bible* I (Philadelphia: Jewish Publication Society, 1909), 316.

2. See *I Maccabees* 1: 14–15 and II 4: 14–17 for Hasmonean castigations of their opponents. On staunch criticisms of those who participated and watched sporting events, see also Michael Poliakoff, "Jacob, Job, and Other Wrestlers: Reception of Greek Athletics by Jews and Christians in Antiquity," *Journal of Sports History* 11, no. 2 (Summer, 1984): 48–65.

3. On Jews engaging in a variety of informal sports and/or participating, within

Jewish boundaries, in pagan games, see Poliakoff, "Jacob, Job, and Other Wrestlers," 61–63; Joshua Schwartz, "Ball-Playing in Jewish Society and in the Greco-Roman World," *Proceedings of the Eleventh World Congress of Jewish Studies* (Division B), vol. 1 (1993): 17–24; Salo Wittmayer Baron, *The Jewish Community: Its History and Structure to the American Revolution*, vol. 1 (Philadelphia: Jewish Publication Society, 1948), 92.

4. On the nature of the medieval tournament, see Marc Bloch, *Feudal Society* (Chicago: University of Chicago Press, 1961), 304–5; Alan Young, *Tudor and Jacobean Tournaments* (Dobbs Ferry: Sheridan House, 1987), 1; Urban Tigner Holmes, *Daily Living in the Twelfth Century: Based on Observations of Alexander Neckam in London and Paris* (Madison: University of Wisconsin Press, 1952), 180–81. On the Jews' "right to bear arms" in the Middle Ages and the withdrawal of that right, see Guido Kisch, *The Jews in Medieval Germany: A Study of Their Legal and Social Status*, 2nd ed. (New York: Ktav Publishing House, 1970), 111–28.

5. Israel Abrahams, *Jewish Life in the Middle Ages* (London, 1896), 379–80.

6. Baron, *Jewish Community*, 197–98. For Baron, "sporadic voices in favor of recreational pauses [from study] were as ineffective as those which advocated physical exercises. Northern European Jewry especially had little use for physical education or sports, and paid little heed even to the demand that a father give his son instruction in swimming as a life-saving precaution." The problem with Baron's evaluation, which has been generally accepted as approximating reality, is that the sources he quotes to back his assertion are not from the specific High Middle Ages time and places we are discussing.

7. For an example of such a case, see Irving A. Agus, *Rabbi Meir of Rothenberg: His Life and His Works as Sources for the Religious, Legal and Social History of the Jews of Germany in the Thirteenth Century*, vol. 2 (Philadelphia: Dropsie College, 1947), 659.

8. Patricia Vertinsky, "Body Matters: Race, Gender, and Perceptions of Physical Ability from Goethe to Weininger," in *Identity and Intolerance: Nationalism, Racism, and Xenophobia in Germany and the United States*, ed. Norbert Finzsch and Dietmar Schirmer (Washington, DC: German Historical Institute and Cambridge University Press, 1998), 354–56, 360.

9. See Samson Raphael Hirsch, *Horeb: A Philosophy of Jewish Laws and Observances*, vol. 2, trans. Dayan Dr.I. Grunfeld (London: Soncino Press, 1962), 408. I am also indebted to Professor Mordecai Breuer for his insights on physical training within Hirsch schools in the nineteenth century that he shared with me through Professor Kimmy Caplan on July 29, 2000. See also Aaron Ahrend, "Physical Culture in Rabbinical Literature in Recent Years," *Korot: The Israel Journal of the History of Medicine and Science* 15 (2001): 64–65. Ahrend notes that in the 1920s, Rabbi Yosef Zvi Carlebach, a Hirschian, expanded the sports program in his Hamburg Reali Talmud Torah.

10. For retrospective studies of the socialization and education of children in the shtetl, with emphases on idealizing the scholar, see Mark Zborowski and Elizabeth Herzog, *Life Is with People: The Culture of the Shtetl* (New York: Schocken Books, 1952), 74–77, 341–43, 353, 391, and Emanuel Gamoran, *Changing Conceptions in Jewish Education* (New York: Macmillan Company, 1924), 112–13. Diane K. Roskies and David G. Roskies, *The Shtetl Book* (New York: KTAV, 1975), 150, 158, 211, and passim, notes that the games children played during their heder

years were of the nonphysical type, like tic-tac-toe, memorization games, tag, etc. They do, however, note that sometimes in a heder, youngsters "yelled or fought with each other" (150)—outside the purview of their teachers, we imagine.

11. See R. P. Mankin in *Shaarei Tziyon* (Tammuz-Elul, 5694) [1934], quoted in Ahrend, "Physical Culture in Rabbinical Literature," 63.

12. Ahrend, "Physical Culture in Rabbinical Literature," 63.

13. On Nordau and other Zionist and modern Jewish critiques of the lack of physicality among religious Jews of Eastern Europe, see Howard Eilberg-Schwartz, *People of the Book: Jews and Judaism from an Embodied Perspective* (Albany: State University of New York Press, 1992), 6.

14. On these patterns of religious behavior among first and subsequent generations of East European Jews in America, see Jeffrey S. Gurock, "Twentieth-Century American Orthodoxy's Era of Non-Observance, 1900–1960," *Torah Umada Journal* (2000): 87–107.

15. Interestingly enough, it was this same Rabbi Kagan who in 1894 strongly admonished East European Jewry against migration to America, lest they lose their cultural distinctiveness and identity in this land of freedom. In a sense, the many thousands of Orthodox-practicing Jews who did not hear or listen to his voice, were a self-selecting group that was predisposed toward a degree of comfort with the libertine American religious environment. See Rabbi Israel Mayer ha-Kohen Kagan, *Niddehei Yisrael* (Warsaw, 1894), 129–30.

16. On the public schools as an Americanizing institution for all Jewish youngsters, see Stephan F. Brumberg, *Going to America, Going to School: The Jewish Immigrant Public School Encounter in Turn-of-the-Century New York* (New York: Praeger, 1986), especially 9 and 78, which note the importance of physical training and hygiene as part of the school curriculum. See also Cary Goodman, *Choosing Sides: Playground Life and Street Life on the Lower East Side* (New York: Schocken Books, 1979), for a discussion of settlement houses and other formal play areas that were designed to help Americanize immigrants.

17. Abraham Cahan, "The New Writers of the Ghetto," *The Bookman* 39 (August, 1914): 633. This source is an account by Cahan of an untitled Yiddish story written by Aaron Weitzman.

18. The most comprehensive study of the role of ancillary activities—including sports activities—within American synagogue life is David Kaufman, *Shul with a Pool: The "Synagogue-Center" in American Jewish Life* (Waltham, MA: Brandeis University Press, 1999). Kaufman correctly notes that this idea did not begin with Jewish Theological Seminary students at the turn of the twentieth century, but with Reform rabbis a decade or so earlier. Still, its efflorescence and multifaceted programs clearly date from this immigrant era encounter. See Kaufman, *Shul with a Pool*, 10–50, on the earliest manifestations of synagogue center activities.

19. On the history of these activities within institutions that defined themselves as Orthodox and how these activities help us define the nature of that traditional denomination in the beginning decades of the twentieth century, see Kaufman, *Shul with a Pool*, 164–205, and Gurock, *American Jewish Orthodoxy in Historical Perspective* (Hoboken: KTAV, 1996), chapters 1, 2, 8, and 10.

20. On the young Kaplan's interest in sports as well as the sports-related incident that, in part, led him to found the Jewish Center, see Jeffrey S. Gurock and Jacob J. Schacter, *A Modern Heretic and a Traditional Community: Mordecai*

M. Kaplan, Orthodoxy and American Judaism (New York: Columbia University Press, 1997), 25, 91–92.

21. On the early history of Etz Chaim's curriculum, see Gurock, *The Men and Women of Yeshiva: Higher Education, Orthodoxy and American Judaism* (New York: Columbia University Press, 1988), 14–17. On the amount of time allocated to general education, including physical education as opposed to religious study, in Etz Chaim and its sister schools the Rabbi Jacob Joseph Yeshiva, Yeshiva of Harlem, and Yeshiva Chaim Berlin, see Alexander Dushkin, *Jewish Education in New York City* (New York: Bureau of Jewish Education, 1918), 326–28.

22. See Gurock, *Men and Women of Yeshiva*, 47–54. See also Seth Taylor, *Between Tradition and Modernity: A History of the Marsha Stern Talmudical Academy* (New York: Yeshiva University High School, 1991), 9–10, and passim.

23. Safir served as the academy's principal from 1919 to 1963. On Safir's goals for the school and its students, see Shelley R. Safir, "Our Next Step," *The Elchanite* (June, 1925): 13–14. On the qualifications of the academy's gym teacher, see "Annual Report of the Board of Trustees of Talmudical Academy for the School Year Ending July 31, 1919, to the University of the State of New York" (Norman Abrams Collection, Yeshiva University Archives). For a report on the faculty-student ball game, see *The Annual Elchanite* (1923), 23. On Safir's interest in tennis, see *The Commentator* (hereafter *Comm*) (March 18, 1935): 4.

24. See *The Elchanite Jr.* (January, 1925), 43, for students' pride in their scholastic and athletic balances. For Safir's report on athletic facilities, see his "[Report to] [t]he University of the State of New York, the State Department of Education, Albany" (May, 1921) (Norman Abrams Collection, Yeshiva University Archives).

25. For Revel's views of "harmonization" or "synthesis" as a goal of education at his modern yeshiva, see Gurock, *Men and Women of Yeshiva*, 90–91, and passim.

26. See below for a discussion of the proposed building of a physical culture building as part of Revel's master plan for his Americanized yeshiva as evidence of his understanding student and community needs for athletics. It is noteworthy that although Revel's Talmud faculty—his Roshei Yeshiva—were certainly not sportsmen, one of his respected faculty members, Rabbi Solomon Polachek, who taught for him from 1922 to 1929, did express a positive view of yeshiva students being physically fit. Rabbi Mayer Berlin recorded in his autobiography that he and Polachek once happened upon some youngsters from a gymnasium school in Brisk, Lithuania, and observed them running and jumping around happily in athletic activity. Polachek reportedly remarked "with sorrow, why didn't we have this [activity] when we were youngsters. It would not have hurt our ability to study if we permitted ourselves some time every day to run and jump around." See Mayer Bar Ilan Berlin, *M'Volozhin ad Yerushalayim*, vol. 1, new ed. (Tel Aviv: Foundation for the Publication of the Writings of Rabbi Mayer Bar Ilan, 1971).

27. Zvi Yaron, *The Philosophy of Rabbi Kook* (Jerusalem: Department for Torah Education and Culture in the Diaspora of the World Zionist Organization, 1991), 104–7; Ahrend, "Physical Culture in Rabbinical Literature," 70.

28. For a discussion of ideological and political opposition to Rabbi Kook's views on sports see Ahrend, "Physical Culture in Rabbinical Literature," 13–19.

See Gurock, *Men and Women of Yeshiva,* 67–81, for the history of the integration of a Mizrachi-initiated Teachers Institute within Revel's American yeshiva community.

29. See *The Yeshiva College: What It Is and What It Stands For, a Challenge and a Promise to American Jewry* [1927] (pamphlet on file at the Yeshiva University Archives) for discussions and artist's rendering of the proposed eight-building campus. See also Gurock, *Men and Women of Yeshiva,* 82–89, on the founding of Yeshiva College.

30. Yeshiva College was established in 1928 and was housed in temporary quarters until the opening of the campus in 1929. For information on courses offered in physical education at the college and where the courses were given, see *Yeshiva College Catalogue* (1928–29), 9, 31; (1933–34), 36.

31. Basketball, then generally the most popular sport played by Jews in America, was, likewise, the flagship sport at the Talmudical Academy and Yeshiva College. Periodically, baseball teams were organized, and occasionally there was talk on campus of establishing swimming and tennis teams. Of course, those teams would have to meet away from Washington Heights; Yeshiva had no pool or tennis facility. For more on these "minor" sports, see *The Elchanite* (June, 1938): 82; *Comm* (April 8, 1935): 3.

32. See *Comm* (December 19, 1935): 2 for editorial support for the importance of the basketball team. See also Jack Goldman, "On the Sidelines . . ." *Comm* (September 24, 1938): 3.

33. "A Basketball Angle," *Comm* (January 4, 1939): 4.

34. "A Trumpet for All Israel," *Time,* October 15, 1951, 54. Another version has it that Schechter said a rabbi must "know about baseball." Whichever version is accurate, the importance of the remark remains the same.

35. Bernard Weisberg, "As a Means to an End," *Comm* (January 2, 1944): 5; Myron M. Fenster, "Athletics Promote Synthesis," *Comm* (September 9, 1946): 3.

36. On the early history of students running the sports program and themselves engaging coaches, see Bernie Hoenig, "Yeshiva Sports Celebrates Silver Jubilee as Past History Culminates Bright Era," *Comm* (May 18, 1953): 14. See Lewis N. Ginsberg, "Is Physical Ed. Possible without a Gymnasium," *Comm* (December 13, 1945): 4 for the problems Hurwitz faced in operating his understaffed department with poor facilities. See "Bernard Sarachek to Coach Revamped College Varsity," *Comm* (November 5, 1942): 3 for a report on his hiring. For examples of complaints about the sports facilities, see "Renovate the Gym!" *Comm* (May 23, 1946): 2 and Myron M. Fenster, "Student Body Heartened by Gym Repairs," *Comm* (November 7, 1946): 2.

37. On Belkin's educational background, see Gurock, *Men and Women of Yeshiva,* 137. For a student's sense that Belkin and his administration were unaware of the importance sports played in their lives, see Fenster, "Student Body," 2. See also Gurock's interview with Sam Hartstein, August 2, 2000 (available in Yeshiva University archives), on his role in influencing Belkin. See also the myriad of 1950s press releases and brochures on sports from the public relations files of Yeshiva University. On the role and functions the YUAA played in its early years, see "YUAA Plans for the Coming Year Disclosed by Rabbi Abraham Avrech," *Comm* (September 30, 1948): 3 and Sheldon Rudoff, "Progress and Plans of Y.U.A.A. Lauded; New Ideas Presented," *Comm* (September 27, 1951):

3. On the history of the recruitment of additional coaches for Yeshiva's team, see the retrospective article by Josh Muss, "The Professors," *Comm* (September 20, 1960): 12. See also Seymour Essrog, "They Can Pray and Play," Yeshiva University press release, November 19, 1954, for an example of the coming to fruition of some of the YUAA's dreams. See also a 1953 untitled press release that announces Belkin's appointment of Sarachek as athletic director.

38. Julie Landwirth, "Sound Mind-Sound Body Everybody Preaches It, Who Believes It?" *Comm* (May 10, 1956): 3 for an account of Lookstein's Kookian message.

39. Gurock's interview with Marvin Hershkowitz, August 1, 2000 (available in Yeshiva University archives).

40. On Sarachek's attitude toward Hershkowitz, see Seymour Essrog, "Student Attitudes, Hershko's Last Game," *Comm* (March 25, 1953): 3. See also Gurock's interview with Hershkowitz. On Sarachek as a Belkin loyalist, see Jimmy Powers, "The Powerhouse," *Daily News* (January 21, 1953): 74.

41. On Sarachek's attitudes toward the importance of sports at Yeshiva, see *Comm* (March 25, 1954): 3; (May 25, 1955): 5; (October 19, 1956): 3; and October 24, 1960: 5. See also Gurock's interview with Hartstein.

42. See "Dr. Belkin Discloses New Admissions Plan," *Comm* (February 8, 1956): 1 for the announcement of the founding of the Jewish studies program. For statistics on the record of Yeshiva's basketball team and the composition of the squad during those glory years, see the annual basketball brochures produced by the university's public relations office for the years 1953–54 through 1959–60.

43. On opposition to the founding of JSP, see Joseph Walter Eichenbaum, ed., *James Striar School of General Jewish Studies Bar Mitzvah Journal* (New York: Yeshiva University, 1969), 9. See also Isaac Gottlieb, "Unmitigated Villain Corners Rabbi Besdin . . ." Hamevaser (Sivan, 5724 [1964]), 4, for a reminiscence of how the first students were considered by some to be "non-Jews." See also Gurock, *Men and Women of Yeshiva*, 177–78, on the behavior of JSP ball players and campus attitudes.

44. On the educational background and religious orientation of JSP students as the program matured, see Gurock, *Men and Women of Yeshiva*, 179–185. On the problems the basketball program faced, see Gurock's interview with Jonathan J. Halpert, August 21, 2000 (available in Yeshiva University archives). See also "Cumulative Basketball Statistics Survey," *Comm* (April 4, 1963): 11; see also *Yeshiva College Basketball '88–'89* (Yeshiva University Basketball Program, 1988–89) for statistics on Sarachek's record during the 1960s.

45. For Neil Koslowe's views, see "How to Succeed in Public Relations—By Trying," *Comm* (October 21, 1964): 6; "This Will Be the Year That Will Be," *Comm* (November 5, 1964): 8; "Yeshiva College and the Student Athlete," *Comm* (November 15, 1964): 8; "The Homecoming Weekend Affair—Whither a Yeshiva Generation," *Comm* (December 10, 1964): 8.

46. Chaim Brovender, "Should Yeshiva Condescend to the Level of the Ivy League Colleges?" Hamevaser (Shevat, 5725 [1965]): 7; Richard Hochstein, "Letter to the Editor," *Comm* (December 31, 1964): 9.

47. For the debate over the social implications of the proposed weekend, including the allegation of "*kalus rosh*" and women at Yeshiva socials, see David Ebner, "Letter to the Editor," *Comm* (November 19, 1964): 2; Joseph Isaiah Berlin, "Letter

to the Editors," *Comm* (December 31, 1964): 7, 8; Stern College Students, "Letter to the Editors," *Comm* (December 31, 1964): 2; Anonymous, "Letter to the Editors," *Comm* (February 18, 1965): 6. This debate continued until the end of the academic year. See "Should Yeshiva Sponsor Social Events? The YU Students Voice Their Opinions," *Comm* (May 5, 1964): 4.

48. Koslowe, "The Homecoming," 8. For an attack on Sarachek, see Ephraim Hecht, "Letter to the Editor," *Comm* (December 31, 1964): 2, 8.

49. For defenses of Sarachek, see Moses M. Berlin, "Letter to the Editors," *Comm* (April 8, 1965): 2, and Victor Geller, "Letter to the Editors," *Comm* (February 18, 1965): 6.

50. See Gurock, "Bernard Sarachek, Yeshiva 'Role Model,'" *Yeshiva Review* (Spring, 1995): 36–37, for a discussion of Sarachek's career and reputation in sports circles outside Yeshiva.

51. Gurock's interview with Halpert, August 21, 2000.

CONTRIBUTORS

HARVEY E. GOLDBERG holds the Sarah Allen Shaine chair in the Department of Sociology and Anthropology at the Hebrew University of Jerusalem. He is the author of *Cave Dwellers and Citrus Growers: A Jewish Community in Libya and Israel*; *Jewish Life in Muslim Libya: Rivals and Relatives*; and *Jewish Passages: Cycles of Jewish Life*. He is the editor of *Judaism Viewed from Within and from Without: Anthropological Studies* and *Sephardi and Middle Eastern Jewries: History and Culture in the Modern Era*.

JEFFREY S. GUROCK is the Libby M. Klaperman Professor of Jewish History at Yeshiva University. He is the author or editor of thirteen books including *A Modern Heretic and a Traditional Community: Mordecai M. Kaplan, Orthodoxy and American Judaism*, which in 1998 was awarded the biannual Saul Viener Prize from the American Jewish Historical Society for the best book written in its field. His most recent book is *Judaism's Encounter with American Sports*.

ANAT HELMAN lectures in the Institute of Contemporary Jewry, the Jewish History Department, and the cultural studies program at the Hebrew University. Her forthcoming book describes the development of urban culture in 1920s and 1930s Tel Aviv. Her essays have appeared in *Jewish Quarterly Review*; *Cathedra*; *Historical Journal of Film, Radio and Television*; *Journal of Israeli History*; *Urban History*; and *Zion*.

JOHN HOBERMAN has been active in the sports studies field for twenty-five years. He has taught courses on sport and politics at Harvard University, the University of Chicago, and the University of Texas at Austin, where he is professor of Germanic studies and teaches a course on the history of anti-Semitism for the Jewish Studies Program. He is the author of *Sport and Political Ideology*; *The Olympic Crisis: Sport, Politics, and the Moral Order*; *Mortal Engines: The Science of Performance and the Dehumanization of Sport*; *Darwin's Athletes: How Sport Has Damaged Black America and Preserved the Myth of Race*; and *Testosterone Dreams: Rejuvenation, Aphrodisia, Doping*. His work in progress is a book on masculinity, sport, and the Jews.

JACK JACOBS is a professor of political science in, and deputy executive officer of, the Ph.D./M.A. program in political science of the Graduate Center at the City University of New York (CUNY), and is also a professor of government at John Jay College, CUNY. He is the author of *On Socialists and "the Jewish Question" After Marx* and is the editor of *Jewish Politics in Eastern Europe: The Bund at 100.*

JACK KUGELMASS is the former director of the Jewish Studies Program at Arizona State University and is now the director of the Center for Jewish Studies and holds the Melton Legislative Professorship at the University of Florida, Gainesville. Among other books, he is the editor of *Key Texts in American Jewish Culture,* author of *The Miracle of Intervale Avenue: The Story of a Jewish Congregation in the South Bronx,* and coauthor of *From a Ruined Garden: The Memorial Books of Polish Jewry.* He is currently working on a book on Yiddish travel narratives to Poland after World War II.

ANDRÉ LEVY teaches anthropology in the Department of Behavioral Sciences at Ben-Gurion University of the Negev. He received a Ph.D. from the Hebrew University. His dissertation is titled *Jews among Muslims: Perceptions and Reactions to the End of Casablancan Jewish History* and is based on fieldwork in Casablanca. He is the author of various book chapters and articles that deal with topics such as diasporas, identities, minority-majority relations, and pilgrimages. He recently coedited a book titled *Homelands and Diasporas: Holy Lands and Other Places.*

JOSHUA SHANES is an assistant professor of Jewish studies at College of Charleston. He has taught at the University of Wisconsin, the University of Illinois, and Northwestern University and is currently on faculty at the Spertus Institute of Jewish Studies. His work has appeared in a variety of academic publications, including *Austrian History Yearbook, Polin: Studies in Polish Jewry,* and the forthcoming *YIVO Encyclopedia of East European Jewry.* At present, he is revising his first book on the history of Jewish nationalism in Galicia before World War I.

EDWARD SHAPIRO is professor emeritus at Seton Hall University and associate editor of *American Jewish History.* He is the editor of *The Letters of Sidney Hook: Democracy, Communism, and the Cold War* and is the author of *A Time for Healing: American Jewry Since 1945; We Are Many: Reflections on American Jewish History and Identity;* and *Crown Heights: Blacks, Jews, and the 1991 Brooklyn Riot.*

TAMIR SOREK is an assistant professor of Jewish studies and sociology at the University of Florida, Gainesville. He earned a Ph.D. in sociology and anthropology from the Hebrew University of Jerusalem and was a postdoctoral fellow at the Meyerhoff Center for Jewish Studies at the University of Maryland. His interests center on the processes in which ethnic and national identities are produced and reproduced, the sociology of sport, and commemoration. He has published several articles on the political significance of Arab soccer in Israel and on Palestinian nationalism, and coauthored (with Fabienne Messica) *Refuzniks israéliens,* a book on Israeli soldiers who refuse to serve the occupation.

STEPHEN J. WHITFIELD holds the Max Richter chair in American civilization at Brandeis University. He is the author of *Scott Nearing: Apostle of American Radicalism; Into the Dark: Hannah Arendt and Totalitarianism; Voices of Jacob, Hands of Esau: Jews in American Life and Thought; A Critical American: The Politics of Dwight Macdonald; A Death in the Delta: The Story of Emmett Till; American Space, Jewish Time; The Culture of the Cold War;* and *In Search of American Jewish Culture* and he is the editor of *A Companion to 20th-Century America.*

INDEX

The University of Illinois Press
is a founding member of the
Association of American University Presses.

Composed in 9.5/12.5 Trump Mediaeval
at the University of Illinois Press
Manufactured by Thomson-Shore, Inc.

University of Illinois Press
1325 South Oak Street
Champaign, IL 61820-6903
www.press.uillinois.edu